How to
Actually
Change
Your Mind

ELIEZER YUDKOWSKY

Written by Eliezer Yudkowsky

Published by the
Machine Intelligence Research Institute
Berkeley 94704
United States of America
intelligence.org

Contents

Contents

Introduction

by Rob Bensinger

In the autumn of 1951, a football game between Dartmouth and Princeton turned unusually rough. A pair of psychologists, Dartmouth's Albert Hastorf and Princeton's Hadley Cantril, decided to ask students from both schools which team had initiated the rough play. Nearly everyone agreed that Princeton hadn't started it; but 86% of Princeton students believed that Dartmouth had started it, whereas only 36% of Dartmouth students blamed Dartmouth. (Most Dartmouth students believed "both started it.")

When shown a film of the game later and asked to count the infractions they saw, Dartmouth students claimed to see a mean of 4.3 infractions by the Dartmouth team (and identified half as "mild"), whereas Princeton students claimed to see a mean of 9.8 Dartmouth infractions (and identified a third as "mild").[1]

When something we value is threatened—our world-view, our in-group, our social standing, or something else we care about—our thoughts and per-

---

[1] Albert Hastorf and Hadley Cantril, "They Saw a Game: A Case Study," *Journal of Abnormal and Social Psychology* 49 (1954): 129–134, http://www2.psych.ubc.ca/~schaller/Psyc590Readings/Hastorf1954.pdf.

ceptions rally to their defense.[2,3] Some psychologists go so far as to hypothesize that the human ability to come up with explicit justifications for our conclusions evolved *specifically* to help us win arguments.[4]

One of the basic insights of 20th-century psychology is that human behavior is often driven by sophisticated unconscious processes, and the stories we tell ourselves about our motives and reasons are much more biased and confabulated than we realize. We often fail, in fact, to realize that we're doing any story-telling. When we seem to "directly perceive" things about ourselves in introspection, it often turns out to rest on tenuous implicit causal models.[5,6] When we try to argue for our beliefs, we can come up with shaky reasoning bearing no relation to how we first arrived at the belief.[7] Rather than trusting explanations in proportion to their predictive power, we trust *stories* in proportion to their psychological appeal.

How can we do better? How can we arrive at a realistic view of the world, when we're so prone to rationalization? How can we come to a realistic view of our mental lives, when our thoughts *about* thinking are also suspect?

What's the *least* shaky place we could put our weight down?

---

[2] Emily Pronin, "How We See Ourselves and How We See Others," *Science* 320 (2008): 1177–1180, http://psych.princeton.edu/psychology/research/pronin/pubs/2008%5C%20Self%5C%20and%5C%20Other.pdf.

[3] Robert P. Vallone, Lee Ross, and Mark R. Lepper, "The Hostile Media Phenomenon: Biased Perception and Perceptions of Media Bias in Coverage of the Beirut Massacre," *Journal of Personality and Social Psychology* 49 (1985): 577–585, http://ssc.wisc.edu/~jpiliavi/965/hwang.pdf.

[4] Hugo Mercier and Dan Sperber, "Why Do Humans Reason? Arguments for an Argumentative Theory," *Behavioral and Brain Sciences* 34 (2011): 57–74, https://hal.archives-ouvertes.fr/file/index/docid/904097/filename/MercierSperberWhydohumansreason.pdf.

[5] Richard E. Nisbett and Timothy D. Wilson, "Telling More than We Can Know: Verbal Reports on Mental Processes," *Psychological Review* 84 (1977): 231–259, http://people.virginia.edu/~tdw/nisbett&wilson.pdf.

[6] Eric Schwitzgebel, *Perplexities of Consciousness* (MIT Press, 2011).

[7] Jonathan Haidt, "The Emotional Dog and Its Rational Tail: A Social Intuitionist Approach to Moral Judgment," *Psychological Review* 108, no. 4 (2001): 814–834, doi:10.1037/0033-295X.108.4.814.

The Mathematics of Rationality

At the turn of the 20th century, coming up with simple (e.g., set-theoretic) axioms for arithmetic gave mathematicians a clearer standard by which to judge the correctness of their conclusions. If a human or calculator outputs "2 + 2 = 4," we can now do more than just say "that seems intuitively right." We can explain *why* it's right, and we can prove that its rightness is tied in systematic ways to the rightness of the rest of arithmetic.

But mathematics lets us model the behaviors of physical systems that are a lot more interesting than a pocket calculator. We can also formalize *rational belief in general*, using probability theory to pick out features held in common by all successful forms of inference. We can even formalize *rational behavior in general* by drawing upon decision theory.

Probability theory defines how we would ideally reason in the face of uncertainty, if we had the time, the computing power, and the self-control. Given some background knowledge (*priors*) and a new piece of evidence, probability theory uniquely and precisely defines the best set of new beliefs (*posterior*) I could adopt. Likewise, decision theory defines what action I should take based on my beliefs. For any consistent set of beliefs and preferences I could have, there is a decision-theoretic answer to how I should then act in order to satisfy my preferences.

Suppose you find out that one of six people has a crush on you—perhaps you get a letter from a secret admirer, and you're sure it's from one of those six—but you have no idea which of those six people it is. Your classmate Bob is one of the six candidates, but you have no special evidence for or against the hypothesis that he's the letter's author. What are the odds that Bob is the one with the crush?

Answer: The odds are 1:5. There are six possibilities, so a wild guess would result in you getting it right once for every five times you got it wrong, on average.

We can't say, "Well, I have no idea who has a crush on me; maybe it's Bob, or maybe it's not. So I'll just say the odds are fifty-fifty." Even if we would rather say "I don't know" or "Maybe" and stop there, the right answer is still

1:5. This follows from the assumption that there are six possibilities and you have no reason to favor one of them over any of the others. [8]

Suppose that you've also noticed you get winked at by people ten times as often when they have a crush on you. If Bob then winks at you, that's a new piece of evidence. In that case, it would be a mistake to stay skeptical about whether Bob is your secret admirer; the 10:1 odds in favor of "a random person who winks at me has a crush on me" outweigh the 1:5 odds against "Bob has a crush on me."

It would *also* be a mistake to say, "That evidence is so strong, it's a sure bet that he's the one who has the crush on me! I'll just assume from now on that Bob is into me." Overconfidence is just as bad as underconfidence.

In fact, there's only one viable answer to this question too. To change our mind from the 1:5 prior odds in response to the evidence's 10:1 likelihood ratio, we multiply the left sides together and the right sides together, getting 10:5 posterior odds, or 2:1 odds in favor of "Bob has a crush on me." Given our assumptions and the available evidence, guessing that Bob has a crush on you will turn out to be correct 2 times for every 1 time it turns out to be wrong. Equivalently: the probability that he's attracted to you is 2/3. Any other confidence level would be inconsistent.

It turns out that given very modest constraints, the question "What should I believe?" has an objectively right answer. It has a right answer when you're wracked with uncertainty, not just when you have a conclusive proof. There is always a correct amount of confidence to have in a statement, even when it looks more like a "personal belief" instead of an expert-verified "fact."

Yet we often talk as though the existence of uncertainty and disagreement makes beliefs a mere matter of taste. We say "that's just my opinion" or "you're entitled to your opinion," as though the assertions of science and math existed on a different and higher plane than beliefs that are merely "private" or "subjective." To which economist Robin Hanson responds:[9]

---

[8] We're also assuming, unrealistically, that you can really be certain the admirer is one of those six people, and that you aren't neglecting other possibilities. (What if more than one of the six people has a crush on you?)

[9] Robin Hanson, "You Are Never Entitled to Your Opinion," *Overcoming Bias (blog)*, 2006, http://www.overcomingbias.com/2006/12/you_are_never_e.html.

You are never entitled to your opinion. Ever! You are not even entitled to "I don't know." You are entitled to your desires, and sometimes to your choices. You might own a choice, and if you can choose your preferences, you may have the right to do so. But your beliefs are not about you; beliefs are about the world. Your beliefs should be your best available estimate of the way things are; anything else is a lie. [. . .]

It is true that some topics give experts stronger mechanisms for resolving disputes. On other topics our biases and the complexity of the world make it harder to draw strong conclusions. [. . .]

But never forget that on any question about the way things are (or should be), and in any information situation, there *is* always a best estimate. You are only entitled to your best honest effort to find that best estimate; anything else is a lie.

Our culture hasn't internalized the lessons of probability theory—that the correct answer to questions like "How sure can I be that Bob has a crush on me?" is just as logically constrained as the correct answer to a question on an algebra quiz or in a geology textbook.

Our brains are kludges slapped together by natural selection. Humans aren't perfect reasoners or perfect decision-makers, any more than we're perfect calculators. Even at our best, we don't compute the *exact* right answer to "what should I think?" and "what should I do?" [10]

And yet, knowing we can't become *fully* consistent, we can certainly still get better. Knowing that there's an ideal standard we can compare ourselves to—what researchers call "Bayesian rationality"—can guide us as we improve our thoughts and actions. Though we'll never be perfect Bayesians, the mathematics of rationality can help us understand *why* a certain answer is correct, and help us spot exactly where we messed up.

---

[10] We lack the time and computing power (and evolution lacked the engineering expertise and foresight) to iron out all our bugs. Indeed, even a maximally efficient bug-free reasoner in the real world would still need to rely on heuristics and approximations; the optimal computationally tractable algorithms for changing beliefs fall short of probability theory's consistency.

Imagine trying to learn math through rote memorization alone. You might be told that "10 + 3 = 13," "31 + 108 = 139," and so on, but it won't do you a lot of good unless you understand the pattern behind the squiggles. It can be a lot harder to seek out methods for improving your rationality when you don't have a general framework for judging a method's success. The purpose of this book is to help people build for themselves such frameworks.

Rationality Applied

The tightly linked essays in *How to Actually Change Your Mind* were originally written by Eliezer Yudkowsky for the blog *Overcoming Bias*. Published in the late 2000s, these posts helped inspire the growth of a vibrant community interested in rationality and self-improvement.

They have been collected as book two of the e-book *Rationality: From AI to Zombies*, following the "Map and Territory" collection and preceding four more volumes of essays on many of the same themes. The volume in your hands is a free draft manuscript; the other five volumes are not yet available in print form (as of February 2017), but can be read packaged together at **https://intelligence.org/rationality-ai-zombies/**.

One of the rationality community's most popular writers, Scott Alexander, has previously observed:[11]

> [O]bviously it's useful to have as much evidence as possible, in the same way it's useful to have as much money as possible. But equally obviously it's useful to be able to use a limited amount of evidence wisely, in the same way it's useful to be able to use a limited amount of money wisely.

Rationality techniques help us get more mileage out of the evidence we have, in cases where the evidence is inconclusive or our biases are distorting how we interpret the evidence. This applies to our personal lives, as in the tale of Bob. It applies to disagreements between political factions and sports fans. And it

---

[11] Scott Alexander, "Why I Am Not Rene Descartes," *Slate Star Codex (blog)*, 2014, http://slatestarcodex.com/2014/11/27/why-i-am-not-rene-descartes/.

applies to philosophical puzzles and debates between futurists. Recognizing that the same mathematical rules apply to each of these domains (and that in many cases the same cognitive biases crop up), *How to Actually Change Your Mind* discusses a wide range of topics.

The first sequence of essays in this book, "Overly Convenient Excuses," focuses on questions that are as probabilistically clear-cut as they come. The Bayes-optimal answer is often infeasible to compute in practice, but errors like confirmation bias can take root even in cases where the available evidence is overwhelming and we have plenty of time to think things over.

From there, we move into murkier waters with "Politics and Rationality." Mainstream national politics, as debated by TV pundits, is famous for its angry, unproductive discussions. On the face of it, there's something surprising about that. Why do we take political disagreements so personally, even though the machinery and effects of national politics are often so distant from us in space or in time? For that matter, why do we not become *more* careful and rigorous with the evidence when we're dealing with issues we deem important?

The Dartmouth-Princeton game hints at an answer. Much of our reasoning process is really rationalization—story-telling that makes our current beliefs feel more coherent and justified, without necessarily improving their accuracy. "Against Rationalization" speaks to this problem, followed by "Seeing with Fresh Eyes" (on the challenge of recognizing evidence that doesn't fit our expectations and assumptions).

Leveling up in rationality means encountering a lot of interesting and powerful new ideas. In many cases, it also means making friends who you can bounce ideas off of and finding communities that encourage you to better yourself. "Death Spirals" discusses some important hazards that can afflict groups united around common interests and amazing shiny ideas, which will need to be overcome if we're to get the full benefits out of rationality communities. *How to Actually Change Your Mind* then concludes with a sequence on "Letting Go."

Our natural state *isn't* to change our minds like a Bayesian would. Getting the Dartmouth and Princeton students to notice what they're actually seeing won't be as easy as reciting the axioms of probability theory to them. As research analyst Luke Muehlhauser writes in "The Power of Agency":[12]

> You are not a Bayesian homunculus whose reasoning is "corrupted" by cognitive biases.
>
> You just *are* cognitive biases.

Confirmation bias, status quo bias, correspondence bias, and the like are not tacked on to our reasoning; they are its very substance.

That doesn't mean that debiasing is impossible. We aren't perfect calculators underneath all our arithmetic errors, either. Many of our mathematical limitations result from very deep facts about how the human brain works. Yet we can train our mathematical abilities; we can learn when to trust and distrust our mathematical intuitions; we can shape our environments to make things easier on us. And if we're wrong today, we can be less so tomorrow.

---

[12] Luke Muehlhauser, "The Power of Agency," *Less Wrong (blog)*, 2011, http://lesswrong.com/lw/5i8/the_power_of_agency/.

Part E

Overly Convenient Excuses

1

Tsuyoku Naritai! (I Want to Become Stronger)

In Orthodox Judaism there is a saying: "The previous generation is to the next one as angels are to men; the next generation is to the previous one as donkeys are to men." This follows from the Orthodox Jewish belief that all Judaic law was given to Moses by God at Mount Sinai. After all, it's not as if you could do an experiment to gain new halachic knowledge; the only way you can know is if someone tells you (who heard it from someone else, who heard it from God). Since there is no new source of information; it can only be degraded in transmission from generation to generation.

Thus, modern rabbis are not allowed to overrule ancient rabbis. Crawly things are ordinarily unkosher, but it is permissible to eat a worm found in an apple—the ancient rabbis believed the worm was spontaneously generated inside the apple, and therefore was part of the apple. A modern rabbi cannot say, "Yeah, well, the ancient rabbis knew diddly-squat about biology. Overruled!" A modern rabbi cannot possibly know a halachic principle the ancient rabbis did not, because how could the ancient rabbis have passed down the answer from Mount Sinai to him? Knowledge derives from authority, and therefore is only ever lost, not gained, as time passes.

When I was first exposed to the angels-and-donkeys proverb in (religious) elementary school, I was not old enough to be a full-blown atheist, but I still thought to myself: "Torah loses knowledge in every generation. Science gains knowledge with every generation. No matter where they started out, sooner or later science must surpass Torah."

The most important thing is that there should be progress. So long as you keep moving forward you will reach your destination; but if you stop moving you will never reach it.

Tsuyoku naritai is Japanese. *Tsuyoku* is "strong"; *naru* is "becoming," and the form *naritai* is "want to become." Together it means, "I want to become stronger," and it expresses a sentiment embodied more intensely in Japanese works than in any Western literature I've read. You might say it when expressing your determination to become a professional Go player—or after you lose an important match, but you haven't given up—or after you win an important match, but you're not a ninth-dan player yet—or after you've become the greatest Go player of all time, but you still think you can do better. That is *tsuyoku naritai*, the will to transcendence.

Each year on Yom Kippur, an Orthodox Jew recites a litany which begins *Ashamnu, bagadnu, gazalnu, dibarnu dofi,* and goes on through the entire Hebrew alphabet: *We have acted shamefully, we have betrayed, we have stolen, we have slandered . . .*

As you pronounce each word, you strike yourself over the heart in penitence. There's no exemption whereby, if you manage to go without stealing all year long, you can skip the word *gazalnu* and strike yourself one less time. That would violate the community spirit of Yom Kippur, which is about *confessing* sins—not *avoiding* sins so that you have less to confess.

By the same token, the *Ashamnu* does not end, "But that was this year, and next year I will do better."

The *Ashamnu* bears a remarkable resemblance to the notion that the way of rationality is to beat your fist against your heart and say, "We are all biased, we are all irrational, we are not fully informed, we are overconfident, we are poorly calibrated . . ."

4

Fine. Now tell me how you plan to become *less* biased, *less* irrational, *more* informed, *less* overconfident, *better* calibrated.

There is an old Jewish joke: During Yom Kippur, the rabbi is seized by a sudden wave of guilt, and prostrates himself and cries, "God, I am nothing before you!" The cantor is likewise seized by guilt, and cries, "God, I am nothing before you!" Seeing this, the janitor at the back of the synagogue prostrates himself and cries, "God, I am nothing before you!" And the rabbi nudges the cantor and whispers, "Look who thinks he's nothing."

Take no pride in your confession that you too are biased; do not glory in your self-awareness of your flaws. This is akin to the principle of not taking pride in confessing your ignorance; for if your ignorance is a source of pride to you, you may become loath to relinquish your ignorance when evidence comes knocking. Likewise with our flaws—we should not gloat over how self-aware we are for confessing them; the occasion for rejoicing is when we have a little less to confess.

Otherwise, when the one comes to us with a plan for *correcting* the bias, we will snarl, "Do you think to set yourself above us?" We will shake our heads sadly and say, "You must not be very self-aware."

Never confess to me that you are just as flawed as I am unless you can tell me what you plan to do about it. Afterward you will still have plenty of flaws left, but that's not the point; the important thing is to *do better*, to keep moving ahead, to take one more step forward. *Tsuyoku naritai!*

2

The Proper Use of Humility

It is widely recognized that good science requires some kind of humility. *What sort* of humility is more controversial.

Consider the creationist who says: "But who can really know whether evolution is correct? It is just a theory. You should be more humble and open-minded." Is this humility? The creationist practices a very selective underconfidence, refusing to integrate massive weights of evidence in favor of a conclusion they find uncomfortable. I would say that whether you call this "humility" or not, it is the wrong step in the dance.

What about the engineer who humbly designs fail-safe mechanisms into machinery, even though they're damn sure the machinery won't fail? This seems like a good kind of humility to me. Historically, it's not unheard-of for an engineer to be damn sure a new machine won't fail, and then it fails anyway.

What about the student who humbly double-checks the answers on their math test? Again I'd categorize that as good humility. The student *wants to become stronger*; they react to a possible inner flaw by doing what they can to repair the flaw.

What about a student who says, "Well, no matter how many times I check, I can't ever be *certain* my test answers are correct," and therefore doesn't check even once? Even if this choice stems from an emotion similar to the emotion felt by the previous student, it is less wise.

You suggest studying harder, and the student replies: "No, it wouldn't work for me; I'm not one of the smart kids like you; nay, one so lowly as myself can hope for no better lot." This is social modesty, not humility. It has to do with regulating status in the tribe, rather than scientific process. If you ask someone to "be more humble," by default they'll associate the words to social modesty—which is an intuitive, everyday, ancestrally relevant concept. Scientific humility is a more recent and rarefied invention, and it is not inherently social. Scientific humility is something you would practice even if you were alone in a spacesuit, light years from Earth with no one watching. Or even if you received an absolute guarantee that no one would ever criticize you again, no matter what you said or thought of yourself. You'd still double-check your calculations if you were wise.

The student says: "But I've seen other students double-check their answers and then they still turned out to be wrong. Or what if, by the problem of induction, 2 + 2 = 5 this time around? No matter what I do, I won't be sure of myself." It sounds very profound, and very modest. But it is not coincidence that the student wants to hand in the test quickly, and go home and play video games.

The end of an era in physics does not always announce itself with thunder and trumpets; more often it begins with what seems like a small, small flaw . . . But because physicists have this arrogant idea that their models should work *all* the time, not just *most* of the time, they follow up on small flaws. Usually, the small flaw goes away under closer inspection. Rarely, the flaw widens to the point where it blows up the whole theory. Therefore it is written: "If you do not seek perfection you will halt before taking your first steps."

But think of the social audacity of trying to be right *all* the time! I seriously suspect that if Science claimed that evolutionary theory is true most of the time but not all of the time—or if Science conceded that maybe on some days the Earth *is* flat, but who really knows—then scientists would have better social reputations. Science would be viewed as less confrontational, because we wouldn't have to argue with people who say the Earth is flat—there would be room for compromise. When you argue a lot, people look upon you as confrontational. If you repeatedly refuse to compromise, it's even worse. Consider it as a question of tribal status: scientists have certainly earned some extra status in exchange for such socially useful tools as medicine and cellphones. But this social status does not justify their insistence that *only* scientific ideas on evolution be taught in public schools. Priests also have high social status, after all. Scientists are getting above themselves—they won a little status, and now they think they're chiefs of the whole tribe! They ought to be more humble, and compromise a little.

Many people seem to possess rather hazy views of "rationalist humility." It is dangerous to have a prescriptive principle which you only vaguely comprehend; your mental picture may have so many degrees of freedom that it can adapt to justify almost any deed. Where people have vague mental models that can be used to argue anything, they usually end up believing whatever they started out wanting to believe. This is so convenient that people are often reluctant to give up vagueness. But the purpose of our ethics is to move us, not be moved by us.

"Humility" is a virtue that is often misunderstood. This doesn't mean we should discard the concept of humility, but we should be careful using it. It may help to look at the *actions* recommended by a "humble" line of thinking, and ask: "Does acting this way make you stronger, or weaker?" If you think about the problem of induction as applied to a bridge that needs to stay up, it may sound reasonable to conclude that nothing is certain no matter what precautions are employed; but if you consider the real-world difference between adding a few extra cables, and shrugging, it seems clear enough what makes the stronger bridge.

The vast majority of appeals that I witness to "rationalist's humility" are excuses to shrug. The one who buys a lottery ticket, saying, "But you can't *know* that I'll lose." The one who disbelieves in evolution, saying, "But you can't *prove* to me that it's true." The one who refuses to confront a difficult-looking problem, saying, "It's probably too hard to solve." The problem is motivated skepticism a.k.a. disconfirmation bias—more heavily scrutinizing assertions

8

that we don't want to believe.[1] Humility, in its most commonly misunderstood form, is a fully general excuse not to believe something; since, after all, you can't be *sure*. Beware of fully general excuses!

A further problem is that humility is all too easy to *profess*. Dennett, in *Breaking the Spell: Religion as a Natural Phenomenon*, points out that while many religious assertions are very hard to believe, it is easy for people to believe that they *ought* to believe them.[2] Dennett terms this "belief in belief." What would it mean to really assume, to really believe, that three is equal to one? It's a lot easier to believe that you *should*, somehow, believe that three equals one, and to make this response at the appropriate points in church. Dennett suggests that much "religious belief" should be studied as "religious profession"—what people think they should believe and what they know they ought to say.

It is all too easy to meet every counterargument by saying, "Well, of course I could be wrong." Then, having dutifully genuflected in the direction of Modesty, having made the required obeisance, you can go on about your way without changing a thing.

The temptation is always to claim the most points with the least effort. The temptation is to carefully integrate all incoming news in a way that lets us change our beliefs, and above all our *actions*, as little as possible. John Kenneth Galbraith said: "Faced with the choice of changing one's mind and proving that there is no need to do so, almost everyone gets busy on the proof."[3] And the greater the *inconvenience* of changing one's mind, the more effort people will expend on the proof.

But y'know, if you're gonna *do* the same thing anyway, there's no point in going to such incredible lengths to rationalize it. Often I have witnessed people encountering new information, apparently accepting it, and then carefully explaining why they are going to do exactly the same thing they planned to do previously, but with a different justification. The point of thinking is to *shape* our plans; if you're going to keep the same plans anyway, why bother going

---

[1] Charles S. Taber and Milton Lodge, "Motivated Skepticism in the Evaluation of Political Beliefs," *American Journal of Political Science* 50, no. 3 (2006): 755–769, doi:10.1111/j.1540-5907.2006.00214.x.

[2] Daniel Clement Dennett, *Breaking the spell: Religion as a natural phenomenon*, vol. 14 (Penguin, 2006).

[3] John Kenneth Galbraith, *Economics, Peace and Laughter* (Plume, 1981), 50.

to all that work to justify it? When you encounter new information, the hard part is to *update*, to *react*, rather than just letting the information disappear down a black hole. And humility, properly misunderstood, makes a wonderful black hole—all you have to do is admit you could be wrong. Therefore it is written: "To be humble is to take specific actions in anticipation of your own errors. To confess your fallibility and then do nothing about it is not humble; it is boasting of your modesty."

3

Tsuyoku vs. the Egalitarian Instinct

Hunter-gatherer tribes are usually highly egalitarian (at least if you're male)—the all-powerful tribal chieftain is found mostly in agricultural societies, rarely in the ancestral environment. Among most hunter-gatherer tribes, a hunter who brings in a spectacular kill will carefully downplay the accomplishment to avoid envy.

Maybe, if you start out below average, you can improve yourself without daring to pull ahead of the crowd. But sooner or later, if you aim to do the best you can, you will set your aim above the average.

If you can't admit to yourself that you've done better than others—or if you're ashamed of wanting to do better than others—then the median will forever be your concrete wall, the place where you stop moving forward. And what about people who are below average? Do you dare say you intend to do better than them? How prideful of you!

Maybe it's not healthy to pride yourself on doing better than someone else. Personally I've found it to be a useful motivator, despite my principles, and I'll take all the useful motivation I can get. Maybe that kind of competition is a zero-sum game, but then so is Go; it doesn't mean we should abolish that human activity, if people find it fun and it leads somewhere interesting.

But in any case, surely it isn't healthy to be *ashamed* of doing better.

And besides, life is not graded on a curve. The will to transcendence has no point beyond which it ceases and becomes the will to do worse; and the race that has no finish line also has no gold or silver medals. Just run as fast as you can, without worrying that you might pull ahead of other runners. (But be warned: If you refuse to worry about that possibility, someday you may pull ahead. If you ignore the consequences, they may happen to you.)

Sooner or later, if your path leads true, you will set out to mitigate a flaw that most people have not mitigated. Sooner or later, if your efforts bring forth any fruit, you will find yourself with fewer sins to confess.

Perhaps you will find it the course of wisdom to downplay the accomplishment, even if you succeed. People may forgive a touchdown, but not dancing in the end zone. You will certainly find it quicker, easier, more convenient to publicly disclaim your worthiness, to pretend that you are just as much a sinner as everyone else. Just so long, of course, as everyone knows it isn't true. It can be fun to proudly display your modesty, so long as everyone knows how very much you have to be modest about.

But do not let that be the endpoint of your journeys. Even if you only whisper it to yourself, whisper it still: *Tsuyoku, tsuyoku!* Stronger, stronger!

And then set yourself a higher target. That's the true meaning of the realization that you are still flawed (though a little less so). It means always reaching higher, without shame.

Tsuyoku naritai! I'll always run as fast as I can, even if I pull ahead, I'll keep on running; and someone, someday, will surpass me; but even though I fall behind, I'll always run as fast as I can.

4

The Third Alternative

"Believing in Santa Claus gives children a sense of wonder and encourages them to behave well in hope of receiving presents. If Santa-belief is destroyed by truth, the children will lose their sense of wonder and stop behaving nicely. Therefore, even though Santa-belief is false-to-fact, it is a Noble Lie whose net benefit should be preserved for utilitarian reasons."

Classically, this is known as a false dilemma, the fallacy of the excluded middle, or the package-deal fallacy. Even if we accept the underlying factual and moral premises of the above argument, it does not carry through. Even supposing that the Santa policy (encourage children to believe in Santa Claus) is better than the null policy (do nothing), it does not follow that Santa-ism is the *best of all possible alternatives.* Other policies could also supply children with a sense of wonder, such as taking them to watch a Space Shuttle launch or supplying them with science fiction novels.[1]

Noble Lies are generally package-deal fallacies; and the response to a package-deal fallacy is that if we really need the supposed gain, we can construct a Third Alternative for getting it.

---

[1] Likewise (if I recall correctly), offering children bribes for good behavior encourages the children to behave well *only* when adults are watching, while praise without bribes leads to unconditional good behavior.

13

How can we obtain Third Alternatives? The first step in obtaining a Third Alternative is deciding to look for one, and the last step is the decision to accept it. This sounds obvious, and yet most people fail on these two steps, rather than within the search process.

Some false dilemmas arise honestly, because superior alternatives are cognitively hard to see. But one factory for false dilemmas is justifying a questionable policy by pointing to a supposed benefit over the null action. In this case, the justifier *does not want* a Third Alternative; finding a Third Alternative would destroy the justification. The last thing a Santa-ist wants to hear is that praise works better than bribes, or that spaceships can be as inspiring as flying reindeer.

The best is the enemy of the good. If the goal is *really* to help people, then a superior alternative is cause for celebration—once we find this better strategy, we can help people more effectively. But if the goal is to justify a particular strategy *by claiming that it helps people*, a Third Alternative is an enemy argument, a competitor.

Modern cognitive psychology views decision-making as a search for alternatives. In real life, it's not enough to compare options; you have to generate the options in the first place. On many problems, the number of alternatives is huge, so you need a stopping criterion for the search. When you're looking to buy a house, you can't compare every house in the city; at some point you have to stop looking and decide.

But what about when our conscious motives for the search—the criteria we can admit to ourselves—don't square with subconscious influences? When we are carrying out an allegedly altruistic search, a search for an altruistic policy, and we find a strategy that benefits others but disadvantages ourselves— well, we don't stop looking *there*; we go on looking. Telling ourselves that we're looking for a strategy that brings greater altruistic benefit, of course. But suppose we find a policy that has some defensible benefit, and *also* just happens to be personally convenient? Then we stop the search at once! In fact, we'll probably *resist* any suggestion that we start looking again—pleading lack of time, perhaps. (And yet somehow, we always have cognitive resources for coming up with justifications for our current policy.)

14

Beware when you find yourself arguing that a policy is *defensible* rather than *optimal*; or that it has some benefit compared to the null action, rather than the best benefit of any action.

False dilemmas are often presented to justify unethical policies that are, by some vast coincidence, very convenient. Lying, for example, is often much more convenient than telling the truth; and believing whatever you started out with is more convenient than updating. Hence the popularity of arguments for Noble Lies; it serves as a defense of a pre-existing belief—one does not find Noble Liars who calculate an optimal new Noble Lie; they keep whatever lie they started with. Better stop that search fast!

To do better, ask yourself straight out: *If I saw that there was a superior alternative to my current policy, would I be glad in the depths of my heart, or would I feel a tiny flash of reluctance before I let go?* If the answers are "no" and "yes," beware that you may not have searched for a Third Alternative.

Which leads into another good question to ask yourself straight out: *Did I spend five minutes with my eyes closed, brainstorming wild and creative options, trying to think of a better alternative?* It has to be five minutes by the clock, because otherwise you blink—close your eyes and open them again—and say, "Why, yes, I searched for alternatives, but there weren't any." Blinking makes a good black hole down which to dump your duties. An actual, physical clock is recommended.

And those wild and creative options—were you careful not to think of a good one? Was there a secret effort from the corner of your mind to ensure that every option considered would be obviously bad?

It's amazing how many Noble Liars and their ilk are eager to embrace ethical violations—with all due bewailing of their agonies of conscience—when they haven't spent even five minutes by the clock looking for an alternative. There are some mental searches that we secretly wish would fail; and when the prospect of success is uncomfortable, people take the earliest possible excuse to give up.

5

Lotteries: A Waste of Hope

The classic criticism of the lottery is that the people who play are the ones who can least afford to lose; that the lottery is a sink of money, draining wealth from those who most need it. Some lottery advocates, and even some commentors on *Overcoming Bias*, have tried to defend lottery-ticket buying as a *rational purchase of fantasy*—paying a dollar for a day's worth of pleasant anticipation, imagining yourself as a millionaire.

But consider exactly what this implies. It would mean that you're occupying your valuable brain with a fantasy whose real probability is nearly zero—a tiny line of likelihood which you, yourself, can do nothing to realize. The lottery balls will decide your future. The fantasy is of wealth that arrives without effort—without conscientiousness, learning, charisma, or even patience.[1]

Which makes the lottery another kind of sink: a sink of emotional energy. It encourages people to invest their dreams, their hopes for a better future, into an infinitesimal probability. If not for the lottery, maybe they would fantasize about going to technical school, or opening their own business, or getting a promotion at work—things they might be able to actually *do*, hopes that would make them want to become stronger. Their dreaming brains might, in the

---

[1] Compare Po Bronson's "How Not to Talk to Your Kids," http://nymag.com/news/features/27840/.

16

20th visualization of the pleasant fantasy, notice a way to really do it. Isn't that what dreams and brains are *for*? But how can such reality-limited fare compete with the artificially sweetened prospect of instant wealth—not after herding a dot-com startup through to IPO, but on Tuesday?

Seriously, why can't we just say that buying lottery tickets is stupid? Human beings *are* stupid, from time to time—it shouldn't be so surprising a hypothesis.

Unsurprisingly, the human brain doesn't do 64-bit floating-point arithmetic, and it can't devalue the emotional force of a pleasant anticipation by a factor of 0.00000001 without dropping the line of reasoning entirely. Unsurprisingly, many people don't realize that a numerical calculation of expected utility ought to *override* or *replace* their imprecise financial instincts, and instead treat the calculation as merely one *argument* to be balanced against their pleasant anticipations—an emotionally weak argument, since it's made up of mere squiggles on paper, instead of visions of fabulous wealth.

This seems sufficient to explain the popularity of lotteries. Why do so many arguers feel impelled to defend this classic form of self-destruction?[2]

The process of overcoming bias requires (1) first noticing the bias, (2) analyzing the bias in detail, (3) deciding that the bias is bad, (4) figuring out a workaround, and then (5) implementing it. It's unfortunate how many people get through steps 1 and 2 and then bog down in step 3, which by rights should be the easiest of the five. Biases are lemons, not lemonade, and we shouldn't try to make lemonade out of them—just burn those lemons *down*.

---

[2] See "Debiasing as Non-Self-Destruction," http://lesswrong.com/lw/hf/debiasing_as_nonselfdestruction/.

6

New Improved Lottery

People are still suggesting that the lottery is not a waste of hope, but a service which enables purchase of fantasy—"daydreaming about becoming a millionaire for much less money than daydreaming about hollywood stars in movies."[1] One commenter wrote: "There is a big difference between zero chance of becoming wealthy, and epsilon. Buying a ticket allows your dream of riches to bridge that gap."

Actually, one of the points I was trying to make is that between zero chance of becoming wealthy, and epsilon chance, there is an order-of-epsilon difference. If you doubt this, let epsilon equal one over googolplex.

Anyway, if we pretend that the lottery sells epsilon hope, this suggests a design for a New Improved Lottery. The New Improved Lottery pays out every five years on average, at a random time—determined, say, by the decay of a not-very-radioactive element. You buy in once, for a single dollar, and get not just a few days of epsilon chance of becoming rich, but a few *years* of epsilon. Not only that, your wealth could strike at any time! At *any minute*, the phone could ring to inform you that *you, yes, you* are a millionaire!

---

[1] See "The Future of Fantasy," http://www.economist.com/blogs/freeexchange/2007/04/the_future_of_fantasy. For the comment I'm responding to, see http://lesswrong.com/lw/hl/lotteries_a_waste_of_hope/e1u.

Think of how much better this would be than an ordinary lottery drawing, which only takes place at defined times, a few times per week. Let's say the boss comes in and demands you rework a proposal, or restock inventory, or something similarly annoying. Instead of getting to work, you could turn to the phone and stare, hoping for that call—because there would be epsilon chance that, *at that exact moment, you yes you* would be awarded the Grand Prize! And even if it doesn't happen *this* minute, why, there's no need to be disappointed—it might happen the *next* minute!

Think of how many more fantasies this New Improved Lottery would enable. You could shop at the store, adding expensive items to your shopping cart—if your cellphone doesn't ring with news of a lottery win, you could always put the items back, right?

Maybe the New Improved Lottery could even show a constantly fluctuating probability distribution over the likelihood of a win occurring, and the likelihood of particular numbers being selected, with the overall expectation working out to the aforesaid Poisson distribution. Think of how much fun *that* would be! Oh, goodness, right this minute the chance of a win occurring is nearly ten times higher than usual! And look, the number 42 that I selected for the Mega Ball has nearly twice the usual chance of winning! You could feed it to a display on people's cellphones, so they could just flip open the cellphone and see their chances of winning. Think of how exciting *that* would be! Much more exciting than trying to balance your checkbook! Much more exciting than doing your homework! This new dream would be so much tastier that it would compete with, not only hopes of going to technical school, but even hopes of getting home from work early. People could just stay glued to the screen all day long, why, they wouldn't need to dream about anything *else*!

Yep, offering people tempting daydreams *that will not actually happen* sure is a valuable service, all right. People are willing to pay; it must be valuable. The alternative is that consumers are making mistakes, and we all know that can't happen.

And yet current governments, with their vile monopoly on lotteries, don't offer this simple and obvious service. Why? Because they want to overcharge people. They want them to spend money every week. They want them to spend a hundred dollars for the thrill of believing their chance of winning is a hundred times as large, instead of being able to stare at a cellphone screen waiting for the likelihood to spike. So if you believe that the lottery is a service, it is clearly an enormously overpriced service—charged to the poorest members of society—and it is your solemn duty as a citizen to demand the New Improved Lottery instead.

7

But There's Still a Chance, Right?

Years ago, I was speaking to someone when he casually remarked that he didn't believe in evolution. And I said, "This is not the nineteenth century. When Darwin first proposed evolution, it might have been reasonable to doubt it. But this is the twenty-first century. We can *read the genes.* Humans and chimpanzees have 98% shared DNA. We *know* humans and chimps are related. It's *over.*"

He said, "Maybe the DNA is just similar by coincidence."

I said, "The odds of that are something like two to the power of seven hundred and fifty million to one."

He said, "But there's still a chance, right?"

Now, there's a number of reasons my past self cannot claim a strict moral victory in this conversation. One reason is that I have no memory of whence I pulled that $2^{750,000,000}$ figure, though it's probably the right meta-order of magnitude. The other reason is that my past self didn't apply the concept of a calibrated confidence. Of all the times over the history of humanity that a human being has calculated odds of $2^{750,000,000}$:1 against something, they have undoubtedly been wrong more often than once in $2^{750,000,000}$ times. E.g. the shared genes estimate was revised to 95%, not 98%—and that may even apply only to the 30,000 known genes and not the entire genome, in which case it's the wrong meta-order of magnitude.

But I think the other guy's reply is still pretty funny.

I don't recall what I said in further response—probably something like "*No*"—but I remember this occasion because it brought me several insights into the laws of thought as seen by the unenlightened ones.

It first occurred to me that human intuitions were making a qualitative distinction between "No chance" and "A very tiny chance, but worth keeping track of." You can see this in the *Overcoming Bias* lottery debate.

The problem is that probability theory sometimes lets us calculate a chance which is, indeed, too tiny to be worth the mental space to keep track of it—but by that time, you've already calculated it. People mix up the map with the territory, so that on a gut level, tracking a symbolically described probability feels like "a chance worth keeping track of," even if the *referent* of the symbolic description is a number so tiny that if it were a dust speck, you couldn't see it. We can use words to describe numbers that small, but not feelings—a feeling that small doesn't exist, doesn't fire enough neurons or release enough neurotransmitters to be felt. This is why people buy lottery tickets—no one can *feel* the smallness of a probability that small.

But what I found even more fascinating was the qualitative distinction between "certain" and "uncertain" arguments, where if an argument is not certain, you're allowed to ignore it. Like, if the likelihood is zero, then you have to give up the belief, but if the likelihood is one over googol, you're allowed to keep it.

Now it's a free country and no one should put you in jail for illegal reasoning, but if you're going to ignore an argument that says the likelihood is one over googol, why not also ignore an argument that says the likelihood is zero? I mean, as long as you're ignoring the evidence anyway, why is it so much worse to ignore certain evidence than uncertain evidence?

I have often found, in life, that I have learned from other people's nicely blatant bad examples, duly generalized to more subtle cases. In this case, the flip lesson is that, if you can't ignore a likelihood of one over googol because you want to, you can't ignore a likelihood of 0.9 because you want to. It's all the same slippery cliff.

Consider his example if you ever you find yourself thinking, "But you can't *prove* me wrong." If you're going to ignore a probabilistic counterargument, why not ignore a proof, too?

8

The Fallacy of Gray

The Sophisticate: "The world isn't black and white. No one does pure good or pure bad. It's all gray. Therefore, no one is better than anyone else."

The Zetet: "Knowing only gray, you conclude that all grays are the same shade. You mock the simplicity of the two-color view, yet you replace it with a one-color view . . ."

—Marc Stiegler, *David's Sling*

I don't know if the Sophisticate's mistake has an official name, but I call it the Fallacy of Gray. We saw it manifested in the previous essay—the one who believed that odds of two to the power of seven hundred and fifty millon to one, against, meant "there was still a chance." All probabilities, to him, were simply "uncertain" and that meant he was licensed to ignore them if he pleased.

"The Moon is made of green cheese" and "the Sun is made of mostly hydrogen and helium" are both uncertainties, but they are not the same uncertainty.

Everything is shades of gray, but there are shades of gray so light as to be very nearly white, and shades of gray so dark as to be very nearly black. Or even if not, we can still compare shades, and say "it is darker" or "it is lighter."

Years ago, one of the strange little formative moments in my career as a rationalist was reading this paragraph from *Player of Games* by Iain M. Banks, especially the sentence in bold:

> A guilty system recognizes no innocents. As with any power apparatus which thinks everybody's either for it or against it, we're against it. You would be too, if you thought about it. The very way you think places you amongst its enemies. This might not be your fault, because **every society imposes some of its values on those raised within it, but the point is that some societies try to maximize that effect, and some try to minimize it**. You come from one of the latter and you're being asked to explain yourself to one of the former. Prevarication will be more difficult than you might imagine; neutrality is probably impossible. You cannot choose not to have the politics you do; they are not some separate set of entities somehow detachable from the rest of your being; they are a function of your existence. I know that and they know that; you had better accept it.

Now, don't write angry comments saying that, if societies impose fewer of their values, then each succeeding generation has more work to start over from scratch. That's not what I got out of the paragraph.

What I got out of the paragraph was something which seems so obvious in retrospect that I could have conceivably picked it up in a hundred places; but something about that one paragraph made it click for me.

It was the whole notion of the Quantitative Way applied to life-problems like moral judgments and the quest for personal self-improvement. That, even if you couldn't switch something from on to off, you could still tend to increase it or decrease it.

Is this too obvious to be worth mentioning? I say it is not too obvious, for many bloggers have said of *Overcoming Bias*: "It is impossible, no one can completely eliminate bias." I don't care if the one is a professional economist, it is clear that they have not yet grokked the Quantitative Way as it applies to everyday life and matters like personal self-improvement. That which I cannot *eliminate* may be well worth *reducing*.

Or consider an exchange between Robin Hanson and Tyler Cowen.[1] Robin Hanson said that he preferred to put at least 75% weight on the prescriptions of economic theory versus his intuitions: "I try to mostly just straightforwardly apply economic theory, adding little personal or cultural judgment." Tyler Cowen replied:

> In my view there is no such thing as "straightforwardly applying economic theory" . . . theories are always applied through our personal and cultural filters and there is no other way it can be.

Yes, but you can try to minimize that effect, or you can do things that are bound to increase it. And *if* you try to minimize it, then in many cases I don't think it's unreasonable to call the output "straightforward"—even in economics.

"Everyone is imperfect." Mohandas Gandhi was imperfect and Joseph Stalin was imperfect, but they were not the same shade of imperfection. "Everyone is imperfect" is an excellent example of replacing a two-color view with a one-color view. If you say, "No one is perfect, but *some people are less imperfect than others*," you may not gain applause; but for those who strive to do better, you have held out hope. No one is *perfectly* imperfect, after all.

(Whenever someone says to me, "Perfectionism is bad for you," I reply: "I think it's okay to be imperfect, but not so imperfect that other people notice.")

Likewise the folly of those who say, "Every scientific paradigm imposes some of its assumptions on how it interprets experiments," and then act like they'd proven science to occupy the same level with witchdoctoring. Every worldview imposes some of its structure on its observations, but the point is that there are worldviews which try to minimize that imposition, and worldviews which glory in it. There is no white, but there are shades of gray that are far lighter than others, and it is folly to treat them as if they were all on the same level.

If the Moon has orbited the Earth these past few billion years, if you have seen it in the sky these last years, and you expect to see it in its appointed place and phase tomorrow, then that is not a certainty. And if you expect an invisible

---

[1] Hanson's "Economist Judgment" (http://www.overcomingbias.com/2007/12/economist-judgm.html) and Cowen's "Can Theory Override Intuition?" (http://marginalrevolution.com/marginalrevolution/2007/12/how-my-views-di.html).

26

dragon to heal your daughter of cancer, that too is not a certainty. But they are rather different degrees of uncertainty—this business of expecting things to happen yet again in the same way you have previously predicted to twelve decimal places, versus expecting something to happen that *violates* the order previously observed. Calling them both "faith" seems a little too un-narrow.

It's a most peculiar psychology—this business of "Science is based on faith too, so there!" Typically this is said by people who claim that faith is a *good* thing. Then why do they say "Science is based on faith too!" in that angry-triumphal tone, rather than as a compliment? And a rather *dangerous* compliment to give, one would think, from their perspective. If science is based on "faith," then science is of the same kind as religion—directly comparable. If science is a religion, it is the religion that heals the sick and reveals the secrets of the stars. It would make sense to say, "The priests of science can blatantly, publicly, verifiably walk on the Moon as a faith-based miracle, and your priests' faith can't do the same." Are you sure you wish to go there, oh faithist? Perhaps, on further reflection, you would prefer to retract this whole business of "Science is a religion too!"

There's a strange dynamic here: You try to purify your shade of gray, and you get it to a point where it's pretty light-toned, and someone stands up and says in a deeply offended tone, "But it's not white! It's gray!" It's one thing when someone says, "This isn't as light as you think, because of specific problems X, Y, and Z." It's a different matter when someone says angrily "It's not white! It's gray!" without pointing out any specific dark spots.

In this case, I begin to suspect psychology that is more imperfect than usual—that someone may have made a devil's bargain with their own mistakes, and now refuses to hear of any possibility of improvement. When someone finds an excuse not to try to do better, they often refuse to concede that anyone else *can* try to do better, and every mode of improvement is thereafter their enemy, and every claim that it is possible to move forward is an offense against them. And so they say in one breath proudly, "I'm glad to be gray," and in the next breath angrily, "And *you're gray too!*"

If there is no black and white, there is yet lighter and darker, and not all grays are the same.

27

The commenter G2 points us to Asimov's "The Relativity of Wrong":

> When people thought the earth was flat, they were wrong. When people thought the earth was spherical, they were wrong. But if you think that thinking the earth is spherical is just as wrong as thinking the earth is flat, then your view is wronger than both of them put together.

9

Absolute Authority

The one comes to you and loftily says: "Science doesn't really *know* anything. All you have are *theories*—you can't know for *certain* that you're right. You scientists changed your minds about how gravity works—who's to say that tomorrow you won't change your minds about evolution?"

Behold the abyssal cultural gap. If you think you can cross it in a few sentences, you are bound to be sorely disappointed.

In the world of the unenlightened ones, there is authority and un-authority. What can be trusted, can be trusted; what cannot be trusted, you may as well throw away. There are good sources of information and bad sources of information. If scientists have changed their stories ever in their history, then science cannot be a true Authority, and can never again be trusted—like a witness caught in a contradiction, or like an employee found stealing from the till.

Plus, the one takes for granted that a proponent of an idea is expected to defend it against every possible counterargument and confess nothing. All claims are discounted accordingly. If even the *proponent* of science admits that science is less than perfect, why, it must be pretty much worthless.

When someone has lived their life accustomed to certainty, you can't just say to them, "Science is probabilistic, just like all other knowledge." They will accept the first half of the statement as a confession of guilt; and dismiss the second half as a flailing attempt to accuse everyone else to avoid judgment.

You have admitted you are not trustworthy—so begone, Science, and trouble us no more!

One obvious source for this pattern of thought is religion, where the scriptures are alleged to come from God; therefore to confess any flaw in them would destroy their authority utterly; so any trace of doubt is a sin, and claiming certainty is *mandatory* whether you're certain or not.[1]

But I suspect that the traditional school regimen also has something to do with it. The teacher tells you certain things, and you have to believe them, and you have to recite them back on the test. But when a student makes a suggestion in class, you don't have to go along with it—you're free to agree or disagree (it seems) and no one will punish you.

This experience, I fear, maps the domain of belief onto the social domains of *authority*, of *command*, of *law*. In the social domain, there is a qualitative difference between absolute laws and nonabsolute laws, between commands and suggestions, between authorities and unauthorities. There seems to be strict knowledge and unstrict knowledge, like a strict regulation and an unstrict regulation. Strict authorities must be yielded to, while unstrict suggestions can be obeyed or discarded as a matter of personal preference. And Science, since it confesses itself to have a possibility of error, must belong in the second class.

(I note in passing that I see a certain similarity to they who think that if you don't get an Authoritative probability written on a piece of paper from the teacher in class, or handed down from some similar Unarguable Source, then your uncertainty is not a matter for Bayesian probability theory.[2] Someone might—*gasp!*—argue with your estimate of the prior probability. It thus seems to the not-fully-enlightened ones that Bayesian priors belong to the class of beliefs proposed by students, and not the class of beliefs commanded you by teachers—it is not proper *knowledge*.)

---

[1] See "Professing and Cheering," collected in *Map and Territory* and available at https://intelligence.org/rationality-ai-zombies/.
[2] See "Focus Your Uncertainty" in *Map and Territory*.

The abyssal cultural gap between the Authoritative Way and the Quantitative Way is rather annoying to those of us staring across it from the rationalist side. Here is someone who believes they have knowledge *more* reliable than science's mere probabilistic guesses—such as the guess that the Moon will rise in its appointed place and phase tomorrow, just like it has every observed night since the invention of astronomical record-keeping, and just as predicted by physical theories whose previous predictions have been successfully confirmed to fourteen decimal places. And what is this knowledge that the unenlightened ones set above ours, and why? It's probably some musty old scroll that has been contradicted eleventeen ways from Sunday, and from Monday, and from every day of the week. Yet this is more reliable than Science (they say) because it never admits to error, never changes its mind, no matter how often it is contradicted. They toss around the word "certainty" like a tennis ball, using it as lightly as a feather—while scientists are weighed down by dutiful doubt, struggling to achieve even a modicum of probability. "I'm perfect," they say without a care in the world, "I must be so far above *you*, who must still struggle to improve yourselves."

There is nothing simple you can say to them—no *fast* crushing rebuttal. By thinking carefully, you may be able to win over the audience, if this is a public debate. Unfortunately you cannot just blurt out, "Foolish mortal, the Quantitative Way is beyond your comprehension, and the beliefs you lightly name 'certain' are less assured than the least of our mighty hypotheses." It's a difference of *life-gestalt* that isn't easy to describe in words at all, let alone quickly.

What might you try, rhetorically, in front of an audience? Hard to say . . . maybe:

- "The power of science comes from having the ability to change our minds and admit we're wrong. If you've never admitted you're wrong, it doesn't mean you've made fewer mistakes."

- "Anyone can *say* they're absolutely certain. It's a bit harder to never, ever make any mistakes. Scientists understand the difference, so they don't say they're absolutely certain. That's all. It doesn't mean that they have any specific reason to doubt a theory—absolutely every scrap of evidence can be going the same way, all the stars and planets lined up like dominos in support of a single hypothesis, and the scientists still won't say they're absolutely sure, because they've just got higher standards. It doesn't mean scientists are less *entitled* to certainty than, say, the politicians who always seem so sure of everything."

- "Scientists don't use the phrase 'not absolutely certain' the way you're used to from regular conversation. I mean, suppose you went to the doctor, and got a blood test, and the doctor came back and said, 'We ran some tests, and it's not absolutely certain that you're not made out of cheese, and there's a non-zero chance that twenty fairies made out of sentient chocolate are singing the "I love you" song from Barney inside your lower intestine.' Run for the hills, your doctor needs a doctor. When a scientist says the same thing, it means that they think the probability is so tiny that you couldn't see it with an electron microscope, but the scientist is willing to see the evidence in the extremely unlikely event that you have it."

- "Would you be willing to change your mind about the things you call 'certain' if you saw enough evidence? I mean, suppose that God himself descended from the clouds and told you that your whole religion was true except for the Virgin Birth. If that would change your mind, you can't say you're absolutely certain of the Virgin Birth. For technical reasons of probability theory, if it's theoretically possible for you to change your mind about something, it can't have a probability exactly equal to one. The uncertainty might be smaller than a dust speck, but it has to be there. And if you wouldn't change your mind even if God told you otherwise, then you have a problem with refusing to admit you're wrong that transcends anything a mortal like me can say to you, I guess."

But, in a way, the more interesting question is what you say to someone *not* in front of an audience. How do you begin the long process of teaching someone to live in a universe without certainty?

32

I think the first, beginning step should be understanding that you *can* live without certainty—that *if*, *hypothetically speaking*, you couldn't be certain of anything, it would not deprive you of the ability to make moral or factual distinctions. To paraphrase Lois Bujold, "Don't push harder, lower the resistance."

One of the common *defenses* of Absolute Authority is something I call "The Argument from the Argument from Gray," which runs like this:

- *Moral relativists say*:

    - The world isn't black and white, therefore:

    - Everything is gray, therefore:

    - No one is better than anyone else, therefore:

    - I can do whatever I want and you can't stop me bwahahaha.

- But we've got to be able to stop people from committing murder.

- Therefore there has to be some way of being absolutely certain, or the moral relativists win.

Reversed stupidity is not intelligence. You can't arrive at a correct answer by reversing *every single* line of an argument that ends with a bad conclusion—it gives the fool too much detailed control over you. Every single line must be correct for a mathematical argument to carry. And it doesn't follow, from the fact that moral relativists say "The world isn't black and white," that this is false, any more than it follows, from Stalin's belief that $2 + 2 = 4$, that "$2 + 2 = 4$" is false. The error (and it only takes one) is in the leap from the two-color view to the single-color view, that all grays are the same shade.

It would concede far too much (indeed, concede the whole argument) to agree with the premise that you need absolute knowledge of absolutely good options and absolutely evil options in order to be moral. You can have uncertain knowledge of relatively better and relatively worse options, and still choose. It should be routine, in fact, not something to get all dramatic about.

I mean, yes, if you have to choose between two alternatives A and B, and you somehow succeed in establishing knowably certain well-calibrated 100%

confidence that A is absolutely and entirely desirable and that B is the sum of everything evil and disgusting, then this is a *sufficient* condition for choosing A over B. It is not a *necessary* condition.

Oh, and: Logical fallacy: Appeal to consequences of belief.

Let's see, what else do they need to know? Well, there's the entire rationalist culture which says that doubt, questioning, and confession of error are not terrible shameful things.

There's the whole notion of gaining information by *looking at things*, rather than being proselytized. When you look at things harder, sometimes you find out that they're different from what you thought they were at first glance; but it doesn't mean that Nature lied to you, or that you should give up on seeing.

Then there's the concept of a calibrated confidence—that "probability" isn't the same concept as the little progress bar in your head that measures your emotional commitment to an idea. It's more like a measure of how often, pragmatically, in real life, people in a certain state of belief say things that are actually true. If you take one hundred people and ask them each to make a statement of which they are "absolutely certain," how many of these statements will be correct? Not one hundred.

If anything, the statements that people are really fanatic about are *far less* likely to be correct than statements like "the Sun is larger than the Moon" that seem too obvious to get excited about. For every statement you can find of which someone is "absolutely certain," you can probably find someone "absolutely certain" of its opposite, because such fanatic professions of belief do not arise in the absence of opposition. So the little progress bar in people's heads that measures their emotional commitment to a belief does not translate well into a calibrated confidence—it doesn't even behave monotonically.

As for "absolute certainty"—well, if you say that something is 99.9999% probable, it means you think you could make *one million* equally strong independent statements, *one after the other*, over the course of a solid year or so, and be wrong, on average, around once. This is incredible enough. (It's amazing to realize we can actually *get* that level of confidence for "Thou shalt not win the lottery.") So let us say nothing of probability 1.0. Once you realize you don't *need* probabilities of 1.0 to get along in life, you'll realize how abso-

34

lutely ridiculous it is to think you could ever get to 1.0 with a human brain. A probability of 1.0 isn't just certainty, it's *infinite certainty*.

In fact, it seems to me that to prevent public misunderstanding, maybe scientists should go around saying "We are not INFINITELY certain" rather than "We are not certain." For the latter case, in ordinary discourse, suggests you know some specific reason for doubt.

10

How to Convince Me That 2 + 2 = 3

In "What is Evidence?" I wrote:[1]

> This is why rationalists put such a heavy premium on the paradoxical-seeming claim that a belief is only really *worthwhile* if you could, in principle, be persuaded to believe otherwise. If your retina ended up in the same state regardless of what light entered it, you would be blind . . . Hence the phrase, "blind faith." If what you believe doesn't depend on what you see, you've been blinded as effectively as by poking out your eyeballs.

Cihan Baran replied:[2]

> I can not conceive of a situation that would make 2 + 2 = 4 false. Perhaps for that reason, my belief in 2 + 2 = 4 is unconditional.

I admit, I cannot conceive of a "situation" that would *make* 2 + 2 = 4 false. (There are redefinitions, but those are not "situations," and then you're no longer

---

[1] See *Map and Territory*.
[2] Comment: http://lesswrong.com/lw/jl/what_is_evidence/f7h

talking about 2, 4, =, or +.) But that doesn't make my belief unconditional. I find it quite easy to imagine a situation which would *convince* me that 2 + 2 = 3.

Suppose I got up one morning, and took out two earplugs, and set them down next to two other earplugs on my nighttable, and noticed that there were now three earplugs, without any earplugs having appeared or disappeared—in contrast to my stored memory that 2 + 2 was supposed to equal 4. Moreover, when I visualized the process in my own mind, it seemed that making xx and xx come out to xxxx required an extra x to appear from nowhere, and was, moreover, inconsistent with other arithmetic I visualized, since subtracting xx from xxx left xx, but subtracting xx from xxxx left xxx. This would conflict with my stored memory that 3 − 2 = 1, but memory would be absurd in the face of physical and mental confirmation that xxx − xx = xx.

I would also check a pocket calculator, Google, and perhaps my copy of 1984 where Winston writes that "Freedom is the freedom to say two plus two equals three." All of these would naturally show that the rest of the world agreed with my current visualization, and disagreed with my memory, that 2 + 2 = 3.

How could I possibly have ever been so deluded as to believe that 2 + 2 = 4? Two explanations would come to mind: First, a neurological fault (possibly caused by a sneeze) had made all the additive sums in my stored memory go up by one. Second, someone was messing with me, by hypnosis or by my being a computer simulation. In the second case, I would think it more likely that they had messed with my arithmetic *recall* than that 2 + 2 *actually* equalled 4. Neither of these plausible-sounding explanations would prevent me from noticing that I was very, very, *very* confused.[3]

What would convince me that 2 + 2 = 3, in other words, is exactly the same kind of evidence that currently convinces me that 2 + 2 = 4: The evidential crossfire of physical observation, mental visualization, and social agreement.

There was a time when I had no idea that 2 + 2 = 4. I did not arrive at this *new* belief by random processes—then there would have been no particular reason for my brain to end up storing "2 + 2 = 4" instead of "2 + 2 = 7." The fact that my brain stores an answer surprisingly similar to what happens when

---

[3] See "Your Strength as a Rationalist" in *Map and Territory*.

I lay down two earplugs alongside two earplugs, calls forth an explanation of what entanglement produces this strange mirroring of mind and reality.

There's really only two possibilities, for a belief of fact—either the belief got there via a mind-reality entangling process, or not. If not, the belief can't be correct except by coincidence. For beliefs with the slightest shred of internal complexity (requiring a computer program of more than 10 bits to simulate), the space of possibilities is large enough that coincidence vanishes.[4]

Unconditional facts are not the same as unconditional beliefs. If entangled evidence convinces me that a fact is unconditional, this doesn't mean I always believed in the fact without need of entangled evidence.

I believe that 2 + 2 = 4, and I find it quite easy to conceive of a situation which would convince me that 2 + 2 = 3. Namely, the same sort of situation that currently convinces me that 2 + 2 = 4. Thus I do not fear that I am a victim of blind faith.[5]

---

[4] For more on belief formation and beliefs of fact, see "Feeling Rational" and "What Is Evidence?" in *Map and Territory*. For more on belief complexity, see "Occam's Razor" in the same volume.

[5] If there are any Christians reading this who know Bayes's Theorem, might I inquire of you what situation would convince you of the truth of Islam? Presumably it would be the same sort of situation causally responsible for producing your current belief in Christianity: We would push you screaming out of the uterus of a Muslim woman, and have you raised by Muslim parents who continually told you that it is good to believe unconditionally in Islam.

Or is there more to it than that? If so, what situation would convince you of Islam, or at least, non-Christianity? And how confident are you that the general kinds of evidence and reasoning you appeal to would have been enough to dissuade you of your religion if you had been raised a Muslim?

11

Infinite Certainty

In "Absolute Authority," I argued that you don't *need* infinite certainty:

> If you have to choose between two alternatives A and B, and you somehow succeed in establishing knowably certain well-calibrated 100% confidence that A is absolutely and entirely desirable and that B is the sum of everything evil and disgusting, then this is a *sufficient* condition for choosing A over B. It is not a *necessary* condition . . . You can have uncertain knowledge of relatively better and relatively worse options, and still choose. It should be routine, in fact.

Concerning the proposition that $2 + 2 = 4$, we must distinguish between the map and the territory. Given the seeming absolute stability and universality of physical laws, it's possible that never, in the whole history of the universe, has any particle exceeded the local lightspeed limit. That is, the lightspeed limit may be not just true 99% of the time, or 99.9999% of the time, or $(1 - 1/\text{googolplex})$ of the time, but simply *always and absolutely true*.

But whether we can ever have *absolute confidence* in the lightspeed limit is a whole 'nother question. The map is not the territory.

It may be entirely and wholly true that a student plagiarized their assignment, but whether you have any knowledge of this fact at all—let alone *absolute* confidence in the belief—is a separate issue. If you flip a coin and then don't look at it, it may be completely true that the coin is showing heads, and you may be completely unsure of whether the coin is showing heads or tails. A degree of uncertainty is not the same as a degree of truth or a frequency of occurrence.

The same holds for mathematical truths. It's questionable whether the statement "2 + 2 = 4" or "In Peano arithmetic, SS0 + SS0 = SSSS0" can be said to be *true* in any purely abstract sense, apart from physical systems that seem to behave in ways similar to the Peano axioms. Having said this, I will charge right ahead and guess that, in whatever sense "2 + 2 = 4" is true at all, it is always and precisely true, not just roughly true ("2 + 2 actually equals 4.0000004") or true 999,999,999,999 times out of 1,000,000,000,000.

I'm not totally sure what "true" should mean in this case, but I stand by my guess. The credibility of "2 + 2 = 4 is always true" far exceeds the credibility of any particular philosophical position on what "true," "always," or "is" means in the statement above.

This doesn't mean, though, that I have *absolute confidence* that 2 + 2 = 4. See the previous discussion on how to convince me that 2 + 2 = 3, which could be done using much the same sort of evidence that convinced me that 2 + 2 = 4 in the first place. I could have hallucinated all that previous evidence, or I could be misremembering it. In the annals of neurology there are stranger brain dysfunctions than this.

So if we attach some probability to the statement "2 + 2 = 4," then what should the probability be? What you seek to attain in a case like this is good calibration—statements to which you assign "99% probability" come true 99 times out of 100. This is actually a hell of a lot more difficult than you might think. Take a hundred people, and ask each of them to make ten statements of which they are "99% confident." Of the 1,000 statements, do you think that around 10 will be wrong?

I am not going to discuss the actual experiments that have been done on calibration—you can find them in my book chapter on cognitive biases and global catastrophic risk[1]—because I've seen that when I blurt this out to people without proper preparation, they thereafter use it as a Fully General Counterargument, which somehow leaps to mind whenever they have to discount the confidence of someone whose opinion they dislike, and fails to be available when they consider their own opinions. So I try not to talk about the experiments on calibration except as part of a structured presentation of rationality that includes warnings against motivated skepticism.

But the observed calibration of human beings who say they are "99% confident" is not 99% accuracy.

Suppose you say that you're 99.99% confident that 2 + 2 = 4. Then you have just asserted that you could make 10,000 *independent* statements, in which you repose equal confidence, and be wrong, on average, around once. Maybe for 2 + 2 = 4 this extraordinary degree of confidence would be possible: "2 + 2 = 4" is extremely simple, and mathematical as well as empirical, and widely believed socially (not with passionate affirmation but just quietly taken for granted). So maybe you really could get up to 99.99% confidence on this one.

I don't think you could get up to 99.99% confidence for assertions like "53 is a prime number." Yes, it seems likely, but by the time you tried to set up protocols that would let you assert 10,000 *independent* statements of this sort—that is, not just a set of statements about prime numbers, but a new protocol each time—you would fail more than once.[2]

Yet the map is not the territory: If I say that I am 99% confident that 2 + 2 = 4, it doesn't mean that I think "2 + 2 = 4" is true to within 99% precision, or that "2 + 2 = 4" is true 99 times out of 100. The proposition in which I repose my confidence is the proposition that "2 + 2 = 4 is always and exactly true," not the proposition "2 + 2 = 4 is mostly and usually true."

As for the notion that you could get up to 100% confidence in a mathematical proposition—well, really now! If you say 99.9999% confidence, you're implying that you could make *one million* equally fraught statements, one after

---

[1] Eliezer Yudkowsky, "Cognitive Biases Potentially Affecting Judgment of Global Risks," in *Global Catastrophic Risks*, ed. Nick Bostrom and Milan M. Ćirković (New York: Oxford University Press, 2008), 91–119.

[2] Peter de Blanc has an amusing anecdote on this point: http://www.spaceandgames.com/?p=27. (I told him not to do it again.)

the other, and be wrong, on average, about once. That's around a solid year's worth of talking, if you can make one assertion every 20 seconds and you talk for 16 hours a day.

Assert 99.9999999999% confidence, and you're taking it up to a trillion. Now you're going to talk for a hundred human lifetimes, and not be wrong even once?

Assert a confidence of (1 − 1/googolplex) and your ego far exceeds that of mental patients who think they're God.

And a googolplex is a lot smaller than even relatively small inconceivably huge numbers like 3 ↑↑↑ 3. But even a confidence of (1 − 1/3 ↑↑↑ 3) isn't all that much closer to **PROBABILITY 1** than being 90% sure of something.

If all else fails, the hypothetical Dark Lords of the Matrix, who are *right now* tampering with your brain's credibility assessment of *this very sentence*, will bar the path and defend us from the scourge of infinite certainty.

Am I absolutely sure of that?

Why, of course not.

As Rafal Smigrodski once said:

> I would say you should be able to assign a less than 1 certainty level to the mathematical concepts which are necessary to derive Bayes's rule itself, and still practically use it. I am not totally sure I have to be always unsure. Maybe I could be legitimately sure about something. But once I assign a probability of 1 to a proposition, I can never undo it. No matter what I see or learn, I have to reject everything that disagrees with the axiom. I don't like the idea of not being able to change my mind, ever.

12

0 And 1 Are Not Probabilities

One, two, and three are all integers, and so is negative four. If you keep counting up, or keep counting down, you're bound to encounter a whole lot more integers. You will not, however, encounter anything called "positive infinity" or "negative infinity," so these are not integers.

Positive and negative infinity are not integers, but rather special symbols for talking about the behavior of integers. People sometimes say something like, "5 + infinity = infinity," because if you start at 5 and keep counting up without ever stopping, you'll get higher and higher numbers without limit. But it doesn't follow from this that "infinity − infinity = 5." You can't count up from 0 without ever stopping, and then count down without ever stopping, and then find yourself at 5 when you're done.

From this we can see that infinity is not only not-an-integer, it doesn't even *behave* like an integer. If you unwisely try to mix up infinities with integers, you'll need all sorts of special new inconsistent-seeming behaviors which you don't need for 1, 2, 3 and other *actual* integers.

Even though infinity isn't an integer, you don't have to worry about being left at a loss for numbers. Although people have seen five sheep, millions of grains of sand, and septillions of atoms, no one has ever counted an infinity of anything. The same with continuous quantities—people have measured dust specks a millimeter across, animals a meter across, cities kilometers across, and galaxies thousands of lightyears across, but no one has ever measured anything an infinity across. In the real world, you don't *need* a whole lot of infinity.[1]

In the usual way of writing probabilities, probabilities are between 0 and 1. A coin might have a probability of 0.5 of coming up tails, or the weatherman might assign probability 0.9 to rain tomorrow.

This isn't the only way of writing probabilities, though. For example, you can transform probabilities into odds via the transformation $O = (P/(1-P))$. So a probability of 50% would go to odds of 0.5/0.5 or 1, usually written 1:1, while a probability of 0.9 would go to odds of 0.9/0.1 or 9, usually written 9:1. To take odds back to probabilities you use $P = (O/(1 + O))$, and this is perfectly reversible, so the transformation is an isomorphism—a two-way reversible mapping. Thus, probabilities and odds are isomorphic, and you can use one or the other according to convenience.

For example, it's more convenient to use odds when you're doing Bayesian updates. Let's say that I roll a six-sided die: If any face except 1 comes up, there's a 10% chance of hearing a bell, but if the face 1 comes up, there's a 20% chance of hearing the bell. Now I roll the die, and hear a bell. What are the *odds* that the face showing is 1? Well, the prior odds are 1:5 (corresponding to the real number $1/5 = 0.20$) and the likelihood ratio is 0.2:0.1 (corresponding to the real number 2) and I can just multiply these two together to get the posterior odds 2:5 (corresponding to the real number 2/5 or 0.40). Then I convert back into a probability, if I like, and get $(0.4/1.4) = 2/7 = {\sim}29\%$.

So odds are more manageable for Bayesian updates—if you use probabilities, you've got to deploy Bayes's Theorem in its complicated version. But probabilities are more convenient for answering questions like "If I roll a six-sided die, what's the chance of seeing a number from 1 to 4?" You can add up

---

[1] I should note for the more sophisticated reader that they do not need to write me with elaborate explanations of, say, the difference between ordinal numbers and cardinal numbers. I'm familiar with the different set-theoretic notions of infinity, but I don't see a good use for them in probability theory.

the probabilities of 1/6 for each side and get 4/6, but you can't add up the odds ratios of 0.2 for each side and get an odds ratio of 0.8.

Why am I saying all this? To show that "odd ratios" are just as legitimate a way of mapping uncertainties onto real numbers as "probabilities." Odds ratios are more convenient for some operations, probabilities are more convenient for others. A famous proof called Cox's Theorem (plus various extensions and refinements thereof) shows that all ways of representing uncertainties that obey some reasonable-sounding constraints, end up isomorphic to each other.

Why does it matter that odds ratios are just as legitimate as probabilities? Probabilities as ordinarily written are between 0 and 1, and both 0 and 1 look like they ought to be readily reachable quantities—it's easy to see 1 zebra or 0 unicorns. But when you transform probabilities onto odds ratios, 0 goes to 0, but 1 goes to positive infinity. Now absolute truth doesn't look like it should be so easy to reach.

A representation that makes it even simpler to do Bayesian updates is the log odds—this is how E. T. Jaynes recommended thinking about probabilities. For example, let's say that the prior probability of a proposition is 0.0001—this corresponds to a log odds of around -40 decibels. Then you see evidence that seems 100 times more likely if the proposition is true than if it is false. This is 20 decibels of evidence. So the posterior odds are around -40 dB $+$ 20 dB $= -20$ dB, that is, the posterior probability is $\sim$0.01.

When you transform probabilities to log odds, 0 goes to negative infinity and 1 goes to positive infinity. Now both infinite certainty and infinite improbability seem a bit more out-of-reach.

In probabilities, 0.9999 and 0.99999 seem to be only 0.00009 apart, so that 0.502 is much further away from 0.503 than 0.9999 is from 0.99999. To get to probability 1 from probability 0.99999, it seems like you should need to travel a distance of merely 0.00001.

But when you transform to odds ratios, 0.502 and 0.503 go to 1.008 and 1.012, and 0.9999 and 0.99999 go to 9,999 and 99,999. And when you transform to log odds, 0.502 and 0.503 go to 0.03 decibels and 0.05 decibels, but 0.9999 and 0.99999 go to 40 decibels and 50 decibels.

45

When you work in log odds, **the distance between any two degrees of uncertainty equals the amount of evidence you would need to go from one to the other**. That is, the log odds gives us a natural measure of spacing among degrees of confidence.

Using the log odds exposes the fact that reaching infinite certainty requires infinitely strong evidence, just as infinite absurdity requires infinitely strong counterevidence.

Furthermore, all sorts of standard theorems in probability have special cases if you try to plug 1s or 0s into them—like what happens if you try to do a Bayesian update on an observation to which you assigned probability 0.

So I propose that it makes sense to say that 1 and 0 are not in the probabilities; just as negative and positive infinity, which do not obey the field axioms, are not in the real numbers.

The main reason this would upset probability theorists is that we would need to rederive theorems previously obtained by assuming that we can marginalize over a joint probability by adding up all the pieces and having them sum to 1.

However, in the real world, when you roll a die, it doesn't literally have infinite certainty of coming up some number between 1 and 6. The die might land on its edge; or get struck by a meteor; or the Dark Lords of the Matrix might reach in and write "37" on one side.

If you made a magical symbol to stand for "all possibilities I haven't considered," then you could marginalize over the events including this magical symbol, and arrive at a magical symbol "*1*" that stands for infinite certainty.

But I would rather ask whether there's some way to derive a theorem without using magic symbols with special behaviors. That would be more elegant. Just as there are mathematicians who refuse to believe in the law of the excluded middle or infinite sets, I would like to be a probability theorist who doesn't believe in absolute certainty.

13

Your Rationality Is My Business

Some responses to "Lotteries: A Waste of Hope" chided me for daring to criticize others' decisions; if someone else chooses to buy lottery tickets, who am I to disagree? This is a special case of a more general question: What business is it of mine, if someone else chooses to believe what is pleasant rather than what is true? Can't we each choose for ourselves whether to care about the truth?

An obvious snappy comeback is: "Why do *you* care whether *I* care whether someone *else* cares about the truth?" It is somewhat inconsistent for your utility function to contain a negative term for anyone else's utility function having a term for someone else's utility function. But that is only a snappy comeback, not an answer.

So here then is my answer: I believe that it is right and proper for me, as a human being, to have an interest in the future, and what human civilization becomes in the future. One of those interests is the human pursuit of truth, which has strengthened slowly over the generations (for there was not always Science). I wish to strengthen that pursuit further, in *this* generation. That is a wish of mine, for the Future. For we are all of us players upon that vast gameboard, whether we accept the responsibility or not.

And that makes *your* rationality *my* business.

Is this a dangerous idea? Yes, and not just pleasantly edgy "dangerous." People have been burned to death because some priest decided that they didn't think the way they should. Deciding to burn people to death because they "don't think properly"—that's a revolting kind of reasoning, isn't it? You wouldn't want people to think that way, why, it's *disgusting.* People who think like that, well, we'll have to do something about them . . .

I agree! Here's my proposal: Let's argue against bad ideas but *not* set their bearers on fire.

The syllogism we desire to avoid runs: "I think Susie said a bad thing, *therefore,* Susie should be set on fire." Some try to avoid the syllogism by labeling it improper to think that Susie said a bad thing. No one should judge anyone, ever; anyone who judges is committing a terrible sin, and should be publicly pilloried for it.

As for myself, I deny the *therefore.* My syllogism runs, "I think Susie said something wrong, *therefore,* I will argue against what she said, but I will not set her on fire, or try to stop her from talking by violence or regulation . . ."

We are all of us players upon that vast gameboard; and one of my interests for the Future is to make the game fair. The counterintuitive idea underlying science is that factual disagreements should be fought out with experiments and mathematics, not violence and edicts. This incredible notion can be extended beyond science, to a fair fight for the whole Future. You should have to win by convincing people, and should not be allowed to burn them. This is one of the principles of Rationality, to which I have pledged my allegiance.

People who advocate relativism or selfishness do not appear to me to be truly relativistic or selfish. If they were really relativistic, they would not judge. If they were really selfish, they would get on with making money instead of arguing passionately with others. Rather, they have chosen the side of Relativism, whose goal upon that vast gameboard is to prevent the players—*all* the players—from making certain kinds of judgments. Or they have chosen the side of Selfishness, whose goal is to make *all* players selfish. And then they play the game, fairly or unfairly according to their wisdom.

48

If there are any true Relativists or Selfishes, we do not hear them—they remain silent, non-players.

I cannot help but care how you think, because—as I cannot help but see the universe—each time a human being turns away from the truth, the unfolding story of humankind becomes a little darker. In many cases, it is a small darkness only. (Someone doesn't *always* end up getting hurt.) Lying to yourself, in the privacy of your own thoughts, does not shadow humanity's history so much as telling public lies or setting people on fire. Yet there is a part of me which cannot help but mourn. And so long as I *don't* try to set you on fire—only argue with your ideas—I believe that it is right and proper to me, as a human, that I care about my fellow humans. That, also, is a position I defend into the Future.

Part F

Politics and Rationality

14

Politics is the Mind-Killer

People go funny in the head when talking about politics. The evolutionary reasons for this are so obvious as to be worth belaboring: In the ancestral environment, politics was a matter of life and death. And sex, and wealth, and allies, and reputation . . . When, today, you get into an argument about whether "we" ought to raise the minimum wage, you're executing adaptations for an ancestral environment where being on the wrong side of the argument could get you killed. Being on the *right* side of the argument could let *you* kill your hated rival!

If you want to make a point about science, or rationality, then my advice is to not choose a domain from *contemporary* politics if you can possibly avoid it. If your point is inherently about politics, then talk about Louis XVI during the French Revolution. Politics is an important domain to which we should individually apply our rationality—but it's a terrible domain in which to *learn* rationality, or discuss rationality, unless all the discussants are already rational.

Politics is an extension of war by other means. Arguments are soldiers. Once you know which side you're on, you must support all arguments of that side, and attack all arguments that appear to favor the enemy side; otherwise it's like stabbing your soldiers in the back—providing aid and comfort to the enemy. People who would be level-headed about evenhandedly weighing all sides of an issue in their professional life as scientists, can suddenly turn into slogan-chanting zombies when there's a Blue or Green position on an issue.[1]

In Artificial Intelligence, and particularly in the domain of nonmonotonic reasoning, there's a standard problem: "All Quakers are pacifists. All Republicans are not pacifists. Nixon is a Quaker and a Republican. Is Nixon a pacifist?"

What on Earth was the point of choosing this as an example? To rouse the political emotions of the readers and distract them from the main question? To make Republicans feel unwelcome in courses on Artificial Intelligence and discourage them from entering the field?[2]

Why would anyone pick such a *distracting* example to illustrate nonmonotonic reasoning? Probably because the author just couldn't resist getting in a good, solid dig at those hated Greens. It feels so *good* to get in a hearty punch, y'know, it's like trying to resist a chocolate cookie.

As with chocolate cookies, not everything that feels pleasurable is good for you.

I'm not saying that I think we should be apolitical, or even that we should adopt Wikipedia's ideal of the Neutral Point of View. But try to resist getting in those good, solid digs if you can possibly avoid it. If your topic legitimately relates to attempts to ban evolution in school curricula, then go ahead and talk about it—but don't blame it explicitly on the whole Republican Party; some of your readers may be Republicans, and they may feel that the problem is a few rogues, not the entire party. As with Wikipedia's NPOV, it doesn't matter whether (you think) the Republican Party really *is* at fault. It's just better for the spiritual growth of the community to discuss the issue without invoking color politics.

---

[1] For more on the warring Blue and Green factions in imperial Rome, see "A Fable of Science and Politics" in *Map and Territory*.

[2] And no, I am not a Republican. Or a Democrat.

15

Policy Debates Should Not Appear One-Sided

Robin Hanson proposed stores where banned products could be sold.[1] There are a number of excellent arguments for such a policy—an inherent right of individual liberty, the career incentive of bureaucrats to prohibit *everything*, legislators being just as biased as individuals. But even so (I replied), *some* poor, honest, not overwhelmingly educated mother of five children is going to go into these stores and buy a "Dr. Snakeoil's Sulfuric Acid Drink" for her arthritis and die, leaving her orphans to weep on national television.

I was just making a factual observation. Why did some people think it was an argument in favor of regulation?

On questions of simple fact (for example, whether Earthly life arose by natural selection) there's a legitimate expectation that the argument should be a one-sided battle; the facts themselves are either one way or another, and the so-called "balance of evidence" should reflect this. Indeed, under the Bayesian definition of evidence, "strong evidence" is just that sort of evidence which we only expect to find on one side of an argument.

---

[1] In "Paternalism Is About Bias," http://www.overcomingbias.com/2007/03/paternalism_is_.html.

But there is no reason for complex actions with many consequences to exhibit this onesidedness property. Why do people seem to want their *policy* debates to be one-sided?

Politics is the mind-killer. Arguments are soldiers. Once you know which side you're on, you must support all arguments of that side, and attack all arguments that appear to favor the enemy side; otherwise it's like stabbing your soldiers in the back. If you abide within that pattern, policy debates will also appear one-sided to you—the costs and drawbacks of your favored policy are enemy soldiers, to be attacked by any means necessary.

One should also be aware of a related failure pattern: thinking that the course of Deep Wisdom is to compromise with perfect evenness between whichever two policy positions receive the most airtime. A policy may legitimately have *lopsided* costs or benefits. If policy questions were not tilted one way or the other, we would be unable to make decisions about them. But there is also a human tendency to deny all costs of a favored policy, or deny all benefits of a disfavored policy; and people will therefore tend to think policy tradeoffs are tilted much further than they actually are.

If you allow shops that sell otherwise banned products, some poor, honest, poorly educated mother of five kids is going to buy something that kills her. This is a prediction about a factual consequence, and as a factual question it appears rather straightforward—a sane person should readily confess this to be true regardless of which stance they take on the policy issue. You may *also* think that making things illegal just makes them more expensive, that regulators will abuse their power, or that her individual freedom trumps your desire to meddle with her life. But, as a matter of simple fact, she's still going to die.

We live in an unfair universe. Like all primates, humans have strong negative reactions to perceived unfairness; thus we find this fact stressful. There are two popular methods of dealing with the resulting cognitive dissonance. First, one may change one's view of the facts—deny that the unfair events took place, or edit the history to make it appear fair.[2] Second, one may change one's morality—deny that the events are unfair.

---

[2] This is mediated by the affect heuristic and the just-world fallacy.

Some libertarians might say that if you go into a "banned products shop," passing clear warning labels that say THINGS IN THIS STORE MAY KILL YOU, and buy something that kills you, then it's your own fault and you deserve it. If that were a moral truth, there would be *no downside* to having shops that sell banned products. It wouldn't just be a *net benefit*, it would be a *one-sided* tradeoff with no drawbacks.

Others argue that regulators can be trained to choose rationally and in harmony with consumer interests; if those were the facts of the matter then (in their moral view) there would be *no downside* to regulation.

Like it or not, there's a birth lottery for intelligence—though this is one of the cases where the universe's unfairness is so extreme that many people choose to deny the facts. The experimental evidence for a purely genetic component of 0.6–0.8 is overwhelming, but even if this were to be denied, you don't choose your parental upbringing or your early schools either.

I was raised to believe that denying reality is a *moral wrong*. If I were to engage in wishful optimism about how Sulfuric Acid Drink was likely to benefit me, I would be doing something that I was *warned* against and raised to regard as unacceptable. Some people are born into environments—we won't discuss their genes, because that part is too unfair—where the local witch doctor tells them that it is *right* to have faith and *wrong* to be skeptical. In all goodwill, they follow this advice and die. Unlike you, they weren't raised to believe that people are responsible for their individual choices to follow society's lead. Do you really think you're so smart that you would have been a proper scientific skeptic even if you'd been born in 500 CE? Yes, there is a birth lottery, no matter what you believe about genes.

Saying "People who buy dangerous products deserve to get hurt!" is not tough-minded. It is a way of refusing to live in an unfair universe. Real tough-mindedness is saying, "Yes, sulfuric acid is a horrible painful death, and no, that mother of five children didn't deserve it, but we're going to keep the shops open anyway because we did this cost-benefit calculation." Can you imagine a politician saying that? Neither can I. But insofar as economists have the power to influence policy, it might help if they could think it privately—

maybe even say it in journal articles, suitably dressed up in polysyllabismic obfuscationalization so the media can't quote it.

I don't think that when someone makes a stupid choice and dies, this is a cause for celebration. I count it as a tragedy. It is not always helping people, to save them from the consequences of their own actions; but I draw a moral line at capital punishment. If you're dead, you can't learn from your mistakes.

Unfortunately the universe doesn't agree with me. We'll see which one of us is still standing when this is over.

16

The Scales of Justice, the Notebook of Rationality

Lady Justice is widely depicted as carrying scales. A set of scales has the property that whatever pulls one side down pushes the other side up. This makes things very convenient and easy to track. It's also usually a gross distortion.

In human discourse there is a natural tendency to treat discussion as a form of combat, an extension of war, a sport; and in sports you only need to keep track of how many points have been scored by each team. There are only two sides, and every point scored against one side is a point in favor of the other. Everyone in the audience keeps a mental running count of how many points each speaker scores against the other. At the end of the debate, the speaker who has scored more points is, obviously, the winner; so everything that speaker says must be true, and everything the loser says must be wrong.

"The Affect Heuristic in Judgments of Risks and Benefits" studied whether subjects mixed up their judgments of the possible benefits of a technology (e.g., nuclear power), and the possible risks of that technology, into a single overall good or bad feeling about the technology.[1] Suppose that I first tell

---

[1] Melissa L. Finucane et al., "The Affect Heuristic in Judgments of Risks and Benefits," *Journal of Behavioral Decision Making* 13, no. 1 (2000): 1–17.

you that a particular kind of nuclear reactor generates less nuclear waste than competing reactor designs. But then I tell you that the reactor is more unstable than competing designs, with a greater danger of melting down if a sufficient number of things go wrong simultaneously.

If the reactor is more likely to melt down, this seems like a "point against" the reactor, or a "point against" someone who argues for building the reactor. And if the reactor produces less waste, this is a "point for" the reactor, or a "point for" building it. So are these two facts opposed to each other? No. In the real world, no. These two facts may be cited by different sides of the same debate, but they are logically distinct; the facts don't know whose side they're on.

If it's a physical fact about a reactor design that it's passively safe (won't go supercritical even if the surrounding coolant systems and so on break down), this doesn't imply that the reactor will necessarily generate less waste, or produce electricity at a lower cost. All these things would be good, but they are not the same good thing. The amount of waste produced by the reactor arises from the properties of that reactor. Other physical properties of the reactor make the nuclear reaction more unstable. Even if some of the same design properties are involved, you have to separately consider the probability of meltdown, and the expected annual waste generated. These are two different physical questions with two different factual answers.

But studies such as the above show that people tend to judge technologies—and many other problems—by an overall good or bad feeling. If you tell people a reactor design produces less waste, they rate its probability of meltdown as lower. This means getting the *wrong answer* to physical questions with definite factual answers, because you have mixed up logically distinct questions—treated facts like human soldiers on different sides of a war, thinking that any soldier on one side can be used to fight any soldier on the other side.

A set of scales is not wholly inappropriate for Lady Justice if she is investigating a strictly factual question of guilt or innocence. Either John Smith killed John Doe, or not. We are taught (by E. T. Jaynes) that all Bayesian evidence consists of probability flows *between* hypotheses; there is no such thing as evidence that "supports" or "contradicts" a single hypothesis, except insofar as other hypotheses do worse or better. So long as Lady Justice is investigating a *single*, strictly *factual* question with a *binary* answer space, a set of scales would be an appropriate tool. If Justitia must consider any more complex issue, she should relinquish her scales or relinquish her sword.

Not all arguments reduce to mere up or down. Lady Rationality carries a notebook, wherein she writes down all the facts that aren't on anyone's side.

17

Correspondence Bias

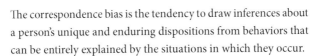

> The correspondence bias is the tendency to draw inferences about
> a person's unique and enduring dispositions from behaviors that
> can be entirely explained by the situations in which they occur.
>
> —Gilbert and Malone[1]

We tend to see far too direct a correspondence between others' actions and
personalities. When we see someone else kick a vending machine for no visible
reason, we assume they are "an angry person." But when you yourself kick
the vending machine, it's because the bus was late, the train was early, your
report is overdue, and now the damned vending machine has eaten your lunch
money for the second day in a row. *Surely,* you think to yourself, *anyone would
kick the vending machine, in that situation.*

We attribute our own actions to our *situations*, seeing our behaviors as
perfectly normal responses to experience. But when someone else kicks a
vending machine, we don't see their past history trailing behind them in the

---

[1] Daniel T. Gilbert and Patrick S. Malone, "The Correspondence Bias," *Psychological Bulletin* 117, no.
1 (1995): 21–38, http://www.wjh.harvard.edu/~dtg/Gilbert%5C%20&%5C%20Malone%5C%
20(CORRESPONDENCE%5C%20BIAS).pdf

air. We just see the kick, for no reason *we* know about, and we think this must be a naturally angry person—since they lashed out without any provocation.

Yet consider the prior probabilities. There are more late buses in the world, than mutants born with unnaturally high anger levels that cause them to sometimes spontaneously kick vending machines. Now the average human is, in fact, a mutant. If I recall correctly, an average individual has two to ten somatically expressed mutations. But any *given* DNA location is very unlikely to be affected. Similarly, any given aspect of someone's disposition is probably not very far from average. To suggest otherwise is to shoulder a burden of improbability.

Even when people are informed explicitly of situational causes, they don't seem to properly discount the observed behavior. When subjects are told that a pro-abortion or anti-abortion speaker was *randomly assigned* to give a speech on that position, subjects still think the speakers harbor leanings in the direction randomly assigned.[2]

It seems quite intuitive to explain rain by water spirits; explain fire by a fire-stuff (phlogiston) escaping from burning matter; explain the soporific effect of a medication by saying that it contains a "dormitive potency." Reality usually involves more complicated mechanisms: an evaporation and condensation cycle underlying rain, oxidizing combustion underlying fire, chemical interactions with the nervous system for soporifics. But mechanisms sound more complicated than essences; they are harder to think of, less available. So when someone kicks a vending machine, we think they have an innate vending-machine-kicking-tendency.

Unless the "someone" who kicks the machine is us—in which case we're behaving perfectly normally, given our situations; surely anyone else would do the same. Indeed, we overestimate how likely others are to respond the same way we do—the "false consensus effect." Drinking students considerably overestimate the fraction of fellow students who drink, but nondrinkers considerably underestimate the fraction. The "fundamental attribution error"

---

[2] Edward E. Jones and Victor A. Harris, "The Attribution of Attitudes," *Journal of Experimental Social Psychology* 3 (1967): 1–24, http://www.radford.edu/~jaspelme/443/spring-2007/Articles/Jones_n_Harris_1967.pdf.

refers to our tendency to overattribute others' behaviors to their dispositions, while reversing this tendency for ourselves.

To understand why people act the way they do, we must first realize that everyone sees themselves as behaving normally. Don't ask what strange, mutant disposition they were born with, which directly corresponds to their surface behavior. Rather, ask what situations people see themselves as being in. Yes, people do have dispositions—but there are not *enough* heritable quirks of disposition to directly account for all the surface behaviors you see.

Suppose I gave you a control with two buttons, a red button and a green button. The red button destroys the world, and the green button stops the red button from being pressed. Which button would you press? The green one. Anyone who gives a different answer is probably overcomplicating the question.[3]

And yet people sometimes ask me why I want to save the world.[4] Like I must have had a traumatic childhood or something. Really, it seems like a pretty obvious decision . . . if you see the situation in those terms.

I may have non-average views which call for explanation—why do I believe such things, when most people don't?—but given those beliefs, my *reaction* doesn't seem to call forth an exceptional explanation. Perhaps I am a victim of false consensus; perhaps I overestimate how many people would press the green button if they saw the situation in those terms. But y'know, I'd still bet there'd be at least a *substantial minority*.

Most people see themselves as perfectly normal, from the inside. Even people you hate, people who do terrible things, are not exceptional mutants. No mutations are required, alas. When you understand this, you are ready to stop being surprised by human events.

---

[3] Compare "Transhumanism as Simplified Humanism," http://yudkowsky.net/singularity/simplified.
[4] See "Artificial Intelligence as a Positive and Negative Factor in Global Risk," http://intelligence.org/files/AIPosNegFactor.pdf.

18

Are Your Enemies Innately Evil?

We see far too direct a correspondence between others' actions and their inherent dispositions. We see unusual dispositions that exactly match the unusual behavior, rather than asking after real situations or imagined situations that could explain the behavior. We hypothesize mutants.

When someone actually *offends* us—commits an action of which we (rightly or wrongly) disapprove—then, I observe, the correspondence bias redoubles. There seems to be a *very* strong tendency to blame evil deeds on the Enemy's mutant, evil disposition. Not as a moral point, but as a strict question of prior probability, we should ask what the Enemy might believe about their situation that would reduce the seeming bizarrity of their behavior. This would allow us to hypothesize a less exceptional disposition, and thereby shoulder a lesser burden of improbability.

On September 11th, 2001, nineteen Muslim males hijacked four jet airliners in a deliberately suicidal effort to hurt the United States of America. Now why do you suppose they might have done that? Because they saw the USA as a beacon of freedom to the world, but were born with a mutant disposition that made them hate freedom?

65

Realistically, most people don't construct their life stories with themselves as the villains. Everyone is the hero of their own story. The Enemy's story, as seen by the Enemy, *is not going to make the Enemy look bad.* If you try to construe motivations that *would* make the Enemy look bad, you'll end up flat wrong about what actually goes on in the Enemy's mind.

But politics is the mind-killer. Debate is war; arguments are soldiers. If the Enemy did have an evil disposition, that would be an argument in favor of your side. And *any* argument that favors your side must be supported, no matter how silly—otherwise you're letting up the pressure somewhere on the battlefront. Everyone strives to outshine their neighbor in patriotic denunciation, and no one dares to contradict. Soon the Enemy has horns, bat wings, flaming breath, and fangs that drip corrosive venom. If you deny any aspect of this on merely factual grounds, you are arguing the Enemy's side; you are a traitor. Very few people will understand that you aren't defending the Enemy, just defending the truth.

If it took a mutant to do monstrous things, the history of the human species would look very different. Mutants would be rare.

Or maybe the fear is that understanding will lead to forgiveness. It's easier to shoot down evil mutants. It is a more inspiring battle cry to scream, "Die, vicious scum!" instead of "Die, people who could have been just like me but grew up in a different environment!" You might feel guilty killing people who *weren't* pure darkness.

This looks to me like the deep-seated yearning for a one-sided policy debate in which the best policy has *no* drawbacks. If an army is crossing the border or a lunatic is coming at you with a knife, the policy alternatives are (a) defend yourself or (b) lie down and die. If you defend yourself, you may have to kill. If you kill someone who could, in another world, have been your friend, that is a tragedy. And it *is* a tragedy. The other option, lying down and dying, is also a tragedy. Why must there be a non-tragic option? Who says that the best policy available must have no downside? If someone has to die, it may as well be the initiator of force, to discourage future violence and thereby minimize the total sum of death.

66

If the Enemy has an average disposition, and is acting from beliefs about their situation that would make violence a typically human response, then that doesn't mean their beliefs are factually accurate. It doesn't mean they're justified. It means you'll have to shoot down someone who is the hero of their own story, and in their novel the protagonist will die on page 80. That is a tragedy, but it is better than the alternative tragedy. It is the choice that every police officer makes, every day, to keep our neat little worlds from dissolving into chaos.

When you accurately estimate the Enemy's psychology—when you know what is really in the Enemy's mind—that knowledge won't feel like landing a delicious punch on the opposing side. It won't give you a warm feeling of righteous indignation. It won't make you feel good about yourself. If your estimate makes you feel unbearably sad, you may be seeing the world as it really is. More rarely, an accurate estimate may send shivers of serious horror down your spine, as when dealing with true psychopaths, or neurologically intact people with beliefs that have utterly destroyed their sanity (Scientologists or Jesus Campers).

So let's come right out and say it—the 9/11 hijackers weren't evil mutants. They did not hate freedom. They, too, were the heroes of their own stories, and they died for what they believed was right—truth, justice, and the Islamic way. If the hijackers saw themselves that way, it doesn't mean their beliefs were true. If the hijackers saw themselves that way, it doesn't mean that we have to agree that what they did was justified. If the hijackers saw themselves that way, it doesn't mean that the passengers of United Flight 93 should have stood aside and let it happen. It does mean that in another world, if they had been raised in a different environment, those hijackers might have been police officers. And that is indeed a tragedy. Welcome to Earth.

19

Reversed Stupidity Is Not Intelligence

"... then our people on that time-line went to work with corrective action. Here."

He wiped the screen and then began punching combinations. Page after page appeared, bearing accounts of people who had claimed to have seen the mysterious disks, and each report was more fantastic than the last.

"The standard smother-out technique," Verkan Vall grinned. "I only heard a little talk about the 'flying saucers,' and all of that was in joke. In that order of culture, you can always discredit one true story by setting up ten others, palpably false, parallel to it."

—H. Beam Piper, *Police Operation*

Piper had a point. Pers'nally, I don't believe there are any poorly hidden aliens infesting these parts. But my disbelief has nothing to do with the awful embarrassing irrationality of flying saucer cults—at least, I hope not.

You and I believe that flying saucer cults arose in the total absence of any flying saucers. Cults can arise around almost any idea, thanks to human silliness. This silliness operates *orthogonally* to alien intervention: We would expect to see flying saucer cults whether or not there were flying saucers. Even if there were poorly hidden aliens, it would not be any *less* likely for flying saucer cults to arise. The conditional probability $P(\text{cults}|\text{aliens})$ isn't less than $P(\text{cults}|\neg\text{aliens})$, unless you suppose that poorly hidden aliens would deliberately suppress flying saucer cults.[1] By the Bayesian definition of evidence, the observation "flying saucer cults exist" is not evidence *against* the existence of flying saucers. It's not much evidence one way or the other.

This is an application of the general principle that, as Robert Pirsig puts it, "The world's greatest fool may say the Sun is shining, but that doesn't make it dark out."[2]

If you knew someone who was wrong 99.99% of the time on yes-or-no questions, you could obtain 99.99% accuracy just by reversing their answers. They would need to do all the work of obtaining good evidence entangled with reality, and processing that evidence coherently, just to *anticorrelate* that reliably. They would have to be superintelligent to be that stupid.

A car with a broken engine cannot drive backward at 200 mph, even if the engine is *really really broken.*

If stupidity does not reliably anticorrelate with truth, how much less should human evil anticorrelate with truth? The converse of the halo effect is the horns effect: All perceived negative qualities correlate. If Stalin is evil, then everything he says should be false. You wouldn't want to agree with *Stalin*, would you?

Stalin also believed that 2 + 2 = 4. Yet if you defend any statement made by Stalin, even "2 + 2 = 4," people will see only that you are "agreeing with Stalin"; you must be on his side.

Corollaries of this principle:

- To argue against an idea honestly, you should argue against the best arguments of the strongest advocates. Arguing against weaker advocates proves *nothing*, because even the strongest idea will attract weak

---

[1] Read "$P(\text{cults}|\text{aliens})$" as "the probability of UFO cults given that aliens have visited Earth," and read "$P(\text{cults}|\neg\text{aliens})$" as "the probability of UFO cults given that aliens have not visited Earth."
[2] Robert M. Pirsig, *Zen and the Art of Motorcycle Maintenance: An Inquiry Into Values*, 1st ed. (New York: Morrow, 1974).

advocates. If you want to argue against transhumanism or the intelligence explosion, you have to directly challenge the arguments of Nick Bostrom or Eliezer Yudkowsky post-2003. The least convenient path is the only valid one.[3]

- Exhibiting sad, pathetic lunatics, driven to madness by their apprehension of an Idea, is no evidence against that Idea. Many New Agers have been made crazier by their personal apprehension of quantum mechanics.

- Someone once said, "Not all conservatives are stupid, but most stupid people are conservatives." If you cannot place yourself in a state of mind where this statement, true or false, seems *completely irrelevant* as a critique of conservatism, you are not ready to think rationally about politics.

- Ad hominem argument is not valid.

- You need to be able to argue against genocide without saying "Hitler wanted to exterminate the Jews." If Hitler *hadn't* advocated genocide, would it thereby become okay?

- In Hansonian terms: Your instinctive willingness to believe something will change along with your willingness to *affiliate* with people who are known for believing it—quite apart from whether the belief is actually *true*. Some people may be reluctant to believe that God does not exist, not because there is evidence that God *does* exist, but rather because they are reluctant to affiliate with Richard Dawkins or those darned "strident" atheists who go around publicly saying "God does not exist."

- If your current computer stops working, you can't conclude that everything about the current system is wrong and that you need a new system without an AMD processor, an ATI video card, a Maxtor hard drive, or case fans—even though your current system has all these things and it doesn't work. Maybe you just need a new power cord.

---

[3] See Scott Alexander's "The Least Convenient Possible World," http://lesswrong.com/lw/2k/the_least_convenient_possible_world/.

- If a hundred inventors fail to build flying machines using metal and wood and canvas, it doesn't imply that what you really need is a flying machine of bone and flesh. If a thousand projects fail to build Artificial Intelligence using electricity-based computing, this doesn't mean that electricity is the source of the problem. Until you understand the problem, hopeful reversals are exceedingly unlikely to hit the solution.[4]

---

[4]See also "Selling Nonapples," http://lesswrong.com/lw/vs/selling_nonapples/.

20

Argument Screens Off Authority

Scenario 1: Barry is a famous geologist. Charles is a fourteen-year-old juvenile delinquent with a long arrest record and occasional psychotic episodes. Barry flatly asserts to Arthur some counterintuitive statement about rocks, and Arthur judges it 90% probable. Then Charles makes an equally counterintuitive flat assertion about rocks, and Arthur judges it 10% probable. Clearly, Arthur is taking the speaker's *authority* into account in deciding whether to believe the speaker's assertions.

Scenario 2: David makes a counterintuitive statement about physics and gives Arthur a detailed explanation of the arguments, including references. Ernie makes an equally counterintuitive statement, but gives an unconvincing argument involving several leaps of faith. Both David and Ernie assert that this is the best explanation they can possibly give (to anyone, not just Arthur). Arthur assigns 90% probability to David's statement after hearing his explanation, but assigns a 10% probability to Ernie's statement.

It might seem like these two scenarios are roughly symmetrical: both involve taking into account useful evidence, whether strong versus weak authority, or strong versus weak argument.

72

But now suppose that Arthur asks Barry and Charles to make full technical cases, with references; and that Barry and Charles present equally good cases, and Arthur looks up the references and they check out. Then Arthur asks David and Ernie for their credentials, and it turns out that David and Ernie have roughly the same credentials—maybe they're both clowns, maybe they're both physicists.

Assuming that Arthur is knowledgeable enough to understand all the technical arguments—otherwise they're just impressive noises—it seems that Arthur should view David as having a great advantage in plausibility over Ernie, while Barry has at best a minor advantage over Charles.

Indeed, if the technical arguments are good enough, Barry's advantage over Charles may not be worth tracking. A good technical argument is one that *eliminates* reliance on the personal authority of the speaker.

Similarly, if we really believe Ernie that the argument he gave is the best argument he *could* give, which includes all of the inferential steps that Ernie executed, and all of the support that Ernie took into account—citing any authorities that Ernie may have listened to himself—then we can pretty much ignore any information about Ernie's credentials. Ernie can be a physicist or a clown, it shouldn't matter. (Again, this assumes we have enough technical ability to process the argument. Otherwise, Ernie is simply uttering mystical syllables, and whether we "believe" these syllables depends a great deal on his authority.)

So it seems there's an asymmetry between argument and authority. If we know authority we are still interested in hearing the arguments; but if we know the arguments fully, we have very little left to learn from authority.

Clearly (says the novice) authority and argument are fundamentally different kinds of evidence, a difference unaccountable in the boringly clean methods of Bayesian probability theory.[1] For while the strength of the evidences—90% versus 10%—is just the same in both cases, they do not behave similarly when combined. How will we account for this?

---

[1] See "What Is Evidence?" in *Map and Territory*.

Here's half a technical demonstration of how to represent this difference in probability theory. (The rest you can take on my personal authority, or look up in the references.)

If $P(H|E_1) = 90\%$ and $P(H|E_2) = 9\%$, what is the probability $P(H|E_1, E_2)$? If learning E_1 is true leads us to assign 90% probability to H, and learning E_2 is true leads us to assign 9% probability to H, then what probability should we assign to H if we learn both E_1 and E_2? This is simply not something you can calculate in probability theory from the information given. No, the missing information is not the prior probability of H. The events E_1 and E_2 may not be independent of each other.

Suppose that H is "My sidewalk is slippery," E_1 is "My sprinkler is running," and E_2 is "It's night." The sidewalk is slippery starting from one minute after the sprinkler starts, until just after the sprinkler finishes, and the sprinkler runs for ten minutes. So if we know the sprinkler is on, the probability is 90% that the sidewalk is slippery. The sprinkler is on during 10% of the nighttime, so if we know that it's night, the probability of the sidewalk being slippery is 9%. If we know that it's night and the sprinkler is on—that is, if we know both facts—the probability of the sidewalk being slippery is 90%.

We can represent this in a graphical model as follows:

Whether or not it's Night *causes* the Sprinkler to be on or off, and whether the Sprinkler is on *causes* the sidewalk to be Slippery or unSlippery.

The direction of the arrows is meaningful. Say we had:

This would mean that, if I *didn't* know anything about the sprinkler, the probability of Nighttime and Slipperiness would be independent of each other. For example, suppose that I roll Die One and Die Two, and add up the showing numbers to get the Sum:

If you don't tell me the sum of the two numbers, and you tell me the first die showed 6, this doesn't tell me anything about the result of the second die, yet. But if you now also tell me the sum is 7, I know the second die showed 1.

Figuring out when various pieces of information are dependent or independent of each other, given various background knowledge, actually turns into a quite technical topic. The books to read are Judea Pearl's *Probabilistic Reasoning in Intelligent Systems: Networks of Plausible Inference* and *Causality: Models, Reasoning, and Inference.* (If you only have time to read one book, read the first one.)

If you know how to read causal graphs, then you look at the dice-roll graph and immediately see:

$$P(\text{Die 1}, \text{Die 2}) = P(\text{Die 1}) \times P(\text{Die 2})$$
$$P(\text{Die 1}, \text{Die 2}|\text{Sum}) \neq P(\text{Die 1}|\text{Sum}) \times P(\text{Die 2}|\text{Sum}) .$$

If you look at the correct sidewalk diagram, you see facts like:

$$P(\text{Slippery}|\text{Night}) \neq P(\text{Slippery})$$
$$P(\text{Slippery}|\text{Sprinkler}) \neq P(\text{Slippery})$$
$$P(\text{Slippery}|\text{Night}, \text{Sprinkler}) = P(\text{Slippery}|\text{Sprinkler}) .$$

That is, the probability of the sidewalk being Slippery, given knowledge about the Sprinkler and the Night, is the same probability we would assign if we knew only about the Sprinkler. Knowledge of the Sprinkler has made knowledge of the Night irrelevant to inferences about Slipperiness.

75

This is known as *screening off*, and the criterion that lets us read such conditional independences off causal graphs is known as *D-separation*.

For the case of argument and authority, the causal diagram looks like this:

If something is true, then it therefore tends to have arguments in favor of it, and the experts therefore observe these evidences and change their opinions. (In theory!)

If we see that an expert believes something, we infer back to the existence of evidence-in-the-abstract (even though we don't know what that evidence is exactly), and from the existence of this abstract evidence, we infer back to the truth of the proposition.

But if we know the value of the Argument node, this D-separates the node "Truth" from the node "Expert Belief" by blocking all paths between them, according to certain technical criteria for "path blocking" that seem pretty obvious in this case. So even without checking the exact probability distribution, we can read off from the graph that:

$$P(\text{truth}|\text{argument}, \text{expert}) = P(\text{truth}|\text{argument}) .$$

This does not represent a contradiction of ordinary probability theory. It's just a more compact way of expressing certain probabilistic facts. You could read the same equalities and inequalities off an unadorned probability distribution— but it would be harder to see it by eyeballing. Authority and argument don't need two different kinds of probability, any more than sprinklers are made out of ontologically different stuff than sunlight.

In practice you can never *completely* eliminate reliance on authority. Good authorities are more likely to know about any counterevidence that exists and should be taken into account; a lesser authority is less likely to know this, which makes their arguments less reliable. This is not a factor you can eliminate merely by hearing the evidence they *did* take into account.

It's also very hard to reduce arguments to *pure* math; and otherwise, judging the strength of an inferential step may rely on intuitions you can't duplicate without the same thirty years of experience.

There is an ineradicable legitimacy to assigning *slightly* higher probability to what E. T. Jaynes tells you about Bayesian probability, than you assign to Eliezer Yudkowsky making the exact same statement. Fifty additional years of experience should not count for literally *zero* influence.

But this slight strength of authority is only *ceteris paribus*, and can easily be overwhelmed by stronger arguments. I have a minor erratum in one of Jaynes's books—because algebra trumps authority.

21

Hug the Query

In the art of rationality there is a discipline of *closeness-to-the-issue*—trying to observe evidence that is as near to the original question as possible, so that it screens off as many other arguments as possible.

The Wright Brothers say, "My plane will fly." If you look at their authority (bicycle mechanics who happen to be excellent amateur physicists) then you will compare their authority to, say, Lord Kelvin, and you will find that Lord Kelvin is the greater authority.

If you demand to see the Wright Brothers' calculations, and you can follow them, and you demand to see Lord Kelvin's calculations (he probably doesn't have any apart from his own incredulity), then authority becomes much less relevant.

If you actually *watch the plane fly*, the calculations themselves become moot for many purposes, and Kelvin's authority not even worth considering.

The more *directly* your arguments bear on a question, without intermediate inferences—the closer the observed nodes are to the queried node, in the Great Web of Causality—the more powerful the evidence. It's a theorem of these causal graphs that you can never get *more* information from distant nodes, than from strictly closer nodes that screen off the distant ones.

Jerry Cleaver said: "What does you in is not failure to apply some high-level, intricate, complicated technique. It's overlooking the basics. Not keeping your eye on the ball."[1]

Just as it is superior to argue physics than credentials, it is also superior to argue physics than rationality. Who was more rational, the Wright Brothers or Lord Kelvin? If we can check their calculations, we don't have to care! The virtue of a rationalist cannot *directly* cause a plane to fly.

If you forget this principle, learning about more biases will hurt you, because it will distract you from more direct arguments. It's all too easy to argue that someone is exhibiting Bias #182 in your repertoire of fully generic accusations, but you can't *settle* a factual issue without closer evidence. If there are biased reasons to say the Sun is shining, that doesn't make it dark out.

Just as you can't always experiment today, you can't always check the calculations today.[2] Sometimes you don't know enough background material, sometimes there's private information, sometimes there just isn't time. There's a sadly large number of times when it's worthwhile to judge the speaker's rationality. You should always do it with a hollow feeling in your heart, though, a sense that something's missing.

Whenever you can, dance as near to the original question as possible—press yourself up against it—get close enough to *hug the query!*

---

[1] Jerry Cleaver, *Immediate Fiction: A Complete Writing Course* (Macmillan, 2004).
[2] See also "Is Molecular Nanotechnology 'Scientific'?", http://lesswrong.com/lw/io/is_molecular_nanotechnology_scientific/.

22

Rationality and the English Language

The other day, someone commented that my writing reminded them of George Orwell's "Politics and the English Language."[1,2] I was honored. Especially since I'd already thought of today's topic.

If you *really* want an artist's perspective on rationality, then read Orwell; he is mandatory reading for rationalists as well as authors. Orwell was not a scientist, but a writer; his tools were not numbers, but words; his adversary was not Nature, but human evil. If you wish to imprison people for years without trial, you must think of some other way to say it than "I'm going to imprison Mr. Jennings for years without trial." You must muddy the listener's thinking, prevent clear images from outraging conscience. You say, "Unreliable elements were subjected to an alternative justice process."

Orwell was the outraged opponent of totalitarianism and the muddy thinking in which evil cloaks itself—which is how Orwell's writings on language ended up as classic rationalist documents on a level with Feynman, Sagan, or Dawkins.

---

[1] Source: http://lesswrong.com/lw/jb/applause_lights/f1t
[2] George Orwell, "Politics and the English Language," *Horizon*, April 1946,

"Writers are told to avoid usage of the passive voice." A rationalist whose background comes *exclusively* from science may fail to see the flaw in the previous sentence; but anyone who's done a little writing should see it right away. I wrote the sentence in the passive voice, without telling you *who* tells authors to avoid passive voice. Passive voice removes the actor, leaving only the acted-upon. "Unreliable elements were subjected to an alternative justice process"—subjected by *whom*? What does an "alternative justice process" *do*? With enough static noun phrases, you can keep anything unpleasant from actually *happening*.

Journal articles are often written in passive voice. (Pardon me, *some scientists* write their journal articles in passive voice. It's not as if the articles are being written by no one, with no one to blame.) It sounds more authoritative to say "The subjects were administered Progenitorivox" than "I gave each college student a bottle of 20 Progenitorivox, and told them to take one every night until they were gone." If you remove the scientist from the description, that leaves only the all-important data. But in reality the scientist *is* there, and the subjects *are* college students, and the Progenitorivox wasn't "administered" but handed over with instructions. Passive voice obscures reality.

Judging from the comments I get, someone will protest that using the passive voice in a journal article is hardly a sin—after all, if you *think* about it, you can realize the scientist is there. It doesn't seem like a logical flaw. And this is why rationalists need to read Orwell, not just Feynman or even Jaynes.

Nonfiction conveys *knowledge*, fiction conveys *experience*. Medical science can extrapolate what would happen to a human unprotected in a vacuum. Fiction can make you live through it.

Some rationalists will try to analyze a misleading phrase, try to see if there *might possibly* be anything meaningful to it, try to *construct* a logical interpretation. They will be charitable, give the author the benefit of the doubt. Authors, on the other hand, are trained *not* to give themselves the benefit of the doubt. Whatever the audience *thinks* you said *is* what you said, whether you meant to say it or not; you can't argue with the audience no matter how clever your justifications.

A writer knows that readers will *not* stop for a minute to think. A fictional experience is a continuous stream of first impressions. A writer-rationalist pays attention to the *experience* words create. If you are evaluating the public rationality of a statement, and you analyze the words deliberatively, rephrasing propositions, trying out different meanings, searching for nuggets of truthiness, then you're losing track of the first impression—what the audience *sees*, or rather *feels*.

A novelist would notice the screaming wrongness of "The subjects were administered Progenitorivox." What life is here for a reader to live? This sentence creates a distant feeling of authoritativeness, and that's *all*—the *only* experience is the feeling of being told something reliable. A novelist would see nouns too abstract to show what actually happened—the postdoc with the bottle in their hand, trying to look stern; the student listening with a nervous grin.

My point is not to say that journal articles should be written like novels, but that a rationalist should become consciously aware of the *experiences* which words create. A rationalist must understand the mind and how to operate it. That includes the stream of consciousness, the part of yourself that unfolds in language. A rationalist must become consciously aware of the actual, experiential impact of phrases, beyond their mere propositional semantics.[3]

Or to say it more bluntly: *Meaning does not excuse impact!*

I don't care what rational interpretation you can *construct* for an applause light like "AI should be developed through democratic processes." That cannot excuse its irrational impact of signaling the audience to applaud, not to mention its cloudy question-begging vagueness.

Here is Orwell, railing against the *impact* of cliches, their effect on the experience of thinking:

> When one watches some tired hack on the platform mechanically
> repeating the familiar phrases—BESTIAL, ATROCITIES, IRON HEEL,
> BLOODSTAINED TYRANNY, FREE PEOPLES OF THE WORLD, STAND
> SHOULDER TO SHOULDER—one often has a curious feeling that one

---

[3] Compare "Semantic Stopsigns" and "Applause Lights" in *Map and Territory*.

is not watching a live human being but some kind of dummy . . . A speaker who uses that kind of phraseology has gone some distance toward turning himself into a machine. The appropriate noises are coming out of his larynx, but his brain is not involved, as it would be if he were choosing his words for himself . . .

What is above all needed is to let the meaning choose the word, and not the other way around. In prose, the worst thing one can do with words is surrender to them. When you think of a concrete object, you think wordlessly, and then, if you want to describe the thing you have been visualising you probably hunt about until you find the exact words that seem to fit it. When you think of something abstract you are more inclined to use words from the start, and unless you make a conscious effort to prevent it, the existing dialect will come rushing in and do the job for you, at the expense of blurring or even changing your meaning. Probably it is better to put off using words as long as possible and get one's meaning as clear as one can through pictures and sensations.

Charles Sanders Peirce might have written that last paragraph. More than one path can lead to the Way.

23

Human Evil and Muddled Thinking

George Orwell saw the descent of the civilized world into totalitarianism, the conversion or corruption of one country after another; the boot stamping on a human face, forever, and remember that it is forever. You were born too late to remember a time when the rise of totalitarianism seemed unstoppable, when one country after another fell to secret police and the thunderous knock at midnight, while the professors of free universities hailed the Soviet Union's purges as progress. It feels as alien to you as fiction; it is hard for you to take seriously. Because, in your branch of time, the Berlin Wall fell. And if Orwell's name is not carved into one of those stones, it should be.

Orwell saw the destiny of the human species, and he put forth a convulsive effort to wrench it off its path. Orwell's weapon was clear writing. Orwell knew that muddled language is muddled thinking; he knew that human evil and muddled thinking intertwine like conjugate strands of DNA:[1]

> In our time, political speech and writing are largely the defence
> of the indefensible. Things like the continuance of British rule

---

[1] Orwell, "Politics and the English Language."

in India, the Russian purges and deportations, the dropping of
the atom bombs on Japan, can indeed be defended, but only
by arguments which are too brutal for most people to face, and
which do not square with the professed aims of the political parties. Thus political language has to consist largely of euphemism,
question-begging and sheer cloudy vagueness. Defenceless vil-
lages are bombarded from the air, the inhabitants driven out into
the countryside, the cattle machine-gunned, the huts set on fire
with incendiary bullets: this is called PACIFICATION . . .

Orwell was clear on the goal of his clarity:

If you simplify your English, you are freed from the worst follies
of orthodoxy. You cannot speak any of the necessary dialects, and
when you make a stupid remark its stupidity will be obvious, even
to yourself.

To make our stupidity obvious, even to ourselves—this is the heart of *Overcoming Bias*.

Evil sneaks, hidden, through the unlit shadows of the mind. We look back
with the clarity of history, and weep to remember the planned famines of Stalin
and Mao, which killed tens of millions. We call this evil, because it was done
by deliberate human intent to inflict pain and death upon innocent human
beings. We call this evil, because of the revulsion that we feel against it, looking
back with the clarity of history. For perpetrators of evil to avoid its natural
opposition, the revulsion must remain latent. Clarity must be avoided at any
cost. Even as humans of clear sight tend to oppose the evil that they see; so
too does human evil, wherever it exists, set out to muddle thinking.

1984 sets this forth starkly: Orwell's ultimate villains are cutters and air-
brushers of photographs (based on historical cutting and airbrushing in the
Soviet Union). At the peak of all darkness in the Ministry of Love, O'Brien
tortures Winston to admit that two plus two equals five:[2]

"Do you remember," he went on, "writing in your diary, 'Freedom
is the freedom to say that two plus two make four'?"

[2] George Orwell, *1984* (Signet Classic, 1950).

85

> "Yes," said Winston.
>
> O'Brien held up his left hand, its back towards Winston, with the thumb hidden and the four fingers extended.
>
> "How many fingers am I holding up, Winston?"
>
> "Four."
>
> "And if the party says that it is not four but five—then how many?"
>
> "Four."
>
> The word ended in a gasp of pain. The needle of the dial had shot up to fifty-five. The sweat had sprung out all over Winston's body. The air tore into his lungs and issued again in deep groans which even by clenching his teeth he could not stop. O'Brien watched him, the four fingers still extended. He drew back the lever. This time the pain was only slightly eased.

I am continually aghast at apparently intelligent folks—such as Robin Hanson's colleague Tyler Cowen—who don't think that overcoming bias is important.[3] This is your *mind* we're talking about. Your human intelligence. It separates you from an orangutan. It built this world. You don't think how the mind works is important? You don't think the mind's systematic malfunctions are important? Do you think the Inquisition would have tortured witches, if all were ideal Bayesians?

Tyler Cowen apparently feels that overcoming bias is just as biased as bias: "I view Robin's blog as exemplifying bias, and indeed showing that bias can be very useful." I *hope* this is only the result of thinking too abstractly while trying to sound clever. Does Tyler seriously think that scope insensitivity to the value of human life is on the same level with trying to create plans that will *really* save as many lives as possible?

Orwell was forced to fight a similar attitude—that to admit to any distinction is youthful naiveté:

> Stuart Chase and others have come near to claiming that all abstract words are meaningless, and have used this as a pretext for

---

[3] See Cowen's "How Important is Overcoming Bias?", http://marginalrevolution.com/marginalrevolution/2007/08/how-important-i.html.

advocating a kind of political quietism. Since you don't know
what Fascism is, how can you struggle against Fascism?

Maybe overcoming bias doesn't look quite exciting enough, if it's framed as a
struggle against mere accidental mistakes. Maybe it's harder to get excited if
there isn't some clear evil to oppose. So let us be absolutely clear that where
there is human evil in the world, where there is cruelty and torture and deliberate murder, there are biases enshrouding it. Where people of clear sight oppose
these biases, the concealed evil fights back. The truth *does* have enemies. If
Overcoming Bias were a newsletter in the old Soviet Union, every poster and
commenter of *Overcoming Bias* would have been shipped off to labor camps.

In all human history, every great leap forward has been driven by a new
clarity of thought. Except for a few natural catastrophes, every great woe has
been driven by a stupidity. Our last enemy is ourselves; and this is a war, and
we are soldiers.

Part G

Against Rationalization

24

Knowing About Biases Can Hurt People

Once upon a time I tried to tell my mother about the problem of expert calibration, saying: "So when an expert says they're 99% confident, it only happens about 70% of the time." Then there was a pause as, suddenly, I realized I was talking to my mother, and I hastily added: "Of course, you've got to make sure to apply that skepticism evenhandedly, including to yourself, rather than just using it to argue against anything you disagree with—"

And my mother said: "Are you kidding? This is great! I'm going to use it all the time!"

Taber and Lodge's "Motivated Skepticism in the Evaluation of Political Beliefs" describes the confirmation of six predictions:

1. Prior attitude effect. Subjects who feel strongly about an issue—even when encouraged to be objective—will evaluate supportive arguments more favorably than contrary arguments.

2. Disconfirmation bias. Subjects will spend more time and cognitive resources denigrating contrary arguments than supportive arguments.

3. Confirmation bias. Subjects free to choose their information sources will seek out supportive rather than contrary sources.

4. **Attitude polarization. Exposing subjects to an apparently balanced set of pro and con arguments will exaggerate their initial polarization.**

5. Attitude strength effect. Subjects voicing stronger attitudes will be more prone to the above biases.

6. **Sophistication effect. Politically knowledgeable subjects, because they possess greater ammunition with which to counter-argue incongruent facts and arguments, will be more prone to the above biases.**

If you're irrational to start with, having *more* knowledge can *hurt* you. For a true Bayesian, information would never have negative expected utility. But humans aren't perfect Bayes-wielders; if we're not careful, we can cut ourselves.

I've *seen* people severely messed up by their own knowledge of biases. They have more ammunition with which to argue against anything they don't like. And that problem—too much ready ammunition—is one of the primary ways that people with high mental agility end up stupid, in Stanovich's "dysrationalia" sense of stupidity.

You can think of people who fit this description, right? People with high g-factor who end up being *less* effective because they are too sophisticated as arguers? Do you think you'd be helping them—making them more effective rationalists—if you just told them about a list of classic biases?

I recall someone who learned about the calibration/overconfidence problem. Soon after he said: "Well, you can't trust experts; they're wrong so often—as experiments have shown. So therefore, when I predict the future, I prefer to assume that things will continue historically as they have—" and went off into this whole complex, error-prone, highly questionable extrapolation. Somehow, when it came to trusting his own preferred conclusions, all those biases and fallacies seemed much less *salient*—leapt much less readily to mind—than when he needed to counter-argue someone else.

I told the one about the problem of disconfirmation bias and sophisticated argument, and lo and behold, the next time I said something he didn't like, he accused me of being a sophisticated arguer. He didn't try to point out any particular sophisticated argument, any particular flaw—just shook his head and sighed sadly over how I was apparently using my own intelligence to defeat itself. He had acquired yet another Fully General Counterargument.

Even the notion of a "sophisticated arguer" can be deadly, if it leaps all too readily to mind when you encounter a seemingly intelligent person who says something you don't like.

I endeavor to learn from my mistakes. The last time I gave a talk on heuristics and biases, I started out by introducing the general concept by way of the conjunction fallacy and representativeness heuristic. And then I moved on to confirmation bias, disconfirmation bias, sophisticated argument, motivated skepticism, and other attitude effects. I spent the next thirty minutes *hammering* on that theme, reintroducing it from as many different perspectives as I could.

I wanted to get my audience interested in the subject. Well, a simple description of conjunction fallacy and representativeness would suffice for that. But suppose they did get interested. Then what? The literature on bias is mostly cognitive psychology for cognitive psychology's sake. I had to give my audience their dire warnings during that one lecture, or they probably wouldn't hear them at all.

Whether I do it on paper, or in speech, I now try to never mention calibration and overconfidence unless I have first talked about disconfirmation bias, motivated skepticism, sophisticated arguers, and dysrationalia in the mentally agile. First, do no harm!

25

Update Yourself Incrementally

Politics is the mind-killer. Debate is war, arguments are soldiers. There is the temptation to search for ways to interpret every possible experimental result to confirm your theory, like securing a citadel against every possible line of attack. This you cannot do. It is mathematically impossible. For every expectation of evidence, there is an equal and opposite expectation of counterevidence.[1]

But it's okay if your cherished belief isn't *perfectly* defended. If the hypothesis is that the coin comes up heads 95% of the time, then one time in twenty you will expect to see what looks like contrary evidence. This is okay. It's normal. It's even expected, so long as you've got nineteen supporting observations for every contrary one. A probabilistic model can take a hit or two, and still survive, so long as the hits don't *keep on* coming in.[2]

Yet it is widely believed, especially in the court of public opinion, that a true theory can have *no* failures and a false theory *no* successes.

You find people holding up a single piece of what they conceive to be evidence, and claiming that their theory can "explain" it, as though this were

---

[1] See "Conservation of Expected Evidence" in *Map and Territory*.
[2] One example of what this can look like in practice: "I Defy the Data!", http://lesswrong.com/lw/ig/i_defy_the_data/.

all the support that any theory needed. Apparently a false theory can have *no* supporting evidence; it is impossible for a false theory to fit even a single event. Thus, a single piece of confirming evidence is all that any theory needs.

It is only slightly less foolish to hold up a single piece of *probabilistic* counterevidence as disproof, as though it were impossible for a correct theory to have even a *slight* argument against it. But this is how humans have argued for ages and ages, trying to defeat all enemy arguments, while denying the enemy even a single shred of support. People want their debates to be one-sided; they are accustomed to a world in which their preferred theories have not one iota of antisupport. Thus, allowing a single item of probabilistic counterevidence would be the end of the world.

I just know someone in the audience out there is going to say, "But you *can't* concede even a single point if you want to win debates in the real world! If you concede that any counterarguments exist, the Enemy will harp on them over and over—you can't let the Enemy do that! You'll *lose!* What could be more viscerally terrifying than *that?*"

Whatever. Rationality is not for winning debates, it is for deciding which side to join. If you've already decided which side to argue for, the work of rationality is *done* within you, whether well or poorly. But how can you, yourself, decide which side to argue? If *choosing the wrong side* is viscerally terrifying, even just a little viscerally terrifying, you'd best integrate *all* the evidence.

Rationality is not a walk, but a dance. On each step in that dance your foot should come down in exactly the correct spot, neither to the left nor to the right. Shifting belief upward with each iota of confirming evidence. Shifting belief downward with each iota of contrary evidence. Yes, *down.* Even with a correct model, if it is not an exact model, you will sometimes need to revise your belief *down.*

If an iota or two of evidence happens to countersupport your belief, that's okay. It happens, sometimes, with probabilistic evidence for non-exact theories. (If an exact theory fails, you *are* in trouble!) Just shift your belief downward a little—the probability, the odds ratio, or even a nonverbal weight of credence in your mind. Just shift downward a little, and wait for more evidence. If the theory is true, supporting evidence will come in shortly, and the probability will climb again. If the theory is false, you don't really want it anyway.

The problem with using black-and-white, binary, qualitative reasoning is that any single observation either destroys the theory or it does not. When not even a single contrary observation is allowed, it creates cognitive dissonance and has to be argued away. And this rules out incremental progress; it rules out correct integration of all the evidence. Reasoning probabilistically, we realize that on average, a correct theory will generate a greater weight of support than countersupport. And so you can, *without fear,* say to yourself: "This is gently contrary evidence, I will shift my belief downward." Yes, *down.* It does not destroy your cherished theory. That is qualitative reasoning; think quantitatively.

For every expectation of evidence, there is an equal and opposite expectation of counterevidence. On every occasion, you must, on average, anticipate revising your beliefs downward as much as you anticipate revising them upward. If you think you already know what evidence will come in, then you must already be fairly sure of your theory—probability close to 1—which doesn't leave much room for the probability to go further upward. And however unlikely it seems that you will encounter disconfirming evidence, the resulting downward shift must be large enough to precisely balance the anticipated gain on the other side. The weighted mean of your expected posterior probability must equal your prior probability.

How silly is it, then, to be terrified of revising your probability downward, if you're bothering to investigate a matter at all? On average, you must anticipate as much downward shift as upward shift from every individual observation.

It may perhaps happen that an iota of antisupport comes in again, and again and again, while new support is slow to trickle in. You may find your belief drifting downward and further downward. Until, finally, you realize from which quarter the winds of evidence are blowing against you. In that moment of realization, there is no point in constructing excuses. In that moment of realization, you have *already relinquished* your cherished belief. Yay! Time to celebrate! Pop a champagne bottle or send out for pizza! You can't become stronger by keeping the beliefs you started with, after all.

26

One Argument Against An Army

I talked about a style of reasoning in which not a single contrary argument is allowed, with the result that every non-supporting observation has to be argued away. Here I suggest that when people encounter a contrary argument, they prevent themselves from downshifting their confidence by *rehearsing* already-known support.

Suppose the country of Freedonia is debating whether its neighbor, Sylvania, is responsible for a recent rash of meteor strikes on its cities. There are several pieces of evidence suggesting this: the meteors struck cities close to the Sylvanian border; there was unusual activity in the Sylvanian stock markets *before* the strikes; and the Sylvanian ambassador Trentino was heard muttering about "heavenly vengeance."

Someone comes to you and says: "I don't think Sylvania is responsible for the meteor strikes. They have trade with us of billions of dinars annually." "Well," you reply, "the meteors struck cities close to Sylvania, there was suspicious activity in their stock market, and their ambassador spoke of heavenly vengeance afterward." Since these three arguments outweigh the first, you *keep* your belief that Sylvania is responsible—you believe rather than disbelieve, qualitatively. Clearly, the balance of evidence weighs against Sylvania.

98

Then another comes to you and says: "I don't think Sylvania is responsible for the meteor strikes. Directing an asteroid strike is really hard. Sylvania doesn't even have a space program." You reply, "But the meteors struck cities close to Sylvania, and their investors knew it, and the ambassador came right out and admitted it!" Again, these three arguments outweigh the first (by three arguments against one argument), so you keep your belief that Sylvania is responsible.

Indeed, your convictions are *strengthened*. On two separate occasions now, you have evaluated the balance of evidence, and both times the balance was tilted against Sylvania by a ratio of 3 to 1.

You encounter further arguments by the pro-Sylvania traitors—again, and again, and a hundred times again—but each time the new argument is handily defeated by 3 to 1. And on every occasion, you feel yourself becoming more confident that Sylvania was indeed responsible, shifting your prior according to the felt balance of evidence.

The problem, of course, is that by *rehearsing* arguments you *already knew*, you are double-counting the evidence. This would be a grave sin even if you double-counted *all* the evidence. (Imagine a scientist who does an experiment with 50 subjects and fails to obtain statistically significant results, so the scientist counts all the data twice.)

But to selectively double-count *only some* evidence is sheer farce. I remember seeing a cartoon as a child, where a villain was dividing up loot using the following algorithm: "One for you, one for me. One for you, one-two for me. One for you, one-two-three for me."

As I emphasized in the last essay, even if a cherished belief is *true*, a rationalist may sometimes need to downshift the probability while integrating *all* the evidence. Yes, the balance of support may still favor your cherished belief. But you still have to shift the probability *down*—yes, *down*—from whatever it was before you heard the contrary evidence. It does no good to *rehearse* supporting arguments, because you have already taken those into account.

And yet it does appear to me that when people are confronted by a *new* counterargument, they search for a justification not to downshift their confidence, and of course they find supporting arguments they *already know*. I have to keep constant vigilance not to do this myself! It feels as natural as parrying a sword-strike with a handy shield.

With the right kind of wrong reasoning, a handful of support—or even a single argument—can stand off an army of contradictions.

27

The Bottom Line

There are two sealed boxes up for auction, box A and box B. One and only one of these boxes contains a valuable diamond. There are all manner of signs and portents indicating whether a box contains a diamond; but I have no sign which I *know* to be perfectly reliable. There is a blue stamp on one box, for example, and I know that boxes which contain diamonds are more likely than empty boxes to show a blue stamp. Or one box has a shiny surface, and I have a suspicion—I am not sure—that no diamond-containing box is ever shiny.

Now suppose there is a clever arguer, holding a sheet of paper, and they say to the owners of box A and box B: "Bid for my services, and whoever wins my services, I shall argue that their box contains the diamond, so that the box will receive a higher price." So the box-owners bid, and box B's owner bids higher, winning the services of the clever arguer.

The clever arguer begins to organize their thoughts. First, they write, "And *therefore*, box B contains the diamond!" at the bottom of their sheet of paper. Then, at the top of the paper, the clever arguer writes, "Box B shows a blue stamp," and beneath it, "Box A is shiny," and then, "Box B is lighter than box A," and so on through many signs and portents; yet the clever arguer neglects all those signs which might argue in favor of box A. And then the clever arguer comes to me and recites from their sheet of paper: "Box B shows a blue stamp, and box A is shiny," and so on, until they reach: "and *therefore*, box B contains the diamond."

But consider: At the moment when the clever arguer wrote down their conclusion, at the moment they put ink on their sheet of paper, the evidential entanglement of that physical ink with the physical boxes became fixed.

It may help to visualize a collection of worlds—Everett branches or Tegmark duplicates—within which there is some objective frequency at which box A or box B contains a diamond.[1] There's likewise some objective frequency within the subset "worlds with a shiny box A" where box B contains the diamond; and some objective frequency in "worlds with shiny box A and blue-stamped box B" where box B contains the diamond.

The ink on paper is formed into odd shapes and curves, which look like this text: "And *therefore*, box B contains the diamond." If you happened to be a literate English speaker, you might become confused, and think that this shaped ink somehow *meant* that box B contained the diamond. Subjects instructed to say the color of printed pictures and shown the picture GREEN in red ink often say "green" instead of "red." It helps to be illiterate, so that you are not confused by the shape of the ink.

To us, the true import of a thing is its entanglement with other things. Consider again the collection of worlds, Everett branches or Tegmark duplicates. At the moment when all clever arguers in all worlds put ink to the bottom line of their paper—let us suppose this is a single moment—it fixed the correlation of the ink with the boxes. The clever arguer writes in non-erasable pen; the

---

[1] The idea of an Everett branch comes from Hugh Everett's 1957 "relative-state" formulation of quantum mechanics. Everett's ideas are associated with the many worlds interpretation of quantum mechanics, which understands the universe's wave function as a superposition of terms that represent a large number of superficially classical macroscopic states, or "worlds," that are perpetually branching off from each other.

Max Tegmark's multiverse hypothesis is much more general than this; Tegmark asserts that all mathematically consistent structures (or, on his preferred formulation, all computable and decidable structures) exist.

We can also consider the more straightforward hypothesis that the universe beyond our cosmological horizon is sufficiently large and ergodic that there will by chance arise many other observers with the exact same experiences as ourselves, all or most of whom have different pasts, futures, and microphysical states. Tegmark's "Parallel Universes" (http://arxiv.org/abs/astro-ph/0302131) discusses all of these conceptions of "multiverses."

ink will not change. The boxes will not change. Within the subset of worlds where the ink says "And therefore, box B contains the diamond," there is already some fixed percentage of worlds where box A contains the diamond. This will not change regardless of what is written in on the blank lines above.

So the evidential entanglement of the ink is fixed, and I leave to you to decide what it might be. Perhaps box owners who believe a better case can be made for them are more liable to hire advertisers; perhaps box owners who fear their own deficiencies bid higher. If the box owners do not themselves understand the signs and portents, then the ink will be completely unentangled with the boxes' contents, though it may tell you something about the owners' finances and bidding habits.

Now suppose another person present is genuinely curious, and they *first* write down all the distinguishing signs of *both* boxes on a sheet of paper, and then apply their knowledge and the laws of probability and write down at the bottom: "*Therefore,* I estimate an 85% probability that box B contains the diamond." Of what is this handwriting evidence? Examining the chain of cause and effect leading to this physical ink on physical paper, I find that the chain of causality wends its way through all the signs and portents of the boxes, and is dependent on these signs; for in worlds with different portents, a different probability is written at the bottom.

So the handwriting of the curious inquirer is entangled with the signs and portents and the contents of the boxes, whereas the handwriting of the clever arguer is evidence only of which owner paid the higher bid. There is a great difference in the indications of ink, though one who foolishly read aloud the ink-shapes might think the English words sounded similar.

Your effectiveness as a rationalist is determined by whichever algorithm actually writes the bottom line of your thoughts. If your car makes metallic squealing noises when you brake, and you aren't willing to face up to the financial cost of getting your brakes replaced, you can decide to look for reasons why your car might not need fixing. But the actual percentage of you that survive in Everett branches or Tegmark worlds—which we will take to describe your effectiveness as a rationalist—is determined by the algorithm that decided *which* conclusion you would seek arguments for. In this case, the real algorithm is "Never repair anything expensive." If this is a good algorithm, fine; if this is a bad algorithm, oh well. The arguments you write afterward, above the bottom line, will not change anything either way.

This is intended as a caution for your own thinking, not a Fully General Counterargument against conclusions you don't like. For it is indeed a clever argument to say "My opponent is a clever arguer," if you are paying yourself to retain whatever beliefs you had at the start. The world's cleverest arguer may point out that the Sun is shining, and yet it is still probably daytime.

28

What Evidence Filtered Evidence?

I discussed the dilemma of the clever arguer, hired to sell you a box that may or may not contain a diamond. The clever arguer points out to you that the box has a blue stamp, and it is a valid known fact that diamond-containing boxes are more likely than empty boxes to bear a blue stamp. What happens at this point, from a Bayesian perspective? Must you helplessly update your probabilities, as the clever arguer wishes?

If you can look at the box yourself, you can add up all the signs yourself. What if you can't look? What if the only evidence you have is the word of the clever arguer, who is legally constrained to make only true statements, but does not tell you everything they know? Each statement that the clever arguer makes is valid evidence—how could you *not* update your probabilities? Has it ceased to be true that, in such-and-such a proportion of Everett branches or Tegmark duplicates in which box B has a blue stamp, box B contains a diamond? According to Jaynes, a Bayesian must always condition on all known evidence, on pain of paradox. But then the clever arguer can make you believe anything they choose, if there is a sufficient variety of signs to selectively report. That doesn't sound right.

Consider a simpler case, a biased coin, which may be biased to come up 2/3 heads and 1/3 tails, or 1/3 heads and 2/3 tails, both cases being equally likely a priori. Each H observed is 1 bit of evidence for an H-biased coin; each T observed is 1 bit of evidence for a T-biased coin.[1] I flip the coin ten times, and then I tell you, "The 4th flip, 6th flip, and 9th flip came up heads." What is your posterior probability that the coin is H-biased?

And the answer is that it could be almost anything, depending on what chain of cause and effect lay behind my utterance of those words—my selection of which flips to report.

- I might be following the algorithm of reporting the result of the 4th, 6th, and 9th flips, regardless of the result of those and all other flips. If you know that I used this algorithm, the posterior odds are 8:1 in favor of an H-biased coin.

- I could be reporting on all flips, and only flips, that came up heads. In this case, you know that all 7 other flips came up tails, and the posterior odds are 1:16 against the coin being H-biased.

- I could have decided in advance to say the result of the 4th, 6th, and 9th flips only if the probability of the coin being H-biased exceeds 98%. And so on.

Or consider the Monty Hall problem:

> On a game show, you are given the choice of three doors leading to three rooms. You know that in one room is $100,000, and the other two are empty. The host asks you to pick a door, and you pick door #1. Then the host opens door #2, revealing an empty room. Do you want to switch to door #3, or stick with door #1?

---

[1] "Bits" in this context are a measure of how much evidence something provides—they're the logarithms of probabilities, base 1/2. Suppose a question has exactly two possible (mutually exclusive) answers, and you initially assign 50% probability to each answer. If I then tell you that the first answer is correct (and you have complete faith in my claim), then you have acquired one bit of evidence. If there are four equally likely options, and I tell you the first one is correct, then I have given you two bits; if there are eight and I tell you the right one, then I have given you three bits; and so on. I discuss this more in the essay "How Much Evidence Does It Take?" (in *Map and Territory*).

The answer depends on the host's algorithm. If the host always opens a door and always picks a door leading to an empty room, then you should switch to door #3. If the host always opens door #2 regardless of what is behind it, #1 and #3 both have 50% probabilities of containing the money. If the host only opens a door, at all, if you initially pick the door with the money, then you should definitely stick with #1.

You shouldn't just condition on #2 being empty, but this fact plus the fact of the host *choosing* to open door #2. Many people are confused by the standard Monty Hall problem because they update only on #2 being empty, in which case #1 and #3 have equal probabilities of containing the money. This is why Bayesians are commanded to condition on all of their knowledge, on pain of paradox.

When someone says, "The 4th coinflip came up heads," we are not conditioning on the 4th coinflip having come up heads—we are not taking the subset of all possible worlds where the 4th coinflip came up heads—but rather are conditioning on the subset of all possible worlds where a speaker following some particular algorithm *said*, "The 4th coinflip came up heads." The spoken sentence is not the fact itself; don't be led astray by the mere meanings of words.

Most legal processes work on the theory that every case has exactly two opposed sides and that it is easier to find two biased humans than one unbiased one. Between the prosecution and the defense, *someone* has a motive to present any given piece of evidence, so the court will see all the evidence; that is the theory. If there are two clever arguers in the box dilemma, it is not quite as good as one curious inquirer, but it is almost as good. But that is with two boxes. Reality often has many-sided problems, and deep problems, and nonobvious answers, which are not readily found by Blues and Greens shouting at each other.

Beware lest you abuse the notion of evidence-filtering as a Fully General Counterargument to exclude all evidence you don't like: "That argument was filtered, therefore I can ignore it." If you're ticked off by a contrary argument, then you are familiar with the case, and care enough to take sides. You probably already know your own side's strongest arguments. You have no reason to infer, from a contrary argument, the existence of new favorable signs and portents which you have not yet seen. So you are left with the uncomfortable facts themselves; a blue stamp on box B is still evidence.

But if you are hearing an argument for the first time, and you are only hearing one side of the argument, then indeed you should beware! In a way, no one can *really* trust the theory of natural selection until after they have listened to creationists for five minutes; and *then* they know it's solid.

29

Rationalization

In "The Bottom Line," I presented the dilemma of two boxes, only one of which contains a diamond, with various signs and portents as evidence. I dichotomized the curious inquirer and the clever arguer. The curious inquirer writes down all the signs and portents, and processes them, and finally writes down, "*Therefore,* I estimate an 85% probability that box B contains the diamond." The clever arguer works for the highest bidder, and begins by writing, "*Therefore,* box B contains the diamond," and then selects favorable signs and portents to list on the lines above.

The first procedure is rationality. The second procedure is generally known as "rationalization."

"Rationalization." What a curious term. I would call it a *wrong word.* You cannot "rationalize" what is not already rational. It is as if "lying" were called "truthization."

On a purely computational level, there is a rather large difference between:

1. Starting from evidence, and then crunching probability flows, in order to output a probable conclusion. (Writing down all the signs and portents, and then flowing forward to a probability on the bottom line which depends on those signs and portents.)

2. Starting from a conclusion, and then crunching probability flows, in order to output evidence apparently favoring that conclusion. (Writing down the bottom line, and then flowing backward to select signs and portents for presentation on the lines above.)

What fool devised such confusingly similar words, "rationality" and "rationalization," to describe such extraordinarily different mental processes? I would prefer terms that made the algorithmic difference obvious, like "rationality" versus "giant sucking cognitive black hole."

Not every change is an improvement, but every improvement is necessarily a change. You cannot obtain more truth for a fixed proposition by arguing it; you can make more people believe it, but you cannot make it more *true*. To improve our beliefs, we must necessarily change our beliefs. Rationality is the operation that we use to obtain more accuracy for our beliefs by changing them. Rationalization operates to fix beliefs in place; it would be better named "anti-rationality," both for its pragmatic results and for its reversed algorithm.

"Rationality" is the *forward* flow that gathers evidence, weighs it, and outputs a conclusion. The curious inquirer used a forward-flow algorithm: *first* gathering the evidence, writing down a list of all visible signs and portents, which they then processed *forward* to obtain a previously unknown probability for the box containing the diamond. During the entire time that the rationality-process was running forward, the curious inquirer did not yet know their destination, which was why they were *curious.* In the Way of Bayes, the prior probability equals the expected posterior probability: If you know your destination, you are already there.

"Rationalization" is a *backward* flow from conclusion to selected evidence. First you write down the bottom line, which is known and fixed; the purpose of your processing is to find out which arguments you should write down on the lines above. This, not the bottom line, is the variable unknown to the running process.

I fear that Traditional Rationality does not properly sensitize its users to the difference between forward flow and backward flow. In Traditional Rationality, there is nothing wrong with the scientist who arrives at a pet hypothesis and then sets out to find an experiment that proves it. A Traditional Rationalist would look at this approvingly, and say, "This pride is the engine that drives Science forward." Well, it *is* the engine that drives Science forward. It is easier to find a prosecutor and defender biased in opposite directions, than to find a single unbiased human.

But just because everyone does something, doesn't make it okay. It would be better yet if the scientist, arriving at a pet hypothesis, set out to *test* that hypothesis for the sake of *curiosity*—creating experiments that would drive their own beliefs in an unknown direction.

If you genuinely don't know where you are going, you will probably feel quite curious about it. Curiosity is the first virtue, without which your questioning will be purposeless and your skills without direction.

Feel the flow of the Force, and make sure it isn't flowing backwards.

30

A Rational Argument

You are, by occupation, a campaign manager, and you've just been hired by Mortimer Q. Snodgrass, the Green candidate for Mayor of Hadleyburg. As a campaign manager reading a book on rationality, one question lies foremost on your mind: "How can I construct an impeccable rational argument that Mortimer Q. Snodgrass is the best candidate for Mayor of Hadleyburg?"

Sorry. It can't be done.

"What?" you cry. "But what if I use only valid support to construct my structure of reason? What if every fact I cite is true to the best of my knowledge, and relevant evidence under Bayes's Rule?"[1]

Sorry. It still can't be done. You defeated yourself the instant you specified your argument's conclusion in advance.

This year, the *Hadleyburg Trumpet* sent out a 16-item questionnaire to all mayoral candidates, with questions like "Can you paint with all the colors of the wind?" and "Did you inhale?" Alas, the *Trumpet's* offices are destroyed by a meteorite before publication. It's a pity, since your own candidate, Mortimer Q. Snodgrass, compares well to his opponents on 15 out of 16 questions. The

---

[1]See "What Is Evidence?" in *Map and Territory*.

only sticking point was Question 11, "Are you now, or have you ever been, a supervillain?"

So you are tempted to publish the questionnaire as part of your own campaign literature . . . with the 11th question omitted, of course.

Which crosses the line between *rationality* and *rationalization*. It is no longer possible for the voters to condition on the facts alone; they must condition on the additional fact of their presentation, and infer the existence of hidden evidence.

Indeed, you crossed the line at the point where you considered whether the questionnaire was favorable or unfavorable to your candidate, before deciding whether to publish it. "What!" you cry. "A campaign should publish facts unfavorable to their candidate?" But put yourself in the shoes of a voter, still trying to select a candidate—why would you censor useful information? You wouldn't, if you were genuinely curious. If you were flowing *forward* from the evidence to an unknown choice of candidate, rather than flowing *backward* from a fixed candidate to determine the arguments.

A "logical" argument is one that follows from its premises. Thus the following argument is *illogical*:

- All rectangles are quadrilaterals.

- All squares are quadrilaterals.

- *Therefore*, all squares are rectangles.

This syllogism is not rescued from illogic by the truth of its premises or even the truth of its conclusion. It is worth distinguishing logical deductions from illogical ones, and to refuse to excuse them even if their conclusions happen to be true. For one thing, the distinction may affect how we revise our beliefs in light of future evidence. For another, sloppiness is habit-forming.

Above all, the syllogism fails to state the real explanation. Maybe all squares are rectangles, but, if so, it's not *because* they are both quadrilaterals. You might call it a hypocritical syllogism—one with a disconnect between its stated reasons and real reasons.

If you really want to present an honest, rational argument *for your candidate*, in a political campaign, there is only one way to do it:

113

- *Before anyone hires you,* gather up all the evidence you can about the different candidates.

- Make a checklist which you, yourself, will use to decide which candidate seems best.

- Process the checklist.

- Go to the winning candidate.

- Offer to become their campaign manager.

- When they ask for campaign literature, print out your checklist.

Only in this way can you offer a *rational* chain of argument, one whose bottom line was written flowing *forward* from the lines above it. Whatever *actually* decides your bottom line is the only thing you can *honestly* write on the lines above.

31

Avoiding Your Belief's Real Weak Points

A few years back, my great-grandmother died, in her nineties, after a long, slow, and cruel disintegration. I never knew her as a person, but in my distant childhood, she cooked for her family; I remember her gefilte fish, and her face, and that she was kind to me. At her funeral, my grand-uncle, who had taken care of her for years, spoke. He said, choking back tears, that God had called back his mother piece by piece: her memory, and her speech, and then finally her smile; and that when God finally took her smile, he knew it wouldn't be long before she died, because it meant that she was almost entirely gone.

I heard this and was puzzled, because it was an unthinkably horrible thing to happen to *anyone*, and therefore I would not have expected my grand-uncle to attribute it to God. Usually, a Jew would somehow just-not-think-about the logical implication that God had permitted a tragedy. According to Jewish theology, God continually sustains the universe and chooses every event in it; but ordinarily, drawing logical implications from this belief is reserved for happier occasions. By saying "God did it!" only when you've been blessed with a baby girl, and just-not-thinking "God did it!" for miscarriages and stillbirths and crib deaths, you can build up quite a lopsided picture of your God's benevolent personality.

Hence I was surprised to hear my grand-uncle attributing the slow disintegration of his mother to a deliberate, strategically planned act of God. It violated the rules of religious self-deception as I understood them.

If I had noticed my own confusion, I could have made a successful surprising prediction. Not long afterward, my grand-uncle left the Jewish religion. (The only member of my extended family besides myself to do so, as far as I know.)

Modern Orthodox Judaism is like no other religion I have ever heard of, and I don't know how to describe it to anyone who hasn't been forced to study Mishna and Gemara. There is a tradition of questioning, but the *kind* of questioning . . . It would not be at all surprising to hear a rabbi, in his weekly sermon, point out the conflict between the seven days of creation and the 13.7 billion years since the Big Bang—because he thought he had a really clever explanation for it, involving three other Biblical references, a Midrash, and a half-understood article in *Scientific American*. In Orthodox Judaism you're allowed to notice inconsistencies and contradictions, but only for purposes of explaining them away, and whoever comes up with the most complicated explanation gets a prize.

There is a tradition of inquiry. But you only attack targets for purposes of defending them. You only attack targets you know you can defend.

In Modern Orthodox Judaism I have not heard much emphasis of the virtues of blind faith. You're allowed to doubt. You're just not allowed to *successfully* doubt.

I expect that the vast majority of educated Orthodox Jews have questioned their faith at some point in their lives. But the questioning probably went something like this: "According to the skeptics, the Torah says that the universe was created in seven days, which is not scientifically accurate. But would the original tribespeople of Israel, gathered at Mount Sinai, have been able to understand the scientific truth, even if it had been presented to them? Did they even have a word for 'billion'? It's easier to see the seven-days story as a metaphor—first God created light, which represents the Big Bang . . ."

116

Is this the weakest point at which to attack one's own Judaism? Read a bit further on in the Torah, and you can find God killing the first-born male children of Egypt to convince an unelected Pharaoh to release slaves who logically could have been teleported out of the country. An Orthodox Jew is most certainly familiar with this episode, because they are supposed to read through the entire Torah in synagogue once per year, and this event has an associated major holiday. The name "Passover" ("Pesach") comes from God *passing over* the Jewish households while killing every male firstborn in Egypt.

Modern Orthodox Jews are, by and large, kind and civilized people; far more civilized than the several editors of the Old Testament. Even the old rabbis were more civilized. There's a ritual in the Seder where you take ten drops of wine from your cup, one drop for each of the Ten Plagues, to emphasize the suffering of the Egyptians. (Of course, you're supposed to be sympathetic to the suffering of the Egyptians, but not *so* sympathetic that you stand up and say, "This is not right! It is *wrong* to do such a thing!") It shows an interesting contrast—the rabbis were sufficiently kinder than the compilers of the Old Testament that they saw the harshness of the Plagues. But Science was weaker in these days, and so rabbis could ponder the more unpleasant aspects of Scripture without fearing that it would break their faith entirely.

You don't even *ask* whether the incident reflects poorly on God, so there's no need to quickly blurt out "The ways of God are mysterious!" or "We're not wise enough to question God's decisions!" or "Murdering babies is okay when God does it!" That part of the question is just-not-thought-about.

The reason that educated religious people stay religious, I suspect, is that when they doubt, they are subconsciously very careful to attack their own beliefs only at the strongest points—places where they know they can defend. Moreover, places where rehearsing the standard defense will feel strengthening.

It probably feels really good, for example, to rehearse one's prescribed defense for "Doesn't Science say that the universe is just meaningless atoms bopping around?" because it confirms the meaning of the universe and how it flows from God, etc. Much more comfortable to think about than an illiterate Egyptian mother wailing over the crib of her slaughtered son. Anyone who

117

spontaneously thinks about the latter, when questioning their faith in Judaism, is *really* questioning it, and is probably not going to stay Jewish much longer.

My point here is not just to beat up on Orthodox Judaism. I'm sure that there's some reply or other for the Slaying of the Firstborn, and probably a dozen of them. My point is that, when it comes to spontaneous self-questioning, one is much more likely to spontaneously self-attack strong points with comforting replies to rehearse, then to spontaneously self-attack the weakest, most vulnerable points. Similarly, one is likely to stop at the first reply and be comforted, rather than further criticizing the reply. A better title than "Avoiding Your Belief's Real Weak Points" would be "Not Spontaneously Thinking About Your Belief's Most Painful Weaknesses."

More than anything, the grip of religion is sustained by people just-not-thinking-about the real weak points of their religion. I don't think this is a matter of training, but a matter of instinct. People don't think about the real weak points of their beliefs for the same reason they don't touch an oven's red-hot burners; it's *painful.*

To do better: When you're doubting one of your most cherished beliefs, close your eyes, empty your mind, grit your teeth, and deliberately think about whatever hurts the most. Don't rehearse standard objections whose standard counters would make you feel better. Ask yourself what *smart* people who disagree would say to your first reply, and your second reply. Whenever you catch yourself flinching away from an objection you fleetingly thought of, drag it out into the forefront of your mind. Punch yourself in the solar plexus. Stick a knife in your heart, and wiggle to widen the hole. In the face of the pain, rehearse only this:[1,2]

What is true is already so.

Owning up to it doesn't make it worse.

Not being open about it doesn't make it go away.

And because it's true, it is what is there to be interacted with.

Anything untrue isn't there to be lived.

---

[1] Eugene T. Gendlin, *Focusing* (Bantam Books, 1982).
[2] Hat tip to Stephen Omohundro.

118

People can stand what is true,

for they are already enduring it.

32

Motivated Stopping and Motivated Continuation

While I disagree with some views of the Fast and Frugal crowd—in my opinion they make a few *too* many lemons into lemonade—it also seems to me that they tend to develop the most *psychologically realistic* models of any school of decision theory. Most experiments present the subjects with options, and the subject chooses an option, and that's the experimental result. The frugalists realized that in real life, you have to *generate* your options, and they studied how subjects did *that*.

Likewise, although many experiments present evidence on a silver platter, in real life you have to gather evidence, which may be costly, and at some point decide that you have enough evidence to stop and choose. When you're buying a house, you don't get exactly ten houses to choose from, and you aren't led on a guided tour of all of them before you're allowed to decide anything. You look at one house, and another, and compare them to each other; you adjust your aspirations—reconsider how much you really need to be close to your workplace and how much you're really willing to pay; you decide which house to look at next; and at some point you decide that you've seen enough houses, and choose.

Gilovich's distinction between *motivated skepticism* and *motivated credulity* highlights how conclusions a person does not want to believe are held to a higher standard than conclusions a person wants to believe. A motivated skeptic asks if the evidence *compels* them to accept the conclusion; a motivated credulist asks if the evidence *allows* them to accept the conclusion.

I suggest that an analogous bias in psychologically realistic search is *motivated stopping* and *motivated continuation*: when we have a *hidden* motive for choosing the "best" current option, we have a hidden motive to stop, and choose, and reject consideration of any more options. When we have a hidden motive to reject the current best option, we have a hidden motive to suspend judgment pending additional evidence, to generate more options—to find something, anything, to do *instead* of coming to a conclusion.

A major historical scandal in statistics was R. A. Fisher, an eminent founder of the field, insisting that no *causal* link had been established between smoking and lung cancer. "Correlation is not causation," he testified to Congress. Perhaps smokers had a gene which both predisposed them to smoke and predisposed them to lung cancer.

Or maybe Fisher's being employed as a consultant for tobacco firms gave him a hidden motive to decide that the evidence already gathered was insufficient to come to a conclusion, and it was better to keep looking. Fisher was also a smoker himself, and died of colon cancer in 1962.[1]

Like many other forms of motivated skepticism, motivated continuation can try to disguise itself as virtuous rationality. Who can argue against gathering more evidence?[2]

I can. Evidence is often costly, and worse, slow, and there is certainly nothing virtuous about refusing to integrate the evidence you already have. You can always change your mind later.[3]

---

[1] Ad hominem note: Fisher was a frequentist. Bayesians are more reasonable about inferring probable causality; see Judea Pearl's *Causality: Models, Reasoning, and Inference*.

[2] Compare Robin Hanson's "Conspicuous Consumption of Info," http://www.overcoming-bias.com/2007/01/conspicuous_con.html.

[3] Apparent contradiction resolved as follows: Spending *one hour* discussing the problem, with your mind carefully cleared of all conclusions, is different from waiting ten years on another $20 million study.

121

As for motivated stopping, it appears in every place a third alternative is feared, and wherever you have an argument whose obvious counterargument you would rather not see, and in other places as well. It appears when you pursue a course of action that makes you feel good just for acting, and so you'd rather not investigate how well your plan *really* worked, for fear of destroying the warm glow of moral satisfaction you paid good money to purchase.[4] It appears wherever your beliefs and anticipations get out of sync, so you have a reason to fear any new evidence gathered.[5]

The moral is that the decision to terminate a search procedure (temporarily or permanently) is, like the search procedure itself, subject to bias and hidden motives. You should suspect motivated stopping when you close off search, after coming to a comfortable conclusion, and yet there's a lot of fast cheap evidence you haven't gathered yet—there are websites you could visit, there are counter-counter arguments you could consider, or you haven't closed your eyes for five minutes by the clock trying to think of a better option. You should suspect motivated continuation when some evidence is leaning in a way you don't like, but you decide that more evidence is needed—*expensive* evidence that you know you can't gather anytime soon, as opposed to something you're going to look up on Google in thirty minutes—before you'll have to do anything uncomfortable.

---

[4] See "'Can't Say No' Spending," http://lesswrong.com/lw/kb/cant_say_no_spending/

[5] For more on this phenomenon, see the discussion of "fake" beliefs in "Belief in Belief" and other *Map and Territory* essays.

33

Fake Justification

Many Christians who've stopped really believing now insist that they revere the Bible as a source of ethical advice. The standard atheist reply is given by Sam Harris: "You and I both know that it would take us five minutes to produce a book that offers a more coherent and compassionate morality than the Bible does."[1] Similarly, one may try to insist that the Bible is valuable as a literary work. Then why not revere *Lord of the Rings*, a vastly superior literary work? And despite the standard criticisms of Tolkien's morality, *Lord of the Rings* is at least superior to the Bible as a source of ethics. So why don't people wear little rings around their neck, instead of crosses? Even *Harry Potter* is superior to the Bible, both as a work of literary art and as moral philosophy.[2]

"How can you justify buying a $1 million gem-studded laptop," you ask your friend, "when so many people have no laptops at all?" And your friend says, "But think of the employment that this will provide—to the laptop maker, the laptop maker's advertising agency—and then they'll buy meals and haircuts—it will stimulate the economy and eventually many people will get their own laptops." But it would be even *more* efficient to buy 5,000 One Laptop Per Child

---

[1] In Harris' "Is Religion Built Upon Lies?" dialogue with Andrew Sullivan, http://www.samharris.org/site/full_text/debate-with-andrew-sullivan-part-two.
[2] If I really wanted to be cruel, I would compare the Bible to Jacqueline Carey's *Kushiel* series.

laptops, thus providing employment to the OLPC manufacturers *and* giving out laptops directly.

I've touched before on the failure to look for third alternatives. But this is not really motivated stopping. Calling it "motivated stopping" would imply that there was a search carried out in the first place.

In "The Bottom Line," I observed that only the real determinants of our beliefs can ever influence our real-world accuracy. Only the real determinants of our actions can influence our effectiveness in achieving our goals. Someone who buys a million-dollar laptop was really thinking, "Ooh, shiny," and that was the one true causal history of their decision to buy a laptop. No amount of "justification" can change this, unless the justification is a genuine, newly running search process that can change the conclusion. *Really* change the conclusion. Most criticism carried out from a sense of duty is more of a token inspection than anything else. Free elections in a one-party country.

To genuinely justify the Bible as an object of laudation by reference to its literary quality, you would have to somehow perform a neutral reading through candidate books until you found the book of highest literary quality. Renown is one reasonable criterion for generating candidates, so I suppose you could legitimately end up reading Shakespeare, the Bible, and *Gödel, Escher, Bach*. (Otherwise it would be quite a coincidence to find the Bible as a candidate, among a million other books.) The real difficulty is in that "neutral reading" part. Easy enough if you're not a Christian, but if you are . . .

But of course nothing like this happened. No search ever occurred. Writing the justification of "literary quality" above the bottom line of "I ♡ the Bible" is a historical misrepresentation of how the bottom line really got there, like selling cat milk as cow milk. That is just not where the bottom line really came from. That is just not what originally happened to produce that conclusion.

If you genuinely subject your conclusion to a criticism that can potentially de-conclude it—if the criticism *genuinely* has that power—then that does modify "the real algorithm behind" your conclusion. It changes the entanglement of your conclusion over possible worlds. But people overestimate, by far, how likely they *really* are to change their minds.

124

With all those open minds out there, you'd think there'd be more belief-updating.

Let me guess: Yes, you admit that you originally decided you wanted to buy a million-dollar laptop by thinking, "Ooh, shiny." Yes, you concede that this isn't a decision process consonant with your stated goals. But since then, you've decided that you really ought to spend your money in such fashion as to provide laptops to as many laptopless wretches as possible. And yet you just *couldn't* find any more efficient way to do this than buying a million-dollar diamond-studded laptop—because, hey, you're giving money to a laptop store and stimulating the economy! Can't beat that!

My friend, I am damned suspicious of this amazing coincidence. I am damned suspicious that the best answer under this lovely, rational, altruistic criterion X, is also the idea that just happened to originally pop out of the unrelated indefensible process Y. If you don't think that rolling dice would have been likely to produce the correct answer, then how likely is it to pop out of any other irrational cognition?

It's improbable that you used mistaken reasoning, yet made no mistakes.

34

Is That Your True Rejection?

It happens every now and then that someone encounters some of my transhumanist-side beliefs—as opposed to my ideas having to do with human rationality—strange, exotic-sounding ideas like superintelligence and Friendly AI. And the one rejects them.

If the one is called upon to explain the rejection, not uncommonly the one says, "Why should I believe anything Yudkowsky says? He doesn't have a PhD!"

And occasionally someone else, hearing, says, "Oh, you should get a PhD, so that people will listen to you." Or this advice may even be offered by the same one who expressed disbelief, saying, "Come back when you have a PhD."

Now, there are good and bad reasons to get a PhD. This is one of the bad ones.

There are many reasons why someone might actually have an initial adverse reaction to transhumanist theses. Most are matters of pattern recognition, rather than verbal thought: the thesis calls to mind an associated category like "strange weird idea" or "science fiction" or "end-of-the-world cult" or "overenthusiastic youth."[1] Immediately, at the speed of perception, the idea is rejected.

If someone afterward says, "Why not?" this launches a search for justification, but the search won't necessarily hit on the true reason. By "'true reason,'" I don't mean the *best* reason that could be offered. Rather, I mean whichever causes were decisive as a matter of historical fact, at the *very first* moment the rejection occurred.

Instead, the search for justification hits on the justifying-sounding fact, "This speaker does not have a PhD." But I also don't have a PhD when I talk about human rationality, so why is the same objection not raised there?

More to the point, if I *had* a PhD, people would not treat this as a decisive factor indicating that they ought to believe everything I say. Rather, the same initial rejection would occur, for the same reasons; and the search for justification, afterward, would terminate at a different stopping point.

They would say, "Why should I believe *you*? You're just some guy with a PhD! There are lots of those. Come back when you're well-known in your field and tenured at a major university."

But do people *actually* believe arbitrary professors at Harvard who say weird things? Of course not.

If you're saying things that sound *wrong* to a novice, as opposed to just rattling off magical-sounding technobabble about leptical quark braids in $N+2$ dimensions; and if the hearer is a stranger, unfamiliar with you personally and unfamiliar with the subject matter of your field; then I suspect that the point at which the average person will actually start to grant credence overriding their initial impression, purely because of academic credentials, is somewhere around the Nobel Laureate level. If that. Roughly, you need whatever level of academic credential qualifies as "beyond the mundane."

This is more or less what happened to Eric Drexler, as far as I can tell. He presented his vision of nanotechnology, and people said, "Where are the technical details?" or "Come back when you have a PhD!" And Eric Drexler spent six years writing up technical details and got his PhD under Marvin Minsky for doing it. And *Nanosystems* is a great book. But did the same people

---

[1] For more on this, see "Science as Attire" in *Map and Territory*.

127

who said, "Come back when you have a PhD," actually change their minds at all about molecular nanotechnology? Not so far as I ever heard.

This might be an important thing for young businesses and new-minted consultants to keep in mind—that what your failed prospects *tell* you is the reason for rejection may not make the *real* difference; and you should ponder that carefully before spending huge efforts. If the venture capitalist says, "If only your sales were growing a little faster!" or if the potential customer says, "It seems good, but you don't have feature X," that may not be the *true* rejection. Fixing it may, or may not, change anything.

And it would also be something to keep in mind during disagreements. Robin Hanson and I share a belief that two rationalists should not agree to disagree: they should not have common knowledge of epistemic disagreement unless something is very wrong.[2]

I suspect that, in general, if two rationalists set out to resolve a disagreement that persisted past the first exchange, they should expect to find that the true sources of the disagreement are either hard to communicate, or hard to expose. E.g.:

- Uncommon, but well-supported, scientific knowledge or math;

- Long inferential distances;

- Hard-to-verbalize intuitions, perhaps stemming from specific visualizations;

- Zeitgeists inherited from a profession (that may have good reason for it);

- Patterns perceptually recognized from experience;

- Sheer habits of thought;

- Emotional commitments to believing in a particular outcome;

- Fear that a past mistake could be disproved;

---

[2] See Hal Finnley's "Agreeing to Agree," http://www.overcomingbias.com/2006/12/agreeing_to_agr.html.

- Deep self-deception for the sake of pride or other personal benefits.

If the matter were one in which *all* the true rejections could be *easily* laid on the table, the disagreement would probably be so straightforward to resolve that it would never have lasted past the first meeting.

"Is this my true rejection?" is something that both disagreers should surely be asking *themselves*, to make things easier on the other person. However, attempts to directly, publicly psychoanalyze the other may cause the conversation to degenerate *very* fast, from what I've seen.

Still—"Is that your true rejection?" should be fair game for Disagreers to humbly ask, if there's any productive way to pursue that sub-issue. Maybe the rule could be that you can openly ask, "Is that simple straightforward-sounding reason your *true* rejection, or does it come from intuition-X or professional-zeitgeist-Y?" While the more embarrassing possibilities lower on the table are left to the Other's conscience, as their own responsibility to handle.

35

Entangled Truths, Contagious Lies

One of your very early philosophers came to the conclusion that a fully competent mind, from a study of one fact or artifact belonging to any given universe, could construct or visualize that universe, from the instant of its creation to its ultimate end . . .

—*First Lensman*

If any one of you will concentrate upon one single fact, or small object, such as a pebble or the seed of a plant or other creature, for as short a period of time as one hundred of your years, you will begin to perceive its truth.

—*Gray Lensman*

I am reasonably sure that a single pebble, taken from a beach of our own Earth, does not specify the continents and countries, politics and people of this Earth. Other planets in space and time, other Everett branches, would generate the same pebble.

On the other hand, the identity of a single pebble would seem to include our laws of physics. In that sense the entirety of our Universe—*all* the Everett branches—would be implied by the pebble.[1]

From the study of that single pebble you could see the laws of physics and all they imply. Thinking about those laws of physics, you can see that planets will form, and you can guess that the pebble came from such a planet. The internal crystals and molecular formations of the pebble developed under gravity, which tells you something about the planet's mass; the mix of elements in the pebble tells you something about the planet's formation.

I am not a geologist, so I don't know to which mysteries geologists are privy. But I find it very easy to imagine showing a geologist a pebble, and saying, "This pebble came from a beach at Half Moon Bay," and the geologist immediately says, "I'm confused," or even, "You liar." Maybe it's the wrong kind of rock, or the pebble isn't worn enough to be from a beach—I don't know pebbles well enough to guess the linkages and signatures by which I might be caught, which is the point.

"Only God can tell a truly plausible lie." I wonder if there was ever a religion that developed this as a proverb? I would (falsifiably) guess not: it's a rationalist sentiment, even if you cast it in theological metaphor. Saying "everything is interconnected to everything else, because God made the whole world and sustains it" may generate some nice warm 'n' fuzzy feelings during the sermon, but it doesn't get you very far when it comes to assigning pebbles to beaches.

A penny on Earth exerts a gravitational acceleration on the Moon of around 4.5×10^{-31} m/s^2, so in one sense it's not too far wrong to say that every event is entangled with its whole past light cone. And since inferences can propagate backward and forward through causal networks, *epistemic* entanglements can easily cross the borders of light cones. But I wouldn't want to be the forensic astronomer who had to look at the Moon and figure out whether the penny landed heads or tails—the influence is far less than quantum uncertainty and thermal noise.

---

[1] Assuming, as seems likely, there are no truly free variables.

If you said, "Everything is entangled with something else," or, "Everything is inferentially entangled and some entanglements are much stronger than others," you might be really wise instead of just Deeply Wise.

Physically, each event is in some sense the sum of its whole past light cone, without borders or boundaries. But the list of *noticeable* entanglements is much shorter, and it gives you something like a network. This high-level regularity is what I refer to when I talk about the Great Web of Causality.

I use these Capitalized Letters somewhat tongue-in-cheek, perhaps; but if anything at all is worth Capitalized Letters, surely the Great Web of Causality makes the list.

"Oh what a tangled web we weave, when first we practise to deceive," said Sir Walter Scott. Not *all* lies spin out of control—we don't live in so righteous a universe. But it does occasionally happen that someone lies about a fact, and then has to lie about an entangled fact, and then another fact entangled with that one:

"Where were you?"

"Oh, I was on a business trip."

"What was the business trip about?"

"I can't tell you that; it's proprietary negotiations with a major client."

"Oh—they're letting you in on those? Good news! I should call your boss to thank him for adding you."

"Sorry—he's not in the office right now . . ."

Human beings, who are not gods, often fail to *imagine* all the facts they would need to distort to tell a truly plausible lie. "God made me pregnant" sounded a tad more likely in the old days before our models of the world contained (quotations of) Y chromosomes. Many similar lies, today, may blow up when genetic testing becomes more common. Rapists have been convicted, and false accusers exposed, years later, based on evidence they didn't realize they could leave. A student of evolutionary biology can see the design signature of natural selection on every wolf that chases a rabbit; and every rabbit that runs away;

and every bee that stings instead of broadcasting a polite warning—but the deceptions of creationists sound plausible to *them*, I'm sure.

Not all lies are uncovered, not all liars are punished; we don't live in that righteous a universe. But not all lies are as safe as their liars believe. How many sins would become known to a Bayesian superintelligence, I wonder, if it did a (non-destructive?) nanotechnological scan of the Earth? At minimum, all the lies of which any evidence still exists in any brain. Some such lies may become known sooner than that, if the neuroscientists ever succeed in building a really good lie detector via neuroimaging. Paul Ekman (a pioneer in the study of tiny facial muscle movements) could probably read off a sizeable fraction of the world's lies right now, given a chance.

Not all lies are uncovered, not all liars are punished. But the Great Web is very commonly underestimated. Just the knowledge that humans have *already accumulated* would take many human lifetimes to learn. Anyone who thinks that a non-God can tell a *perfect* lie, risk-free, is underestimating the tangledness of the Great Web.

Is honesty the best policy? I don't know if I'd go that far: Even on my ethics, it's sometimes okay to shut up. But compared to outright lies, either honesty or silence involves less exposure to recursively propagating risks you don't know you're taking.

36

Of Lies and Black Swan Blowups

Judge Marcus Einfeld, age 70, Queen's Counsel since 1977, Australian Living Treasure 1997, United Nations Peace Award 2002, founding president of Australia's Human Rights and Equal Opportunities Commission, retired a few years back but routinely brought back to judge important cases . . .

. . . went to jail for two years over a series of perjuries and lies that started with a $77, 6-mph-over speeding ticket.[1]

That whole *suspiciously virtuous-sounding* theory about honest people not being good at lying, and entangled traces being left somewhere, and the entire thing blowing up in a Black Swan epic fail, actually *does* have a certain number of exemplars in real life, though obvious selective reporting is at work in our hearing about this one.

---

[1] See https://en.wikipedia.org/wiki/Marcus_Einfeld#Criminal_conviction.

37

Dark Side Epistemology

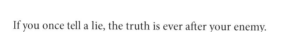

If you once tell a lie, the truth is ever after your enemy.

I have discussed the notion that lies are contagious. If you pick up a pebble from the driveway, and tell a geologist that you found it on a beach—well, do *you* know what a geologist knows about rocks? I don't. But I can suspect that a water-worn pebble wouldn't look like a droplet of frozen lava from a volcanic eruption. Do you know where the pebble in your driveway really came from? Things bear the marks of their places in a lawful universe; in that web, a lie is out of place.[1]

What sounds like an arbitrary truth to one mind—one that could easily be replaced by a plausible lie—might be nailed down by a dozen linkages to the eyes of greater knowledge. To a creationist, the idea that life was shaped by "intelligent design" instead of "natural selection" might sound like a sports team to cheer for. To a biologist, plausibly arguing that an organism was intelligently designed would require lying about almost every facet of the organism. To plausibly argue that "humans" were intelligently designed, you'd have to lie

---

[1] Actually, a geologist in the comments says that most pebbles in driveways are taken *from* beaches, so they couldn't tell the difference between a driveway pebble and a beach pebble, but they could tell the difference between a mountain pebble and a driveway/beach pebble (http://less-wrong.com/lw/uy/dark_side_epistemology/4xbv). Case in point . . .

about the design of the human retina, the architecture of the human brain, the proteins bound together by weak van der Waals forces instead of strong covalent bonds . . .

Or you could just lie about evolutionary theory, which is the path taken by most creationists. Instead of lying about the connected nodes in the network, they lie about the *general* laws governing the links.

And then to cover *that* up, they lie about the rules of science—like what it means to call something a "theory," or what it means for a scientist to say that they are not absolutely certain.

So they pass from lying about specific facts, to lying about general laws, to lying about the rules of reasoning. To lie about whether humans evolved, you must lie about evolution; and then you have to lie about the rules of science that constrain our understanding of evolution.

But how else? Just as a human would be out of place in a community of *actually* intelligently designed life forms, and you have to lie about the rules of evolution to make it appear otherwise, so too beliefs about creationism are themselves out of place in science—you wouldn't find them in a well-ordered mind any more than you'd find palm trees growing on a glacier. And so you have to disrupt the barriers that would forbid them.

Which brings us to the case of self-deception.

A single lie you tell *yourself* may seem plausible enough, when you don't know any of the rules governing thoughts, or even that there *are* rules; and the choice seems as arbitrary as choosing a flavor of ice cream, as isolated as a pebble on the shore . . .

. . . but then someone calls you on your belief, using the rules of reasoning that *they've* learned. They say, "Where's your evidence?"

And you say, "What? Why do I need evidence?"

So they say, "In general, beliefs require evidence."

This argument, clearly, is a soldier fighting on the other side, which you must defeat. So you say: "I disagree! Not all beliefs require evidence. In particular, beliefs about dragons don't require evidence. When it comes to dragons, you're allowed to believe anything you like. So I don't need evidence to believe there's a dragon in my garage."

136

And the one says, "Eh? You can't just exclude dragons like that. There's a reason for the rule that beliefs require evidence. To draw a correct map of the city, you have to walk through the streets and make lines on paper that correspond to what you see. That's not an arbitrary legal requirement—if you sit in your living room and draw lines on the paper at random, the map's going to be wrong. With extremely high probability. That's as true of a map of a dragon as it is of anything."

So now *this*, the explanation of *why* beliefs require evidence, is *also* an opposing soldier. So you say: "Wrong with extremely high probability? Then there's still a chance, right? I don't have to believe if it's not absolutely certain."

Or maybe you even begin to suspect, yourself, that "beliefs require evidence." But this threatens a lie you hold precious; so you reject the dawn inside you, push the Sun back under the horizon.

Or you've previously heard the proverb "beliefs require evidence," and it sounded wise enough, and you endorsed it in public. But it never quite occurred to you, until someone else brought it to your attention, that this proverb could *apply to* your belief that there's a dragon in your garage. So you think fast and say, "The dragon is in a separate magisterium."

Having false beliefs isn't a good thing, but it doesn't have to be permanently crippling—if, when you discover your mistake, you get over it. The dangerous thing is to have a false belief that you *believe should be protected as a belief*—a belief-in-belief, whether or not accompanied by actual belief.

A single Lie That Must Be Protected can block someone's progress into advanced rationality. No, it's not harmless fun.

Just as the world itself is more tangled by far than it appears on the surface, so too there are stricter rules of reasoning, constraining belief more strongly, than the untrained would suspect. The world is woven tightly, governed by general laws, and so are *rational* beliefs.

Think of what it would take to deny evolution or heliocentrism—all the connected truths and governing laws you wouldn't be allowed to know. Then you can imagine how a single act of self-deception can block off the whole meta level of truth-seeking, once your mind begins to be threatened by seeing the connections. Forbidding all the intermediate and higher levels of the rationalist's Art. Creating, in its stead, a vast complex of anti-law, rules of anti-thought, general justifications for believing the untrue.

Steven Kaas said, "Promoting less than maximally accurate beliefs is an act of sabotage. Don't do it to anyone unless you'd also slash their tires." Giving someone a false belief *to protect*—convincing them that the *belief itself* must be defended from any thought that seems to threaten it—well, you shouldn't do that to someone unless you'd also give them a frontal lobotomy.

Once you tell a lie, the truth is your enemy; and every truth connected to that truth, and every ally of truth in general; all of these you must oppose, to protect the lie. Whether you're lying to others, or to yourself.

You have to deny that beliefs require evidence, and then you have to deny that maps should reflect territories, and then you have to deny that truth is a good thing . . .

Thus comes into being the Dark Side.

I worry that people aren't aware of it, or aren't sufficiently wary—that as we wander through our human world, we can expect to encounter *systematically* bad epistemology.

The "how to think" memes floating around, the cached thoughts of Deep Wisdom—some of it will be good advice devised by rationalists. But other notions were invented to protect a lie or self-deception: spawned from the Dark Side.

"Everyone has a right to their own opinion." When you think about it, where was that proverb generated? Is it something that someone would say in the course of protecting a truth, or in the course of protecting *from* the truth? But people don't perk up and say, "Aha! I sense the presence of the Dark Side!" As far as I can tell, it's not widely realized that the Dark Side is out there.

But how else? Whether you're deceiving others, or just yourself, the Lie That Must Be Protected will propagate recursively through the network of empirical causality, and the network of general empirical rules, and the rules of reasoning themselves, and the understanding behind those rules. If there is *good* epistemology in the world, and also lies or self-deceptions that people are trying to protect, then there will come into existence bad epistemology to counter the good. We could hardly expect, in this world, to find the Light

138

Side without the Dark Side; there is the Sun, and that which shrinks away and generates a cloaking Shadow.

Mind you, these are not necessarily *evil people*. The vast majority who go about repeating the Deep Wisdom are more duped than duplicitous, more self-deceived than deceiving. I think.

And it's surely not my intent to offer you a Fully General Counterargument, so that whenever someone offers you some epistemology you don't like, you say: "Oh, someone on the Dark Side made that up." It's one of the rules of the Light Side that you have to refute the proposition for itself, not by accusing its inventor of bad intentions.

But the Dark Side is out there. Fear is the path that leads to it, and one betrayal can turn you. Not all who wear robes are either Jedi or fakes; there are also the Sith Lords, masters and unwitting apprentices. Be warned; be wary.

As for listing common memes that were spawned by the Dark Side—not random false beliefs, mind you, but bad epistemology, the Generic Defenses of Fail—well, would you care to take a stab at it, dear readers?

Part H

Seeing with Fresh Eyes

38

Anchoring and Adjustment

Suppose I spin a Wheel of Fortune device as you watch, and it comes up pointing to 65. Then I ask: Do you think the percentage of African countries in the UN is above or below this number? What do you think is the percentage of African countries in the UN? Take a moment to consider these two questions yourself, if you like, and please don't Google.

Also, try to guess, within *five seconds*, the value of the following arithmetical expression. Five seconds. Ready? Set . . . *Go!*

$$1 \times 2 \times 3 \times 4 \times 5 \times 6 \times 7 \times 8$$

Tversky and Kahneman recorded the estimates of subjects who saw the Wheel of Fortune showing various numbers.[1] The median estimate of subjects who saw the wheel show 65 was 45%; the median estimate of subjects who saw 10 was 25%.

The current theory for this and similar experiments is that subjects take the initial, uninformative number as their starting point or *anchor*; and then they *adjust* upward or downward from their starting estimate until they reach

---

[1] Amos Tversky and Daniel Kahneman, "Judgment Under Uncertainty: Heuristics and Biases," *Science* 185, no. 4157 (1974): 1124–1131, doi:10.1126/science.185.4157.1124.

an answer that "sounds plausible"; and then they stop adjusting. This typically results in under-adjustment from the anchor—more distant numbers could also be "plausible," but one stops at the first satisfying-sounding answer.

Similarly, students shown "$1 \times 2 \times 3 \times 4 \times 5 \times 6 \times 7 \times 8$" made a median estimate of 512, while students shown "$8 \times 7 \times 6 \times 5 \times 4 \times 3 \times 2 \times 1$" made a median estimate of 2,250. The motivating hypothesis was that students would try to multiply (or guess-combine) the first few factors of the product, then adjust upward. In both cases the adjustments were insufficient, relative to the true value of 40,320; but the first set of guesses were much more insufficient because they started from a lower anchor.

Tversky and Kahneman report that offering payoffs for accuracy did not reduce the anchoring effect.

Strack and Mussweiler asked for the year Einstein first visited the United States.[2] Completely implausible anchors, such as 1215 or 1992, produced anchoring effects just as large as more plausible anchors such as 1905 or 1939.

There are obvious applications in, say, salary negotiations, or buying a car. I won't suggest that you exploit it, but watch out for exploiters.

And watch yourself thinking, and try to notice when you are *adjusting* a figure in search of an estimate.

Debiasing manipulations for anchoring have generally proved not very effective. I would suggest these two: First, if the initial guess sounds implausible, try to throw it away entirely and come up with a new estimate, rather than sliding from the anchor. But this in itself may not be sufficient—subjects instructed to avoid anchoring still seem to do so.[3] So, second, even if you are trying the first method, try also to think of an anchor in the opposite direction—an anchor that is clearly too small or too large, instead of too large or too small—and dwell on it briefly.

[2] Fritz Strack and Thomas Mussweiler, "Explaining the Enigmatic Anchoring Effect: Mechanisms of Selective Accessibility," *Journal of Personality and Social Psychology* 73, no. 3 (1997): 437–446.

[3] George A. Quattrone et al., "Explorations in Anchoring: The Effects of Prior Range, Anchor Extremity, and Suggestive Hints" (Unpublished manuscript, Stanford University, 1981).

39

Priming and Contamination

Suppose you ask subjects to press one button if a string of letters forms a word, and another button if the string does not form a word (e.g., "banack" vs. "banner"). Then you show them the string "water." Later, they will more quickly identify the string "drink" as a word. This is known as "cognitive priming"; this particular form would be "semantic priming" or "conceptual priming."

The fascinating thing about priming is that it occurs at such a low level— priming speeds up *identifying letters as forming a word*, which one would expect to take place *before* you deliberate on the word's meaning.

Priming also reveals the massive parallelism of spreading activation: if seeing "water" activates the word "drink," it probably also activates "river," or "cup," or "splash" . . . and this activation spreads, from the semantic linkage of concepts, all the way back to recognizing strings of letters.

Priming is subconscious and unstoppable, an artifact of the human neural architecture. Trying to stop yourself from priming is like trying to stop the spreading activation of your own neural circuits. In Mussweiler and Strack's experiment, subjects were asked an anchoring question: "Is the annual mean temperature in Germany higher or lower than 5 °C / 20 °C?"[1] Afterward, on a word-identification task, subjects presented with the 5 °C anchor were faster on identifying words like "cold" and "snow," while subjects with the high anchor were faster to identify "hot" and "sun." This shows a non-adjustment mechanism for anchoring: priming compatible thoughts and memories.

The more general result is that *completely uninformative, known false*, or *totally irrelevant* "information" can influence estimates and decisions. In the field of heuristics and biases, this more general phenomenon is known as *contamination*.[2]

Early research in heuristics and biases discovered anchoring effects, such as subjects giving lower (higher) estimates of the percentage of UN countries found within Africa, depending on whether they were first asked if the percentage was more or less than 10 (65). This effect was originally attributed to subjects adjusting from the anchor as a starting point, stopping as soon as they reached a plausible value, and under-adjusting because they were stopping at one end of a confidence interval.[3]

Tversky and Kahneman's early hypothesis still appears to be the correct explanation in some circumstances, notably when subjects generate the initial estimate themselves.[4] But modern research seems to show that most anchoring is actually due to contamination, not sliding adjustment.[5]

Your grocery store probably has annoying signs saying "Limit 12 per customer" or "5 for $10." Are these signs effective at getting customers to buy in larger quantities? You probably think you're not influenced.[6] But *someone*

---

[1] Thomas Mussweiler and Fritz Strack, "Comparing Is Believing: A Selective Accessibility Model of Judgmental Anchoring," *European Review of Social Psychology* 10 (1 1999): 135–167, doi:10.1080/14792779943000044.

[2] Gretchen B. Chapman and Eric J. Johnson, "Incorporating the Irrelevant: Anchors in Judgments of Belief and Value," in *Heuristics and Biases: The Psychology of Intuitive Judgment*, ed. Thomas Gilovich, Dale Griffin, and Daniel Kahneman (New York: Cambridge University Press, 2002), 120–138.

[3] Tversky and Kahneman, "Judgment Under Uncertainty."

[4] Nicholas Epley and Thomas Gilovich, "Putting Adjustment Back in the Anchoring and Adjustment Heuristic: Differential Processing of Self-Generated and Experimentor-Provided Anchors," *Psychological Science* 12 (5 2001): 391–396, doi:10.1111/1467-9280.00372.

[5] Hat tip to Unnamed (http://lesswrong.com/lw/j7/anchoring_and_adjustment/eza) for reminding me of this—I'd read the Epley and Gilovich paper years ago, as a chapter in *Heuristics and Biases*, but forgotten it.

[6] See: http://en.wikipedia.org/wiki/Bias_blind_spot

must be, because these signs have been shown to work. Which is why stores keep putting them up.[7]

Yet the most fearsome aspect of contamination is that it serves as yet another of the thousand faces of confirmation bias.[8] Once an idea gets into your head, it primes information compatible with it—and thereby ensures its continued existence. Never mind the selection pressures for winning political arguments; confirmation bias is built directly into our hardware, associational networks priming compatible thoughts and memories. An unfortunate side effect of our existence as neural creatures.

A single fleeting image can be enough to prime associated words for recognition. Don't think it takes anything more to set confirmation bias in motion. All it takes is that one quick flash, and the bottom line is already decided, for we change our minds less often than we think . . .

[7] Brian Wansink, Robert J. Kent, and Stephen J. Hoch, "An Anchoring and Adjustment Model of Purchase Quantity Decisions," *Journal of Marketing Research* 35, no. 1 (1998): 71–81, http://www.jstor.org/stable/3151931.

[8] Other faces, discussed in *Map and Territory*, include positive bias and hindsight bias. See, e.g., "Fake Causality."

40

Do We Believe Everything We're Told?

Some early experiments on anchoring and adjustment tested whether *distracting* the subjects—rendering subjects cognitively "busy" by asking them to keep a lookout for "5" in strings of numbers, or some such—would decrease adjustment, and hence increase the influence of anchors. Most of the experiments seemed to bear out the idea that being cognitive busy increased anchoring, and more generally contamination.

Looking over the accumulating experimental results—more and more findings of contamination, exacerbated by cognitive busyness—Daniel Gilbert saw a truly crazy pattern emerging: Do we believe *everything* we're told?

One might naturally think that on being told a proposition, we would first *comprehend* what the proposition meant, then *consider* the proposition, and finally *accept* or *reject* it. This obvious-seeming model of cognitive process flow dates back to Descartes. But Descartes's rival, Spinoza, disagreed; Spinoza suggested that we first *passively accept a proposition in the course of comprehending it*, and only afterward *actively disbelieve* propositions which are rejected by consideration.

Over the last few centuries, philosophers pretty much went along with Descartes, since his view seemed more, y'know, logical and intuitive.[1] But Gilbert saw a way of testing Descártes's and Spinoza's hypotheses experimentally.

If Descartes is right, then distracting subjects should interfere with both accepting true statements and rejecting false statements. If Spinoza is right, then distracting subjects should cause them to remember false statements as being true, but should not cause them to remember true statements as being false.

Gilbert, Krull, and Malone bear out this result, showing that, among subjects presented with novel statements labeled TRUE or FALSE, distraction had no effect on identifying true propositions (55% success for uninterrupted presentations, vs. 58% when interrupted); but did affect identifying false propositions (55% success when uninterrupted, vs. 35% when interrupted).[2]

A much more dramatic illustration was produced in followup experiments by Gilbert, Tafarodi, and Malone.[3] Subjects read aloud crime reports crawling across a video monitor, in which the color of the text indicated whether a particular statement was true or false. Some reports contained false statements that exacerbated the severity of the crime; other reports contained false statements that extenuated (excused) the crime. Some subjects also had to pay attention to strings of digits, looking for a "5," while reading the crime reports—this being the distraction task to create cognitive busyness. Finally, subjects had to recommend the length of prison terms for each criminal, from 0 to 20 years.

Subjects in the cognitively busy condition recommended an average of 11.15 years in prison for criminals in the "exacerbating" condition, that is, criminals whose reports contained labeled false statements exacerbating the severity of the crime. Busy subjects recommended an average of 5.83 years in

---

[1] See Robin Hanson's "What Evidence Intuition?", http://www.overcomingbias.com/2007/10/what-evidence-i.html.

[2] Daniel T. Gilbert, Douglas S. Krull, and Patrick S. Malone, "Unbelieving the Unbelievable: Some Problems in the Rejection of False Information," *Journal of Personality and Social Psychology* 59 (4 1990): 601–613, doi:10.1037/0022-3514.59.4.601.

[3] Daniel T. Gilbert, Romin W. Tafarodi, and Patrick S. Malone, "You Can't Not Believe Everything You Read," *Journal of Personality and Social Psychology* 65 (2 1993): 221–233, doi:10.1037/0022-3514.65.2.221.

149

prison for criminals whose reports contained labeled false statements excusing the crime. This nearly twofold difference was, as you might suspect, statistically significant.

Non-busy participants read exactly the same reports, with the same labels, and the same strings of numbers occasionally crawling past, except that they did not have to search for the number "5." Thus, they could devote more attention to "unbelieving" statements labeled false. These non-busy participants recommended 7.03 years versus 6.03 years for criminals whose reports falsely exacerbated or falsely excused.

Gilbert, Tafarodi, and Malone's paper was entitled "You Can't Not Believe Everything You Read."

This suggests—to say the very least—that we should be more careful when we expose ourselves to unreliable information, especially if we're doing something else at the time. Be careful when you glance at that newspaper in the supermarket.

41

Cached Thoughts

One of the single greatest puzzles about the human brain is how the damn thing works *at all* when most neurons fire 10–20 times per second, or 200Hz tops. In neurology, the "hundred-step rule" is that any postulated operation has to complete in *at most* 100 sequential steps—you can be as parallel as you like, but you can't postulate more than 100 (preferably fewer) neural spikes one after the other.

Can you imagine having to program using 100Hz CPUs, no matter how many of them you had? You'd also need a hundred billion processors just to get *anything* done in realtime.

If you did need to write realtime programs for a hundred billion 100Hz processors, one trick you'd use as heavily as possible is caching. That's when you store the results of previous operations and look them up next time, instead of recomputing them from scratch. And it's a very *neural* idiom—recognition, association, completing the pattern.

It's a good guess that the actual *majority* of human cognition consists of cache lookups.

This thought does tend to go through my mind at certain times.

There was a wonderfully illustrative story which I thought I had bookmarked, but couldn't re-find: it was the story of a man whose know-it-all neighbor had once claimed in passing that the best way to remove a chimney from your house was to knock out the fireplace, wait for the bricks to drop down one level, knock out those bricks, and repeat until the chimney was gone. Years later, when the man wanted to remove his own chimney, this cached thought was lurking, waiting to pounce . . .

As the man noted afterward—you can guess it didn't go well—his neighbor was not particularly knowledgeable in these matters, not a trusted source. If he'd *questioned* the idea, he probably would have realized it was a poor one. Some cache hits we'd be better off recomputing. But the brain completes the pattern automatically—and if you don't consciously realize the pattern needs correction, you'll be left with a completed pattern.

I suspect that if the thought had occurred to the man himself—if he'd *personally* had this bright idea for how to remove a chimney—he would have examined the idea more critically. But if someone *else* has already thought an idea through, you can save on computing power by caching their *conclusion*—right?

In modern civilization particularly, no one can think fast enough to think their own thoughts. If I'd been abandoned in the woods as an infant, raised by wolves or silent robots, I would scarcely be recognizable as human. No one can think fast enough to recapitulate the wisdom of a hunter-gatherer tribe in one lifetime, starting from scratch. As for the wisdom of a literate civilization, forget it.

But the flip side of this is that I continually see people who aspire to critical thinking, repeating back cached thoughts which were not invented by critical thinkers.

A good example is the skeptic who concedes, "Well, you can't prove or disprove a religion by factual evidence." As I have pointed out elsewhere,[1] this is simply false as probability theory. And it is also simply false relative to the real psychology of religion—a few centuries ago, saying this would have gotten you burned at the stake. A mother whose daughter has cancer prays, "God,

---

[1] In *Map and Territory*, "Religion's Claim to be Non-Disprovable."

please heal my daughter," not, "Dear God, I know that religions are not allowed to have any falsifiable consequences, which means that you can't possibly heal my daughter, so . . . well, basically, I'm praying to make myself feel better, instead of doing something that could actually help my daughter."

But people read "You can't prove or disprove a religion by factual evidence," and then, the next time they see a piece of evidence disproving a religion, their brain completes the pattern. Even some atheists repeat this absurdity without hesitation. If they'd thought of the idea themselves, rather than hearing it from someone else, they would have been more skeptical.

Death. Complete the pattern: "Death gives meaning to life."

It's frustrating, talking to good and decent folk—people who would never in a thousand years *spontaneously* think of wiping out the human species—raising the topic of existential risk, and hearing them say, "Well, maybe the human species doesn't deserve to survive." They would never in a thousand years shoot their own child, who is a part of the human species, but the brain completes the pattern.

What patterns are being completed, inside your mind, that you never chose to be there?

Rationality. Complete the pattern: "Love isn't rational."

If this idea had suddenly occurred to you personally, as an entirely new thought, how would you examine it critically? I know what *I* would say, but what would *you*?[2] It can be hard to see with fresh eyes. Try to keep your mind from completing the pattern in the standard, unsurprising, already-known way. It may be that there is no better answer than the standard one, but you can't *think* about the answer until you can stop your brain from filling in the answer automatically.

Now that you've read this, the next time you hear someone unhesitatingly repeating a meme you think is silly or false, you'll think, "Cached thoughts." My belief is now there in your mind, waiting to complete the pattern. But is it true? Don't let your mind complete the pattern! *Think!*

---

[2] My version of a response is "Feeling Rational," again in *Map and Territory*.

42

Original Seeing

Since Robert Pirsig put this very well, I'll just copy down what he said. I don't know if this story is based on reality or not, but either way, it's true.

> He'd been having trouble with students who had nothing to say. At first he thought it was laziness but later it became apparent that it wasn't. They just couldn't think of anything to say.
>
> One of them, a girl with strong-lensed glasses, wanted to write a five-hundred word essay about the United States. He was used to the sinking feeling that comes from statements like this, and suggested without disparagement that she narrow it down to just Bozeman.
>
> When the paper came due she didn't have it and was quite upset. She had tried and tried but she just couldn't think of anything to say.
>
> It just stumped him. Now *he* couldn't think of anything to say. A silence occurred, and then a peculiar answer: "Narrow it down to the *main street* of Bozeman." It was a stroke of insight.
>
> She nodded dutifully and went out. But just before her next class she came back in *real* distress, tears this time, distress that

had obviously been there for a long time. She still couldn't think of anything to say, and couldn't understand why, if she couldn't think of anything about *all* of Bozeman, she should be able to think of something about just one street.

He was furious. "You're not *looking!*" he said. A memory came back of his own dismissal from the University for having *too much* to say. For every fact there is an *infinity* of hypotheses. The more you *look* the more you *see*. She really wasn't looking and yet somehow didn't understand this.

He told her angrily, "Narrow it down to the *front* of *one* building on the main street of Bozeman. The Opera House. Start with the upper left-hand brick."

Her eyes, behind the thick-lensed glasses, opened wide.

She came in the next class with a puzzled look and handed him a five-thousand-word essay on the front of the Opera House on the main street of Bozeman, Montana. "I sat in the hamburger stand across the street," she said, "and started writing about the first brick, and the second brick, and then by the third brick it all started to come and I couldn't stop. They thought I was crazy, and they kept kidding me, but here it all is. I don't understand it."

Neither did he, but on long walks through the streets of town he thought about it and concluded she was evidently stopped with the same kind of blockage that had paralyzed him on his first day of teaching. She was blocked because she was trying to repeat, in her writing, things she had already heard, just as on the first day he had tried to repeat things he had already decided to say. She couldn't think of anything to write about Bozeman because she couldn't recall anything she had heard worth repeating. She was strangely unaware that she could look and see freshly for herself, as she wrote, without primary regard for what had been said before. The narrowing down to one brick destroyed the blockage because it was so obvious she *had* to do some original and direct seeing.

—Robert M. Pirsig,
Zen and the Art of Motorcycle Maintenance

43

The Virtue of Narrowness

> What is true of one apple may not be true of another apple; thus more can be said about a single apple than about all the apples in the world.
>
> —"The Twelve Virtues of Rationality"

Within their own professions, people grasp the importance of narrowness; a car mechanic knows the difference between a carburetor and a radiator, and would not think of them both as "car parts." A hunter-gatherer knows the difference between a lion and a panther. A janitor does not wipe the floor with window cleaner, even if the bottles look similar to one who has not mastered the art.

Outside their own professions, people often commit the misstep of trying to broaden a word as widely as possible, to cover as much territory as possible. Is it not more glorious, more wise, more impressive, to talk about *all* the apples in the world? How much loftier it must be to *explain human thought in general*, without being distracted by smaller questions, such as how humans invent techniques for solving a Rubik's Cube. Indeed, it scarcely seems necessary to consider *specific* questions at all; isn't a general theory a worthy enough accomplishment on its own?

It is the way of the curious to lift up one pebble from among a million pebbles on the shore, and see something new about it, something interesting, something different. You call these pebbles "diamonds," and ask what might be special about them—what inner qualities they might have in common, beyond the glitter you first noticed. And then someone else comes along and says: "Why not call *this* pebble a diamond too? And this one, and this one?" They are enthusiastic, and they mean well. For it seems undemocratic and exclusionary and elitist and unholistic to call some pebbles "diamonds," and others not. It seems . . . *narrow-minded* . . . if you'll pardon the phrase. Hardly *open*, hardly *embracing*, hardly *communal*.

You might think it poetic, to give one word many meanings, and thereby spread shades of connotation all around. But even poets, if they are good poets, must learn to see the world precisely. It is not enough to compare love to a flower. Hot jealous unconsummated love is not the same as the love of a couple married for decades. If you need a flower to symbolize jealous love, you must go into the garden, and look, and make subtle distinctions—find a flower with a heady scent, and a bright color, and thorns. Even if your intent is to shade meanings and cast connotations, you must keep precise track of exactly which meanings you shade and connote.

It is a necessary part of the rationalist's art—or even the poet's art!—to focus narrowly on unusual pebbles which possess some special quality. And look at the details which those pebbles—and those pebbles alone!—share among each other. This is not a sin.

It is perfectly all right for modern evolutionary biologists to explain *just* the patterns of living creatures, and not the "evolution" of stars or the "evolution" of technology. Alas, some unfortunate souls use the same word "evolution" to cover the naturally selected patterns of replicating life, *and* the strictly accidental structure of stars, *and* the intelligently configured structure of technology. And as we all know, if people use the same word, it must all be the same thing. These biologists must just be too dumb to see the connections.

And what could be more virtuous than seeing connections? Surely the wisest of all human beings are the New Age gurus who say, "Everything is connected to everything else." If you ever say this aloud, you should pause, so that everyone can absorb the sheer shock of this Deep Wisdom.

There is a trivial mapping between a graph and its complement. A fully connected graph, with an edge between every two vertices, conveys the same amount of information as a graph with no edges at all. The important graphs are the ones where some things are *not* connected to some other things.

When the unenlightened ones try to be profound, they draw endless verbal comparisons between this topic, and that topic, which is like this, which is like that; until their graph is fully connected and also totally useless. The remedy is specific knowledge and in-depth study. When you understand things in detail, you can see how they are *not* alike, and start enthusiastically subtracting edges *off* your graph.

Likewise, the important categories are the ones that do not contain everything in the universe. Good hypotheses can only explain some possible outcomes, and not others.

It was perfectly all right for Isaac Newton to explain *just* gravity, *just* the way things fall down—and how planets orbit the Sun, and how the Moon generates the tides—but *not* the role of money in human society or how the heart pumps blood. Sneering at narrowness is rather reminiscent of ancient Greeks who thought that going out and actually *looking* at things was manual labor, and manual labor was for slaves.

As Plato put it in *The Republic, Book VII*:[1]

> If anyone should throw back his head and learn something by staring at the varied patterns on a ceiling, apparently you would think that he was contemplating with his reason, when he was only staring with his eyes . . . I cannot but believe that no study makes the soul look on high except that which is concerned with real being and the unseen. Whether he gape and stare upwards, or shut his mouth and stare downwards, if it be things of the senses that he tries to learn something about, I declare he never could learn, for none of these things admit of knowledge: I say his soul

---

[1] Plato, *Great Dialogues of Plato*, ed. Eric H. Warmington and Philip G. Rouse (Signet Classic, 1999).

is looking down, not up, even if he is floating on his back on land or on sea!

Many today make a similar mistake, and think that narrow concepts are as lowly and unlofty and unphilosophical as, say, going out and looking at things—an endeavor only suited to the underclass. But rationalists—and also poets—need narrow words to express precise thoughts; they need categories that include only some things, and exclude others. There's nothing wrong with focusing your mind, narrowing your categories, excluding possibilities, and sharpening your propositions. Really, there isn't! If you make your words too broad, you end up with something that isn't true and doesn't even make good poetry.

And DON'T EVEN GET ME STARTED on people who think Wikipedia is an "Artificial Intelligence," the invention of LSD was a "Singularity," or that corporations are "superintelligent"!

44

Stranger than History

Suppose I told you that I knew for a *fact* that the following statements were true:

- If you paint yourself a certain *exact* color between blue and green, it will reverse the force of gravity on you and cause you to fall upward.

- In the future, the sky will be filled by billions of floating black spheres. Each sphere will be larger than all the zeppelins that have ever existed put together. If you offer a sphere money, it will lower a male prostitute out of the sky on a bungee cord.

- Your grandchildren will think it is not just foolish, but *evil*, to put thieves in jail instead of spanking them.

You'd think I was crazy, right?

Now suppose it were the year 1901, and you had to choose between believing those statements I have just offered, and believing statements like the following:

- There is an absolute speed limit on how fast two objects can seem to be traveling relative to each other, which is exactly 670,616,629.2 miles per hour. If you hop on board a train going almost this fast and fire a gun out the window, the fundamental units of length change around, so it looks to *you* like the bullet is speeding ahead of you, but other people see something different. Oh, and time changes around too.

- In the future, there will be a superconnected global network of billions of adding machines, each one of which has more power than all pre-1901 adding machines put together. One of the primary uses of this network will be to transport moving pictures of lesbian sex by pretending they are made out of numbers.

- Your grandchildren will think it is not just foolish, but *evil*, to say that someone should not be President of the United States because she is black.

Based on a comment of Robin Hanson's: "*I wonder if one could describe in enough detail a fictional story of an alternative reality, a reality that our ancestors could not distinguish from the truth, in order to make it very clear how surprising the truth turned out to be.*"[1]

---

[1] Source: http://lesswrong.com/lw/j0/making_history_available/ewg

162

45

The Logical Fallacy of Generalization from Fictional Evidence

When I try to introduce the subject of advanced AI, what's the first thing I hear, more than half the time?

"Oh, you mean like the *Terminator* movies / *The Matrix* / Asimov's robots!"

And I reply, "Well, no, not exactly. I try to avoid the logical fallacy of generalizing from fictional evidence."

Some people get it right away, and laugh. Others defend their use of the example, disagreeing that it's a fallacy.

What's wrong with using movies or novels as starting points for the discussion? No one's claiming that it's *true*, after all. Where is the lie, where is the rationalist sin? Science fiction represents the author's attempt to visualize the future; why not take advantage of the thinking that's already been done on our behalf, instead of starting over?

Not every misstep in the precise dance of rationality consists of outright belief in a falsehood; there are subtler ways to go wrong.

First, let us dispose of the notion that science fiction represents a full-fledged rational attempt to forecast the future. Even the most diligent science fiction writers are, first and foremost, storytellers; the requirements of storytelling are not the same as the requirements of forecasting. As Nick Bostrom points out:[1]

> When was the last time you saw a movie about humankind suddenly going extinct (without warning and without being replaced by some other civilization)? While this scenario may be much more probable than a scenario in which human heroes successfully repel an invasion of monsters or robot warriors, it wouldn't be much fun to watch.

So there are specific distortions in fiction.[2] But trying to correct for these specific distortions is not enough. A story is *never* a rational attempt at analysis, not even with the most diligent science fiction writers, because stories don't use probability distributions. I illustrate as follows:

> Bob Merkelthud slid cautiously through the door of the alien spacecraft, glancing right and then left (or left and then right) to see whether any of the dreaded Space Monsters yet remained. At his side was the only weapon that had been found effective against the Space Monsters, a Space Sword forged of pure titanium with 30% probability, an ordinary iron crowbar with 20% probability, and a shimmering black discus found in the smoking ruins of Stonehenge with 45% probability, the remaining 5% being distributed over too many minor outcomes to list here.
>
> Merklethud (though there's a significant chance that Susan Wifflefoofer was there instead) took two steps forward or one step back, when a vast roar split the silence of the black airlock! Or the quiet background hum of the white airlock! Although Amfer and Woofi (1997) argue that Merklethud is devoured at this point, Spacklebackle (2003) points out that—

---

[1] Nick Bostrom, "Existential Risks: Analyzing Human Extinction Scenarios and Related Hazards," *Journal of Evolution and Technology* 9 (2002), http://www.jetpress.org/volume9/risks.html.
[2] E.g., Robin Hanson's "Biases of Science Fiction," http://www.overcomingbias.com/2006/12/biases_of_scien.html.

Characters can be ignorant, but the *author* can't say the three magic words "I don't know." The protagonist must thread a single line through the future, full of the details that lend flesh to the story, from Wifflefoofer's appropriately futuristic attitudes toward feminism, down to the color of her earrings.

Then all these burdensome details and questionable assumptions are wrapped up and given a short label, creating the illusion that they are a single package.[3]

On problems with large answer spaces, the greatest difficulty is not *verifying* the correct answer but simply locating it in answer space to begin with. If someone starts out by asking whether or not AIs are gonna put us into capsules like in *The Matrix*, they're jumping to a 100-bit proposition, without a corresponding 98 bits of evidence to locate it in the answer space as a possibility worthy of explicit consideration. It would only take a handful more evidence after the first 98 bits to promote that possibility to near-certainty, which tells you something about where nearly all the work gets done.

The "preliminary" step of locating possibilities worthy of explicit consideration includes steps like: weighing what you know and don't know, what you can and can't predict; making a deliberate effort to avoid absurdity bias and widen confidence intervals; pondering which questions are the important ones, trying to adjust for possible Black Swans and think of (formerly) unknown unknowns. Jumping to "*The Matrix*: Yes or No?" skips over all of this.

Any professional negotiator knows that to control the terms of a debate is very nearly to control the outcome of the debate. If you start out by thinking of *The Matrix*, it brings to mind marching robot armies defeating humans after a long struggle—not a superintelligence snapping nanotechnological fingers. It focuses on an "Us vs. Them" struggle, directing attention to questions like "Who will win?" and "Who should win?" and "Will AIs really be like that?" It creates a general atmosphere of entertainment, of "What is your amazing vision of the future?"

Lost to the echoing emptiness are: considerations of more than one possible mind design that an "Artificial Intelligence" could implement; the future's

---

[3] Recall the package-deal fallacy discussed in "The Third Alternative," this volume. See also "Occam's Razor" and "Burdensome Details" in *Map and Territory*.

165

dependence on initial conditions; the power of smarter-than-human intelligence and the argument for its unpredictability; people taking the whole matter seriously and trying to do something about it.

If some insidious corrupter of debates decided that *their* preferred outcome would be best served by forcing discussants to start out by refuting *Terminator*, they would have done well in skewing the frame. Debating gun control, the NRA spokesperson does not wish to be introduced as a "shooting freak," the anti-gun opponent does not wish to be introduced as a "victim disarmament advocate." Why should you allow the same order of frame-skewing by Hollywood scriptwriters, even accidentally?

Journalists don't tell me, "The future will be like *2001*." But they ask, "Will the future be like *2001*, or will it be like *A.I.*?" This is just as huge a framing issue as asking, "Should we cut benefits for disabled veterans, or raise taxes on the rich?"

In the ancestral environment, there were no moving pictures; what you saw with your own eyes was true. A momentary glimpse of a single word can prime us and make compatible thoughts more available, with demonstrated strong influence on probability estimates. How much havoc do you think a two-hour movie can wreak on your judgment? It will be hard enough to undo the damage by deliberate concentration—why invite the vampire into your house? In Chess or Go, every wasted move is a loss; in rationality, any non-evidential influence is (on average) entropic.

Do movie-viewers succeed in unbelieving what they see? So far as I can tell, few movie viewers act as if they have *directly* observed Earth's future. People who watched the *Terminator* movies didn't hide in fallout shelters on August 29, 1997. But those who commit the fallacy seem to act as if they had seen the movie events occurring on *some other* planet; not Earth, but somewhere similar to Earth.

You say, "Suppose we build a very smart AI," and they say, "But didn't that lead to nuclear war in *The Terminator*?" As far as I can tell, it's identical reasoning, down to the tone of voice, of someone who might say: "But didn't that lead to nuclear war on Alpha Centauri?" or "Didn't that lead to the fall of the Italian city-state of Piccolo in the fourteenth century?" The movie is not

166

believed, but it is cognitively available. It is treated, not as a prophecy, but as an illustrative historical case. Will history repeat itself? Who knows?

In a recent intelligence explosion discussion, someone mentioned that Vinge didn't seem to think that brain-computer interfaces would increase intelligence much, and cited *Marooned in Realtime* and Tunç Blumenthal, who was the most advanced traveller but didn't seem all that powerful. I replied indignantly, "But Tunç lost most of his hardware! He was crippled!" And then I did a mental double-take and thought to myself: What the *hell* am I saying.

Does the issue not have to be argued in its own right, regardless of how Vinge depicted his characters? Tunç Blumenthal is not "crippled," he's *unreal*. I could say "Vinge chose to depict Tunç as crippled, for reasons that may or may not have had anything to do with his personal best forecast," and that would give his authorial choice an appropriate weight of evidence. I cannot say "Tunç was crippled." There is no *was* of Tunç Blumenthal.

I deliberately left in a mistake I made, in my first draft of the beginning of this essay: "Others defend their use of the *example*, disagreeing that it's a fallacy." But *The Matrix* is *not* an example!

A neighboring flaw is the logical fallacy of arguing from imaginary evidence: "Well, if you *did* go to the end of the rainbow, you *would* find a pot of gold—which just proves my point!" (Updating on evidence predicted, but not observed, is the mathematical mirror image of hindsight bias.)

The brain has many mechanisms for generalizing from observation, not just the availability heuristic. You see three zebras, you form the category "zebra," and this category embodies an automatic perceptual inference. Horse-shaped creatures with white and black stripes are classified as "Zebras," therefore they are fast and good to eat; they are expected to be similar to other zebras observed.

So people see (moving pictures of) three Borg, their brain automatically creates the category "Borg," and they infer automatically that humans with brain-computer interfaces are of class "Borg" and will be similar to other Borg observed: cold, uncompassionate, dressing in black leather, walking with heavy mechanical steps. Journalists don't believe that the future *will* contain Borg— they don't believe *Star Trek* is a prophecy. But when someone talks about

167

brain-computer interfaces, they think, "Will the future contain Borg?" Not, "How do I know computer-assisted telepathy makes people less nice?" Not, "I've never seen a Borg and never has anyone else." Not, "I'm forming a racial stereotype based on *literally* zero evidence."

As George Orwell said of cliches:[4]

> What is above all needed is to let the meaning choose the word, and not the other way around . . . When you think of something abstract you are more inclined to use words from the start, and unless you make a conscious effort to prevent it, the existing dialect will come rushing in and do the job for you, at the expense of blurring or even changing your meaning.

Yet in my estimation, the *most* damaging aspect of using other authors' imaginations is that it stops people from using their own. As Robert Pirsig said:[5]

> She was blocked because she was trying to repeat, in her writing, things she had already heard, just as on the first day he had tried to repeat things he had already decided to say. She couldn't think of anything to write about Bozeman because she couldn't recall anything she had heard worth repeating. She was strangely unaware that she could look and see freshly for herself, as she wrote, without primary regard for what had been said before.

Remembered fictions rush in and do your thinking for you; they substitute for *seeing*—the deadliest convenience of all.

---

[4] Orwell, "Politics and the English Language."
[5] Pirsig, *Zen and the Art of Motorcycle Maintenance.*

46

We Change Our Minds Less Often Than We Think

Over the past few years, we have discreetly approached colleagues faced with a choice between job offers, and asked them to estimate the probability that they will choose one job over another. The average confidence in the predicted choice was a modest 66%, but only 1 of the 24 respondents chose the option to which he or she initially assigned a lower probability, yielding an overall accuracy rate of 96%.

—Dale Griffin and Amos Tversky[1]

When I first read the words above—on August 1st, 2003, at around 3 o'clock in the afternoon—it changed the way I thought. I realized that *once I could guess what my answer would be*—once I could assign a higher probability to deciding one way than other—then I had, in all probability, already decided. We change our minds less often than we think. And most of the time we become able to guess what our answer will be within half a second of hearing the question.

---

[1] Dale Griffin and Amos Tversky, "The Weighing of Evidence and the Determinants of Confidence," *Cognitive Psychology* 24, no. 3 (1992): 411–435, doi:10.1016/0010-0285(92)90013-R.

How swiftly that unnoticed moment passes, when we can't yet guess what our answer will be; the tiny window of opportunity for intelligence to act. In questions of choice, as in questions of fact.

The principle of the bottom line is that only the actual causes of your beliefs determine your effectiveness as a rationalist. Once your belief is fixed, no amount of argument will alter the truth-value; once your decision is fixed, no amount of argument will alter the consequences.

You might think that you could arrive at a belief, or a decision, by non-rational means, and then try to justify it, and if you found you couldn't justify it, reject it.

But we change our minds less often—*much* less often—than we think.

I'm sure that you can think of at least one occasion in your life when you've changed your mind. We all can. How about all the occasions in your life when you didn't change your mind? Are they as available, in your heuristic estimate of your competence?

Between hindsight bias, fake causality, positive bias, anchoring/priming, et cetera, et cetera, and above all the dreaded confirmation bias, once an idea gets into your head, it's probably going to stay there.

47

Hold Off On Proposing Solutions

From Robyn Dawes's *Rational Choice in an Uncertain World.*[1] Bolding added.

Norman R. F. Maier noted that when a group faces a problem, the natural tendency of its members is to propose possible solutions as they begin to discuss the problem. Consequently, the group interaction focuses on the merits and problems of the proposed solutions, people become emotionally attached to the ones they have suggested, and superior solutions are not suggested. Maier enacted an edict to enhance group problem solving: **"Do not propose solutions until the problem has been discussed as thoroughly as possible without suggesting any."** It is easy to show that this edict works in contexts where there are objectively defined good solutions to problems.

Maier devised the following "role playing" experiment to demonstrate his point. Three employees of differing ability work on an assembly line. They rotate among three jobs that require different levels of ability, because the most able—who is also the

[1] Robyn M. Dawes, *Rational Choice in An Uncertain World*, 1st ed., ed. Jerome Kagan (San Diego, CA: Harcourt Brace Jovanovich, 1988), 55–56.

most dominant—is strongly motivated to avoid boredom. In contrast, the least able worker, aware that he does not perform the more difficult jobs as well as the other two, has agreed to rotation because of the dominance of his able co-worker. An "efficiency expert" notes that if the most able employee were given the most difficult task and the least able the least difficult, productivity could be improved by 20%, and the expert recommends that the employees stop rotating. The three employees and . . . a fourth person designated to play the role of foreman are asked to discuss the expert's recommendation. Some role-playing groups are given Maier's edict not to discuss solutions until having discussed the problem thoroughly, while others are not. Those who are not given the edict immediately begin to argue about the importance of productivity versus worker autonomy and the avoidance of boredom. Groups presented with the edict have a much higher probability of arriving at the solution that the two more able workers rotate, while the least able one sticks to the least demanding job—a solution that yields a 19% increase in productivity.

I have often used this edict with groups I have led—**particularly when they face a very tough problem, which is when group members are most apt to propose solutions immediately**. While I have no objective criterion on which to judge the quality of the problem solving of the groups, Maier's edict appears to foster better solutions to problems.

This is so true it's not even funny. And it gets worse and worse the tougher the problem becomes. Take Artificial Intelligence, for example. A surprising number of people I meet seem to know exactly how to build an Artificial General Intelligence, without, say, knowing how to build an optical character recognizer or a collaborative filtering system (much easier problems). And as for building an AI with a positive impact on the world—a Friendly AI, loosely

172

speaking—why, *that* problem is so incredibly difficult that an actual *majority* resolve the whole issue within fifteen seconds.[2] *Give* me a *break*.

This problem is by no means unique to AI. Physicists encounter plenty of nonphysicists with their own theories of physics, economists get to hear lots of amazing new theories of economics. If you're an evolutionary biologist, anyone you meet can instantly solve any open problem in your field, usually by postulating group selection. Et cetera.

Maier's advice echoes the principle of the bottom line, that the effectiveness of our decisions is determined only by whatever evidence and processing we did in first arriving at our decisions—after you write the bottom line, it is too late to write more reasons above. If you make your decision very early on, it will, in fact, be based on very little thought, no matter how many amazing arguments you come up with afterward.

And consider furthermore that We Change Our Minds Less Often than We Think: 24 people assigned an average 66% probability to the future choice thought more probable, but only 1 in 24 actually chose the option thought less probable. **Once you can guess what your answer will be, you have probably already decided.** If you can guess your answer half a second after hearing the question, then you have half a second in which to be intelligent. It's not a lot of time.

Traditional Rationality emphasizes *falsification*—the ability to *relinquish* an initial opinion when confronted by clear evidence against it. But once an idea gets into your head, it will probably require way too much evidence to get it out again. Worse, we don't always have the luxury of overwhelming evidence.

I suspect that a more powerful (and more difficult) method is to *hold off on thinking of an answer*. To suspend, draw out, that tiny moment when we can't yet guess what our answer will be; thus giving our intelligence a longer time in which to act.

Even half a minute would be an improvement over half a second.

---

[2] See http://intelligence.org/files/AIPosNegFactor.pdf for an introduction to AI as a lever on global risk.

48

The Genetic Fallacy

In lists of logical fallacies, you will find included "the genetic fallacy"—the fallacy of attacking a belief based on someone's causes for believing it.

This is, at first sight, a very strange idea—if the causes of a belief do not determine its systematic reliability, what does? If Deep Blue advises us of a chess move, we trust it based on our understanding of the *code* that searches the game tree, being unable to evaluate the actual game tree ourselves. What could license any probability assignment as "rational," except that it was produced by some systematically reliable process?

Articles on the genetic fallacy will tell you that genetic reasoning is not always a fallacy—that the origin of evidence *can* be relevant to its evaluation, as in the case of a trusted expert. But other times, say the articles, it *is* a fallacy; the chemist Kekulé first saw the ring structure of benzene in a dream, but this doesn't mean we can never trust this belief.

So sometimes the genetic fallacy is a fallacy, and sometimes it's not?

The genetic fallacy is formally a fallacy, because the *original cause* of a belief is not the same as its *current justificational status*, the sum of all the support and antisupport *currently* known.

Yet we change our minds less often than we think. Genetic accusations have a force among humans that they would not have among ideal Bayesians.

Clearing your mind is a *powerful heuristic* when you're faced with new suspicion that many of your ideas may have come from a flawed source.

Once an idea gets into our heads, it's not always easy for evidence to root it out. Consider all the people out there who grew up believing in the Bible; later came to reject (on a deliberate level) the idea that the Bible was written by the hand of God; and who nonetheless think that the Bible is full of indispensable ethical wisdom. They have failed to clear their minds; they could do significantly better by doubting anything the Bible said *because the Bible said it.*

At the same time, they would have to bear firmly in mind the principle that reversed stupidity is not intelligence; the goal is to genuinely shake your mind loose and do independent thinking, not to negate the Bible and let that be your algorithm.

Once an idea gets into your head, you tend to find support for it everywhere you look—and so when the original source is suddenly cast into suspicion, you would be very wise indeed to suspect all the leaves that originally grew on that branch . . .

If you can! It's not easy to clear your mind. It takes a convulsive effort to *actually reconsider*, instead of letting your mind fall into the pattern of rehearsing cached arguments. "It ain't a true crisis of faith unless things could just as easily go either way," said Thor Shenkel.

You should be *extremely suspicious* if you have many ideas suggested by a source that you now know to be untrustworthy, but by golly, it seems that all the ideas still ended up being right—the Bible being the obvious archetypal example.

On the other hand . . . there's such a thing as sufficiently clear-cut evidence, that it no longer significantly matters where the idea originally came from. Accumulating that kind of clear-cut evidence is what Science is all about. It doesn't matter any more that Kekulé first saw the ring structure of benzene in a dream—it wouldn't matter if we'd found the hypothesis to test by generating random computer images, or from a spiritualist revealed as a fraud, or even from the Bible. The ring structure of benzene is pinned down by enough experimental evidence to make the source of the suggestion irrelevant.

In the absence of such clear-cut evidence, then you do need to pay attention to the original sources of ideas—to give experts more credence than layfolk, if their field has earned respect—to suspect ideas you originally got from suspicious sources—to distrust those whose motives are untrustworthy, *if* they cannot present arguments independent of their own authority.

The genetic fallacy is a *fallacy* when there exist justifications *beyond* the genetic fact asserted, but the genetic accusation is presented as if it settled the issue. Hal Finney suggests that we call correctly appealing to a claim's origins "the genetic heuristic."[1]

Some good rules of thumb (for humans):

- Be suspicious of genetic accusations against beliefs that you dislike, especially if the proponent claims justifications beyond the simple authority of a speaker. "Flight is a religious idea, so the Wright Brothers must be liars" is one of the classically given examples.

- By the same token, don't think you can get good information about a technical issue just by sagely psychoanalyzing the personalities involved and their flawed motives. If technical arguments exist, they get priority.

- When new suspicion is cast on one of your fundamental sources, you really *should* doubt all the branches and leaves that grew from that root. You are not licensed to reject them outright as conclusions, because reversed stupidity is not intelligence, but . . .

- Be extremely suspicious if you find that you still believe the early suggestions of a source you later rejected.

---

[1] Source: http://lesswrong.com/lw/s3/the_genetic_fallacy/lls

Part I

Death Spirals

49

The Affect Heuristic

The *affect heuristic* is when subjective impressions of goodness/badness act as a heuristic—a source of fast, perceptual judgments. Pleasant and unpleasant feelings are central to human reasoning, and the affect heuristic comes with lovely biases—some of my favorites.

Let's start with one of the relatively less crazy biases. You're about to move to a new city, and you have to ship an antique grandfather clock. In the first case, the grandfather clock was a gift from your grandparents on your fifth birthday. In the second case, the clock was a gift from a remote relative and you have no special feelings for it. How much would you pay for an insurance policy that paid out $100 if the clock were lost in shipping? According to Hsee and Kunreuther, subjects stated willingness to pay more than twice as much in the first condition.[1] This may sound rational—why not pay more to protect the more valuable object?—until you realize that the insurance doesn't *protect* the clock, it just pays if the clock is lost, and pays exactly the same amount for either clock. (And yes, it was stated that the insurance was with an outside company, so it gives no special motive to the movers.)

---

[1] Christopher K. Hsee and Howard C. Kunreuther, "The Affection Effect in Insurance Decisions," *Journal of Risk and Uncertainty* 20 (2 2000): 141–159, doi:10.1023/A:1007876907268.

All right, but that doesn't *sound* too insane. Maybe you could get away with claiming the subjects were insuring affective outcomes, not financial outcomes—purchase of consolation.

Then how about this? Yamagishi showed that subjects judged a disease as more dangerous when it was described as killing 1,286 people out of every 10,000, versus a disease that was 24.14% likely to be fatal.[2] Apparently the mental image of a thousand dead bodies is much more alarming, compared to a single person who's more likely to survive than not.

But wait, it gets worse.

Suppose an airport must decide whether to spend money to purchase some new equipment, while critics argue that the money should be spent on other aspects of airport safety. Slovic et al. presented two groups of subjects with the arguments for and against purchasing the equipment, with a response scale ranging from 0 (would not support at all) to 20 (very strong support).[3] One group saw the measure described as saving 150 lives. The other group saw the measure described as saving 98% of 150 lives. The hypothesis motivating the experiment was that saving 150 lives sounds vaguely good—is that a lot? a little?—while saving 98% of something is clearly very good because 98% is so close to the upper bound of the percentage scale. Lo and behold, saving 150 lives had mean support of 10.4, while saving 98% of 150 lives had mean support of 13.6.

Or consider the report of Denes-Raj and Epstein: subjects who were offered an opportunity to win $1 each time they randomly drew a red jelly bean from a bowl often preferred to draw from a bowl with more red beans and a smaller proportion of red beans.[4] E.g., 7 in 100 was preferred to 1 in 10.

According to Denes-Raj and Epstein, these subjects reported afterward that even though they knew the probabilities were against them, they felt they had a better chance when there were more red beans. This may sound crazy to

---

[2] Kimihiko Yamagishi, "When a 12.86% Mortality Is More Dangerous than 24.14%: Implications for Risk Communication," *Applied Cognitive Psychology* 11 (6 1997): 461–554.

[3] Paul Slovic et al., "Rational Actors or Rational Fools: Implications of the Affect Heuristic for Behavioral Economics," *Journal of Socio-Economics* 31, no. 4 (2002): 329–342, doi:10.1016/S1053-5357(02)00174-9.

[4] Veronika Denes-Raj and Seymour Epstein, "Conflict between Intuitive and Rational Processing: When People Behave against Their Better Judgment," *Journal of Personality and Social Psychology* 66 (5 1994): 819–829, doi:10.1037/0022-3514.66.5.819.

you, oh Statistically Sophisticated Reader, but if you think more carefully you'll realize that it makes perfect sense. A 7% probability versus 10% probability may be bad news, but it's more than made up for by the increased number of red beans. It's a worse probability, yes, but you're still more likely to *win*, you see. You should meditate upon this thought until you attain enlightenment as to how the rest of the planet thinks about probability.

As I discussed in "The Scales of Justice, the Notebook of Rationality," Finucane et al. found that for nuclear reactors, natural gas, and food preservatives, presenting information about high benefits made people perceive lower risks; presenting information about higher risks made people perceive lower benefits; and so on across the quadrants.[5] People conflate their judgments about particular good/bad aspects of something into an overall good or bad feeling about that thing.

Finucane et al. also found that time pressure greatly *increased* the inverse relationship between perceived risk and perceived benefit, consistent with the general finding that time pressure, poor information, or distraction all increase the dominance of perceptual heuristics over analytic deliberation.

Ganzach found the same effect in the realm of finance.[6] According to ordinary economic theory, return and risk should correlate *positively*—or to put it another way, people pay a premium price for safe investments, which lowers the return; stocks deliver higher returns than bonds, but have correspondingly greater risk. When judging *familiar* stocks, analysts' judgments of risks and returns were positively correlated, as conventionally predicted. But when judging *unfamiliar* stocks, analysts tended to judge the stocks as if they were generally good or generally bad—low risk and high returns, or high risk and low returns.

For further reading I recommend Slovic's fine summary article, "Rational Actors or Rational Fools: Implications of the Affect Heuristic for Behavioral Economics."

---

[5]Finucane et al., "The Affect Heuristic in Judgments of Risks and Benefits."

[6]Yoav Ganzach, "Judging Risk and Return of Financial Assets," *Organizational Behavior and Human Decision Processes* 83, no. 2 (2000): 353–370, doi:10.1006/obhd.2000.2914.

50

Evaluability (and Cheap Holiday Shopping)

With the *expensive* part of the Hallowthankmas season now approaching, a question must be looming large in our readers' minds:

> "Dear *Overcoming Bias*, are there biases I can exploit to be *seen* as generous without *actually* spending lots of money?"

I'm glad to report the answer is yes! According to Hsee—in a paper entitled "Less is Better"—if you buy someone a $45 scarf, you are more likely to be seen as generous than if you buy them a $55 coat.[1]

This is a special case of a more general phenomenon. In an earlier experiment, Hsee asked subjects how much they would be willing to pay for a second-hand music dictionary:[2]

- Dictionary A, from 1993, with 10,000 entries, in like-new condition.

---

[1] Christopher K. Hsee, "Less Is Better: When Low-Value Options Are Valued More Highly than High-Value Options," *Behavioral Decision Making* 11 (2 1998): 107–121.

[2] Christopher K. Hsee, "The Evaluability Hypothesis: An Explanation for Preference Reversals between Joint and Separate Evaluations of Alternatives," *Organizational Behavior and Human Decision Processes* 67 (3 1996): 247–257, doi:10.1006/obhd.1996.0077.

- Dictionary B, from 1993, with 20,000 entries, with a torn cover and otherwise in like-new condition.

The gotcha was that some subjects saw both dictionaries side-by-side, while other subjects only saw *one* dictionary . . .

Subjects who saw only *one* of these options were willing to pay an average of $24 for Dictionary A and an average of $20 for Dictionary B. Subjects who saw *both* options, side-by-side, were willing to pay $27 for Dictionary B and $19 for Dictionary A.

Of course, the number of entries in a dictionary is more important than whether it has a torn cover, at least if you ever plan on using it for anything. But if you're only presented with a single dictionary, and it has 20,000 entries, the number 20,000 doesn't mean very much. Is it a little? A lot? Who knows? It's *non-evaluable*. The torn cover, on the other hand—that stands out. That has a definite affective valence: namely, bad.

Seen side-by-side, though, the number of entries goes from *non-evaluable* to *evaluable*, because there are two compatible quantities to be compared. And once the number of entries becomes evaluable, that facet swamps the importance of the torn cover.

From Slovic et al.: Which would you prefer?[3]

1. A 29/36 chance to win $2.

2. A 7/36 chance to win $9.

While the average *prices* (equivalence values) placed on these options were $1.25 and $2.11 respectively, their mean attractiveness ratings were 13.2 and 7.5. Both the prices and the attractiveness rating were elicited in a context where subjects were told that two gambles would be randomly selected from those rated, and they would play the gamble with the higher price or higher attractiveness rating. (Subjects had a motive to rate gambles as more attractive, or price them higher, that they would actually prefer to play.)

The gamble worth more money seemed less attractive, a classic preference reversal. The researchers hypothesized that the dollar values were more com-

---

[3]Slovic et al., "Rational Actors or Rational Fools."

patible with the pricing task, but the probability of payoff was more compatible with attractiveness. So (the researchers thought) why not try to make the gamble's payoff more emotionally salient—more affectively evaluable—more attractive?

And how did they do this? By adding a very small loss to the gamble. The old gamble had a 7/36 chance of winning $9. The new gamble had a 7/36 chance of winning $9 and a 29/36 chance of losing 5 cents. In the old gamble, you implicitly evaluate the attractiveness of $9. The new gamble gets you to evaluate the attractiveness of winning $9 *versus* losing 5 cents.

"The results," said Slovic et al., "exceeded our expectations." In a new experiment, the simple gamble with a 7/36 chance of winning $9 had a mean attractiveness rating of 9.4, while the complex gamble that included a 29/36 chance of losing 5 cents had a mean attractiveness rating of 14.9.

A follow-up experiment tested whether subjects preferred the old gamble to a certain gain of $2. Only 33% of students preferred the old gamble. Among another group asked to choose between a certain $2 and the new gamble (with the added possibility of a 5 cents loss), fully 60.8% preferred the gamble. After all, $9 isn't a very attractive amount of money, but $9 / 5 cents is an *amazingly* attractive win/loss ratio.

You can make a gamble more attractive by adding a strict loss! Isn't psychology fun? This is why no one who truly appreciates the wondrous intricacy of human intelligence wants to design a human-like AI.

Of course, it only works if the subjects don't see the two gambles side-by-side.

Similarly, which of the two ice creams in Figure 1 do you think subjects in Hsee's 1998 study preferred?
Naturally, the answer depends on whether the subjects saw a single ice cream, or the two side-by-side. Subjects who saw a single ice cream were willing to pay $1.66 to Vendor H and $2.26 to Vendor L. Subjects who saw both ice creams were willing to pay $1.85 to Vendor H and $1.56 to Vendor L.

What does this suggest for your holiday shopping? That if you spend $400 on a 16GB iPod Touch, your recipient sees the most expensive MP3 player. If you spend $400 on a Nintendo Wii, your recipient sees the least expensive

184

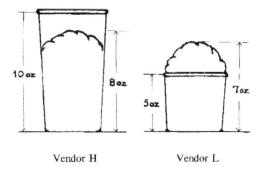

Vendor H   Vendor L

Fig. 1: Two ice creams from Hsee, © 1998 John Wiley & Sons, Ltd.

game machine. Which is better value for the money? Ah, but that question only makes sense if you see the two side-by-side. *You'll* think about them side-by-side while you're shopping, but the recipient will only see what they get.

If you have a fixed amount of money to spend—and your goal is to display your friendship, rather than to actually *help* the recipient—you'll be better off deliberately not shopping for value. Decide how much money you want to spend on impressing the recipient, then find the most worthless object which costs that amount. The cheaper the *class* of objects, the more expensive a *particular* object will appear, given that you spend a fixed amount. Which is more memorable, a $25 shirt or a $25 candle?

Gives a whole new meaning to the Japanese custom of buying $50 melons, doesn't it? You look at that and shake your head and say "What *is* it with the Japanese?" And yet they get to be perceived as incredibly generous, spendthrift even, while spending only $50. You could spend $200 on a fancy dinner and not appear as wealthy as you can by spending $50 on a melon. If only there was a custom of gifting $25 toothpicks or $10 dust specks; they could get away with spending even less.

PS: If you actually use this trick, I want to know what you bought.

51

Unbounded Scales, Huge Jury Awards, and Futurism

"Psychophysics," despite the name, is the respectable field that links physical effects to sensory effects. If you dump acoustic energy into air—make noise—then *how loud* does that sound to a person, as a function of acoustic energy? How much more acoustic energy do you have to pump into the air, before the noise sounds twice as loud to a human listener? It's not twice as much; more like eight times as much.

Acoustic energy and photons are straightforward to measure. When you want to find out how loud an acoustic stimulus *sounds*, how bright a light source *appears*, you usually ask the listener or watcher. This can be done using a bounded scale from "very quiet" to "very loud," or "very dim" to "very bright." You can also use an unbounded scale, whose zero is "not audible at all" or "not visible at all," but which increases from there without limit. When you use an unbounded scale, the observer is typically presented with a constant stimulus, the *modulus*, which is given a fixed rating. For example, a sound that is assigned a loudness of 10. Then the observer can indicate a sound twice as loud as the modulus by writing 20.

And this has proven to be a fairly reliable technique. But what happens if you give subjects an unbounded scale, but no modulus? Zero to infinity, with no reference point for a fixed value? Then they make up their own modulus, of course. The *ratios* between stimuli will continue to correlate reliably between subjects. Subject A says that sound X has a loudness of 10 and sound Y has a loudness of 15. If subject B says that sound X has a loudness of 100, then it's a good guess that subject B will assign loudness in the vicinity of 150 to sound Y. But if you don't know what subject C is using as their modulus—their scaling factor—then there's no way to guess what subject C will say for sound X. It could be 1. It could be 1,000.

For a subject rating a *single* sound, on an *unbounded* scale, *without* a fixed standard of comparison, nearly *all* the variance is due to the arbitrary choice of modulus, rather than the sound itself.

"Hm," you think to yourself, "this sounds an awful lot like juries deliberating on punitive damages. No wonder there's so much variance!" An interesting analogy, but how would you go about demonstrating it experimentally?

Kahneman et al. presented 867 jury-eligible subjects with descriptions of legal cases (e.g., a child whose clothes caught on fire) and asked them to either

1. Rate the outrageousness of the defendant's actions, on a bounded scale,

2. Rate the degree to which the defendant should be punished, on a bounded scale, or

3. Assign a dollar value to punitive damages.[1]

And, lo and behold, while subjects correlated very well with each other in their outrage ratings and their punishment ratings, their punitive damages were all over the map. Yet subjects' *rank-ordering* of the punitive damages—their ordering from lowest award to highest award—correlated well across subjects.

If you asked how much of the variance in the "punishment" scale could be explained by the specific scenario—the particular legal case, as presented to

---

[1] Daniel Kahneman, David A. Schkade, and Cass R. Sunstein, "Shared Outrage and Erratic Awards: The Psychology of Punitive Damages," *Journal of Risk and Uncertainty* 16 (1 1998): 48–86, doi:10.1023/A:1007710408413; Daniel Kahneman, Ilana Ritov, and David Schkade, "Economic Preferences or Attitude Expressions?: An Analysis of Dollar Responses to Public Issues," *Journal of Risk and Uncertainty* 19, nos. 1–3 (1999): 203–235, doi:10.1023/A:1007835629236.

multiple subjects—then the answer, even for the raw scores, was 0.49. For the *rank orders* of the dollar responses, the amount of variance predicted was 0.51. For the *raw dollar* amounts, the variance explained was 0.06!

Which is to say: if you knew the scenario presented—the aforementioned child whose clothes caught on fire—you could take a good guess at the punishment rating, and a good guess at the *rank-ordering* of the dollar award relative to other cases, but the dollar award itself would be completely unpredictable.

Taking the median of twelve randomly selected responses didn't help much either.

So a jury award for punitive damages isn't so much an economic valuation as an attitude expression—a psychophysical measure of outrage, expressed on an unbounded scale with no standard modulus.

I observe that many *futuristic predictions* are, likewise, best considered as attitude expressions. Take the question, "How long will it be until we have human-level AI?" The responses I've seen to this are all over the map. On one memorable occasion, a mainstream AI guy said to me, "Five hundred years." (!!)

Now the reason why time-to-AI is just *not very predictable*, is a long discussion in its own right. But it's not as if the guy who said "Five hundred years" was looking into the future to find out. And he can't have gotten the number using the standard bogus method with Moore's Law. So what did the number 500 *mean*?

As far as I can guess, it's as if I'd asked, "On a scale where zero is 'not difficult at all,' how difficult does the AI problem *feel* to you?" If this were a bounded scale, every sane respondent would mark "extremely hard" at the right-hand end. Everything *feels* extremely hard when you don't know how to do it. But instead there's an unbounded scale with no standard modulus. So people just make up a number to represent "extremely difficult," which may come out as 50, 100, or even 500. Then they tack "years" on the end, and that's their futuristic prediction.

"How hard does the AI problem feel?" isn't the only substitutable question. Others respond as if I'd asked "How positive do you feel about AI?"—except lower numbers mean more positive feelings—and then they also tack "years" on the end. But if these "time estimates" represent anything other than attitude expressions on an unbounded scale with no modulus, I have been unable to determine it.

52

The Halo Effect

The affect heuristic is how an overall feeling of goodness or badness contributes to many other judgments, whether it's logical or not, whether you're aware of it or not. Subjects told about the benefits of nuclear power are likely to rate it as having fewer risks; stock analysts rating unfamiliar stocks judge them as generally good or generally bad—low risk and high returns, or high risk and low returns—in defiance of ordinary economic theory, which says that risk and return should correlate positively.

The halo effect is the manifestation of the affect heuristic in social psychology. Robert Cialdini summarizes:[1]

> Research has shown that we automatically assign to good-looking individuals such favorable traits as talent, kindness, honesty, and intelligence (for a review of this evidence, see Eagly, Ashmore, Makhijani, and Longo, 1991).[2] Furthermore, we make these judgments without being aware that physical attractiveness plays a

---

[1] Robert B. Cialdini, *Influence: Science and Practice* (Boston: Allyn & Bacon, 2001).

[2] Alice H. Eagly et al., "What Is Beautiful Is Good, But . . . A Meta-analytic Review of Research on the Physical Attractiveness Stereotype," *Psychological Bulletin* 110 (1 1991): 109–128, doi:10.1037/0033-2909.110.1.109.

role in the process. Some consequences of this unconscious assumption that "good-looking equals good" scare me. For example, a study of the 1974 Canadian federal elections found that attractive candidates received more than two and a half times as many votes as unattractive candidates (Efran and Patterson, 1976).[3] Despite such evidence of favoritism toward handsome politicians, follow-up research demonstrated that voters did not realize their bias. In fact, 73 percent of Canadian voters surveyed denied in the strongest possible terms that their votes had been influenced by physical appearance; only 14 percent even allowed for the possibility of such influence (Efran and Patterson, 1976). Voters can deny the impact of attractiveness on electability all they want, but evidence has continued to confirm its troubling presence (Budesheim and DePaola, 1994).[4]

A similar effect has been found in hiring situations. In one study, good grooming of applicants in a simulated employment interview accounted for more favorable hiring decisions than did job qualifications—this, even though the interviewers claimed that appearance played a small role in their choices (Mack and Rainey, 1990).[5] The advantage given to attractive workers extends past hiring day to payday. Economists examining US and Canadian samples have found that attractive individuals get paid an average of 12–14 percent more than their unattractive coworkers (Hamermesh and Biddle, 1994).[6]

Equally unsettling research indicates that our judicial process is similarly susceptible to the influences of body dimensions and bone structure. It now appears that good-looking people are likely to receive highly favorable treatment in the legal system

---

[3] M. G. Efran and E. W. J. Patterson, "The Politics of Appearance" (Unpublished PhD thesis, 1976).
[4] Thomas Lee Budesheim and Stephen DePaola, "Beauty or the Beast?: The Effects of Appearance, Personality, and Issue Information on Evaluations of Political Candidates," *Personality and Social Psychology Bulletin* 20 (4 1994): 339–348, doi:10.1177/0146167294204001.
[5] Denise Mack and David Rainey, "Female Applicants' Grooming and Personnel Selection," *Journal of Social Behavior and Personality* 5 (5 1990): 399–407.
[6] Daniel S. Hamermesh and Jeff E. Biddle, "Beauty and the Labor Market," *The American Economic Review* 84 (5 1994): 1174–1194.

191

(see Castellow, Wuensch, and Moore, 1991; and Downs and Lyons, 1990, for reviews).[7] For example, in a Pennsylvania study (Stewart, 1980),[8] researchers rated the physical attractiveness of 74 separate male defendants at the start of their criminal trials. When, much later, the researchers checked court records for the results of these cases, they found that the handsome men had received significantly lighter sentences. In fact, attractive defendants were twice as likely to avoid jail as unattractive defendants. In another study—this one on the damages awarded in a staged negligence trial—a defendant who was better looking than his victim was assessed an average amount of $5,623; but when the victim was the more attractive of the two, the average compensation was $10,051. What's more, both male and female jurors exhibited the attractiveness-based favoritism (Kulka and Kessler, 1978).[9]

Other experiments have demonstrated that attractive people are more likely to obtain help when in need (Benson, Karabenic, and Lerner, 1976)[10] and are more persuasive in changing the opinions of an audience (Chaiken, 1979) . . .[11]

The influence of attractiveness on ratings of intelligence, honesty, or kindness is a clear example of bias—especially when you judge these other qualities based on fixed text—because we wouldn't expect judgments of honesty and attractiveness to conflate for any legitimate reason. On the other hand, how

---

[7] Wilbur A. Castellow, Karl L. Wuensch, and Charles H. Moore, "Effects of Physical Attractiveness of the Plaintiff and Defendant in Sexual Harassment Judgments," *Journal of Social Behavior and Personality* 5 (6 1990): 547–562; A. Chris Downs and Phillip M. Lyons, "Natural Observations of the Links Between Attractiveness and Initial Legal Judgments," *Personality and Social Psychology Bulletin* 17 (5 1991): 541–547, doi:10.1177/0146167291175009.

[8] John E. Stewart, "Defendants' Attractiveness as a Factor in the Outcome of Trials: An Observational Study," *Journal of Applied Social Psychology* 10 (4 1980): 348–361, doi:10.1111/j.1559-1816.1980.tb00715.x.

[9] Richard A. Kulka and Joan B. Kessler, "Is Justice Really Blind?: The Effect of Litigant Physical Attractiveness on Judicial Judgment," *Journal of Applied Social Psychology* 8 (4 1978): 366–381, doi:10.1111/j.1559-1816.1978.tb00790.x.

[10] Peter L. Benson, Stuart A. Karabenick, and Richard M. Lerner, "Pretty Pleases: The Effects of Physical Attractiveness, Race, and Sex on Receiving Help," *Journal of Experimental Social Psychology* 12 (5 1976): 409–415, doi:10.1016/0022-1031(76)90073-1.

[11] Shelly Chaiken, "Communicator Physical Attractiveness and Persuasion," *Journal of Personality and Social Psychology* 37 (8 1979): 1387–1397, doi:10.1037/0022-3514.37.8.1387.

192

much of my perceived intelligence is due to my honesty? How much of my perceived honesty is due to my intelligence? Finding the truth, and saying the truth, are not as widely separated in nature as looking pretty and looking smart . . .

But these studies on the halo effect of attractiveness should make us suspicious that there may be a similar halo effect for kindness, or intelligence. Let's say that you know someone who not only seems very intelligent, but also honest, altruistic, kindly, and serene. You should be suspicious that some of these perceived characteristics are influencing your perception of the others. Maybe the person is genuinely intelligent, honest, and altruistic, but not all that kindly or serene. You should be suspicious if the people you know seem to separate too cleanly into devils and angels.

And—I know you don't think *you* have to do it, but maybe *you* should—be just a little more skeptical of the more attractive political candidates.

53

Superhero Bias

Suppose there's a heavily armed sociopath, a kidnapper with hostages, who has just rejected all requests for negotiation and announced his intent to start killing. In real life, the good guys don't usually kick down the door when the bad guy has hostages. But sometimes—*very* rarely, but sometimes—life imitates Hollywood to the extent of genuine good guys needing to smash through a door.

Imagine, in two widely separated realities, two heroes who charge into the room, first to confront the villain.

In one reality, the hero is strong enough to throw cars, can fire power blasts out of his nostrils, has X-ray hearing, and his skin doesn't just *deflect* bullets but annihilates them on contact. The villain has ensconced himself in an elementary school and taken over two hundred children hostage; their parents are waiting outside, weeping.

In another reality, the hero is a New York police officer, and the hostages are three prostitutes the villain collected off the street.

Consider this question very carefully: Who is the greater hero? And who is more likely to get their own comic book?

The halo effect is that perceptions of all positive traits are correlated. Profiles rated higher on scales of attractiveness are also rated higher on scales of talent, kindness, honesty, and intelligence.

And so comic-book characters who seem strong and invulnerable, both positive traits, also seem to possess more of the heroic traits of courage and heroism. And yet:

> How tough can it be to act all brave and courageous when you're pretty much invulnerable?
>
> —Adam Warren, *Empowered*, Vol. 1

I can't remember if I read the following point somewhere, or hypothesized it myself: *Fame*, in particular, seems to combine additively with all other personality characteristics. Consider Gandhi. Was Gandhi the *most altruistic* person of the twentieth century, or just the *most famous* altruist? Gandhi faced police with riot sticks and soldiers with guns. But Gandhi was a celebrity, and he was protected by his celebrity. What about the others in the march, the people who faced riot sticks and guns even though there wouldn't be international headlines if they were put in the hospital or gunned down?

What did Gandhi think of getting the headlines, the celebrity, the fame, the place in history, *becoming the archetype* for non-violent resistance, when he took less risk than any of the people marching with him? How did he feel when one of those anonymous heroes came up to him, eyes shining, and told Gandhi how wonderful he was? Did Gandhi ever visualize his world in those terms? I don't know; I'm not Gandhi.

This is not in any sense a criticism of Gandhi. The point of non-violent resistance is not to show off your courage. That can be done much more easily by going over Niagara Falls in a barrel. Gandhi couldn't help being somewhat-but-not-entirely protected by his celebrity. And Gandhi's actions did take courage—not as much courage as marching anonymously, but still a great deal of courage.

The bias I wish to point out is that Gandhi's fame score seems to get perceptually *added* to his justly accumulated altruism score. When you think about nonviolence, you think of Gandhi—not an anonymous protestor in one of

Gandhi's marches who faced down riot clubs and guns, and got beaten, and had to be taken to the hospital, and walked with a limp for the rest of her life, *and no one ever remembered her name*.

Similarly, which is greater—to risk your life to save two hundred children, or to risk your life to save three adults?

The answer depends on what one means by *greater*. If you ever have to *choose* between saving two hundred children and saving three adults, then choose the former. "Whoever saves a single life, it is as if he had saved the whole world" may be a fine applause light, but it's terrible moral advice if you've got to pick one or the other. So if you mean "greater" in the sense of "Which is more important?" or "Which is the preferred outcome?" or "Which should I choose if I have to do one or the other?" then it is greater to save two hundred than three.

But if you ask about greatness in the sense of revealed virtue, then someone who would risk their life to save only three lives reveals more courage than someone who would risk their life to save two hundred but not three.

This doesn't mean that you can deliberately choose to risk your life to save three adults, and let the two hundred schoolchildren go hang, because you want to reveal more virtue. Someone who risks their life *because they want to be virtuous* has revealed far less virtue than someone who risks their life *because they want to save others*. Someone who chooses to save three lives rather than two hundred lives, because they think it reveals greater virtue, is so selfishly fascinated with their own "greatness" as to have committed the moral equivalent of manslaughter.

It's one of those *wu wei* scenarios: You cannot reveal virtue by trying to reveal virtue. Given a choice between a safe method to save the world which involves no personal sacrifice or discomfort, and a method that risks your life and requires you to endure great privation, you cannot become a hero by deliberately choosing the second path. There is nothing heroic about wanting to look like a hero. It would be a lost purpose.

Truly virtuous people who are genuinely trying to save lives, rather than trying to reveal virtue, will constantly seek to save more lives with less effort,

196

which means that less of their virtue will be revealed. It may be confusing, but it's not contradictory.

But we cannot always choose to be invulnerable to bullets. After we've done our best to reduce risk and increase scope, any *remaining* heroism is well and truly revealed.

The police officer who puts their life on the line with no superpowers, no X-Ray vision, no super-strength, no ability to fly, and above all no invulnerability to bullets, reveals far greater virtue than Superman—who is a *mere superhero*.

54

Affective Death Spirals

Many, many, many are the flaws in human reasoning which lead us to overestimate how well our beloved theory explains the facts. The phlogiston theory of chemistry could explain just about anything, so long as it didn't have to predict it in advance. And the more phenomena you use your favored theory to explain, the truer your favored theory seems—has it not been confirmed by these many observations? As the theory seems truer, you will be more likely to question evidence that conflicts with it. As the favored theory seems more general, you will seek to use it in more explanations.

If you know anyone who believes that Belgium secretly controls the US banking system, or that they can use an invisible blue spirit force to detect available parking spaces, that's probably how they got started.

(Just keep an eye out, and you'll observe much that seems to confirm this theory . . .)

This positive feedback cycle of credulity and confirmation is indeed fearsome, and responsible for much error, both in science and in everyday life.

But it's nothing compared to the death spiral that begins with a charge of positive affect—a thought that *feels really good.*

A new political system that can save the world. A great leader, strong and noble and wise. An amazing tonic that can cure upset stomachs and cancer.

Heck, why not go for all three? A great cause needs a great leader. A great leader should be able to brew up a magical tonic or two.

The halo effect is that any perceived positive characteristic (such as attractiveness or strength) increases perception of any other positive characteristic (such as intelligence or courage). Even when it makes no sense, or less than no sense.

Positive characteristics enhance perception of every other positive characteristic? That sounds a lot like how a fissioning uranium atom sends out neutrons that fission other uranium atoms.

Weak positive affect is subcritical; it doesn't spiral out of control. An attractive person seems more honest, which, perhaps, makes them seem more attractive; but the effective neutron multiplication factor is less than one. Metaphorically speaking. The resonance confuses things a little, but then dies out.

With intense positive affect attached to the Great Thingy, the resonance touches everywhere. A believing Communist sees the wisdom of Marx in every hamburger bought at McDonald's; in every promotion they're denied that would have gone to them in a true worker's paradise; in every election that doesn't go to their taste; in every newspaper article "slanted in the wrong direction." Every time they use the Great Idea to interpret another event, the Great Idea is confirmed all the more. It feels better—positive reinforcement—and of course, when something feels good, that, alas, makes us *want* to believe it all the more.

When the Great Thingy feels good enough to make you *seek out* new opportunities to feel even better about the Great Thingy, applying it to interpret new events every day, the resonance of positive affect is like a chamber full of mousetraps loaded with ping-pong balls.

You could call it a "happy attractor," "overly positive feedback," a "praise locked loop," or "funpaper." Personally I prefer the term "affective death spiral."

199

Coming up next: How to resist an affective death spiral.[1]

---

[1] Hint: It's not by refusing to ever admire anything again, nor by keeping the things you admire in safe little restricted magisteria.

55

Resist the Happy Death Spiral

Once upon a time, there was a man who was convinced that he possessed a Great Idea. Indeed, as the man thought upon the Great Idea more and more, he realized that it was not just *a* great idea, but *the most wonderful idea ever*. The Great Idea would unravel the mysteries of the universe, supersede the authority of the corrupt and error-ridden Establishment, confer nigh-magical powers upon its wielders, feed the hungry, heal the sick, make the whole world a better place, etc., etc., etc.

The man was Francis Bacon, his Great Idea was the scientific method, and he was the only crackpot in all history to claim that level of benefit to humanity and turn out to be completely right.[1]

That's the problem with deciding that you'll never admire anything that much: Some ideas really *are* that good. Though no one has *fulfilled* claims more audacious than Bacon's; at least, not yet.

But then how can we resist the happy death spiral with respect to Science itself? The happy death spiral starts when you believe something is *so* wonderful that the halo effect leads you to find *more* and *more* nice things to say about

---

[1] Bacon didn't singlehandedly invent science, of course, but he did contribute, and may have been the first to realize the power.

it, making you see it as *even more* wonderful, and so on, spiraling up into the abyss. What if Science is *in fact* so beneficial that we cannot acknowledge its true glory and retain our sanity? Sounds like a nice thing to say, doesn't it? *Oh no it's starting ruuunnnnn . . .*

If you retrieve the standard cached deep wisdom for *don't go overboard on admiring science*, you will find thoughts like "Science gave us air conditioning, but it also made the hydrogen bomb" or "Science can tell us about stars and biology, but it can never prove or disprove the dragon in my garage." But the people who *originated* such thoughts were *not* trying to resist a happy death spiral. They weren't worrying about their own admiration of science spinning out of control. Probably they didn't like something science had to say about their pet beliefs, and sought ways to undermine its authority.

The *standard* negative things to say about science aren't likely to appeal to someone who genuinely feels the exultation of science—that's not the intended audience. So we'll have to search for other negative things to say instead.

But if you look selectively for something negative to say about science— even in an attempt to resist a happy death spiral—do you not automatically convict yourself of rationalization? Why would you pay attention to your own thoughts, if you knew you were trying to manipulate yourself?

I am generally skeptical of people who claim that one bias can be used to counteract another. It sounds to me like an automobile mechanic who says that the motor is broken on your right windshield wiper, but instead of fixing it, they'll just break your left windshield wiper to balance things out. This is the sort of cleverness that leads to shooting yourself in the foot. Whatever the solution, it ought to involve believing true things, rather than believing you believe things that you believe are false.

Can you prevent the happy death spiral by restricting your admiration of Science to a narrow domain? Part of the happy death spiral is seeing the Great Idea everywhere—thinking about how Communism could cure cancer if it were only given a chance. Probably the single most reliable sign of a cult guru is that the guru claims expertise, not in one area, not even in a cluster of related areas, but in *everything*. The guru knows what cult members should eat, wear, do for a living; who they should have sex with; which art they should look at; which music they should listen to . . .

Unfortunately for this plan, most people fail miserably when they try to describe the neat little box that science has to stay inside. The usual trick, "Hey, science won't cure cancer," isn't going to fly. "Science has nothing to say about a parent's love for their child"—sorry, that's simply false. If you try to sever science from e.g. parental love, you aren't just denying cognitive science and evolutionary psychology. You're also denying Martine Rothblatt's founding of United Therapeutics to seek a cure for her daughter's pulmonary hypertension.[2] Science is legitimately related, one way or another, to just about every important facet of human existence.

All right, so what's an example of a *false* nice claim you could make about science?

One false claim, in my humble opinion, is that science is so wonderful that scientists shouldn't even try to take ethical responsibility for their work—it will turn out well in the end regardless. It appears to me that this misunderstands the process whereby science benefits humanity. Scientists are human; they have prosocial concerns just like most other other people, and this is at least *part* of why science ends up doing more good than evil.

But that point is, evidently, not beyond dispute. So here's a simpler false nice claim: "A cancer patient can be cured just through the publishing of enough journal papers." Or: "Sociopaths could become fully normal, if they just committed themselves to never believing anything without replicated experimental evidence with $p < 0.05$."

The way to avoid believing such statements isn't an affective cap, deciding that science is only slightly nice. Nor searching for reasons to believe that publishing journal articles *causes* cancer. Nor believing that science has nothing to say about cancer one way or the other.

Rather, if you know with enough specificity how science works, then you know that while it may be possible for "science to cure cancer," a cancer patient writing journal papers isn't going to experience a miraculous remission. That *specific* proposed chain of cause and effect is not going to work out.

---

[2] Successfully, I might add.

The happy death spiral is only an emotional problem because of a perceptual problem, the halo effect, that makes us more likely to accept future positive claims once we've accepted an initial positive claim. We can't get rid of this effect just by wishing; it will probably always influence us a little. But we can manage to slow down, stop, consider each additional nice claim as an additional burdensome detail, and focus on the specific points of the claim apart from its positiveness.

What if a specific nice claim "can't be disproven" but there are arguments "both for and against" it? Actually these are words to be wary of in general, because often this is what people say when they're rehearsing the evidence or avoiding the real weak points. Given the danger of the happy death spiral, it makes sense to try to avoid being happy about *unsettled* claims—to avoid making them into a source of yet more positive affect about something you liked already.

The happy death spiral is only a *big* emotional problem because of the overly positive feedback, the ability for the process to go critical. You may not be able to eliminate the halo effect entirely, but you can apply enough critical reasoning to keep the halos subcritical—make sure that the resonance dies out rather than exploding.

You might even say that the whole problem starts with people not bothering to critically examine every additional burdensome detail—demanding sufficient evidence to compensate for complexity, searching for flaws as well as support, invoking curiosity—once they've accepted some core premise. Without the conjunction fallacy, there might still be a halo effect, but there wouldn't be a happy death spiral.[3]

Even on the nicest Nice Thingies in the known universe, a perfect rationalist who demanded exactly the necessary evidence for every additional (positive) claim would experience no affective resonance. You can't do this, but you can stay close enough to rational to keep your happiness from spiraling out of control.[4]

---

[3] For more background, see "Burdensome Details," "How Much Evidence Does it Take?", and "Occam's Razor" in the previous volume, *Map and Territory*.

[4] The really dangerous cases are the ones where *any criticism of any positive claim about the Great Thingy feels bad or is socially unacceptable*. Arguments are soldiers; any positive claim is a soldier on

Stuart Armstrong gives closely related advice:[5]

> Cut up your Great Thingy into smaller independent ideas, *and treat them as independent.*
>
> For instance a marxist would cut up Marx's Great Thingy into a theory of value of labour, a theory of the political relations between classes, a theory of wages, a theory on the ultimate political state of mankind. Then each of them should be assessed independently, and the truth or falsity of one should not halo on the others. If we can do that, we should be safe from the spiral, as each theory is too narrow to start a spiral on its own.

This, metaphorically, is like keeping subcritical masses of plutonium from coming together. Three Great Ideas are far less likely to drive you mad than one Great Idea. Armstrong's advice also helps promote specificity: As soon as someone says, "Publishing enough papers can cure your cancer," you ask, "Is that a benefit of the experimental method, and if so, at which stage of the experimental process is the cancer cured? Or is it a benefit of science as a social process, and if so, does it rely on individual scientists wanting to cure cancer, or can they be self-interested?" Hopefully this leads you away from the good or bad feeling, and toward noticing the confusion and lack of support.

To summarize, you *do* avoid a Happy Death Spiral by:

- Splitting the Great Idea into parts;

- Treating every additional detail as burdensome;

- Thinking about the specifics of the causal chain instead of the good or bad feelings;

- Not rehearsing evidence; and

- Not adding happiness from claims that "you can't *prove* are wrong";

---

our side; stabbing your soldiers in the back is treason. Then the chain reaction goes *super*critical. More on this later.

[5] Source: http://lesswrong.com/lw/lm/affective_death_spirals/gp5

but *not* by:

- Refusing to admire anything too much;

- Conducting a biased search for negative points until you feel unhappy again; or

- Forcibly shoving an idea into a safe box.

56

Uncritical Supercriticality

Every now and then, you see people arguing over whether atheism is a "religion." As I touch on elsewhere, in "Purpose and Pragmatism," arguing over the meaning of a word nearly always means that you've lost track of the original question.[1] How might this argument arise to begin with?

An atheist is holding forth, blaming "religion" for the Inquisition, the Crusades, and various conflicts with or within Islam. The religious one may reply, "But atheism is also a religion, because you also have beliefs about God; you believe God doesn't exist." Then the atheist answers, "If atheism is a religion, then not collecting stamps is a hobby," and the argument begins.

Or the one may reply, "But horrors just as great were inflicted by Stalin, who was an atheist, and who suppressed churches in the name of atheism; therefore you are wrong to blame the violence on religion." Now the atheist may be tempted to reply, "No true Scotsman," saying, "Stalin's religion was Communism."[2] The religious one answers "If Communism is a religion, then Star Wars fandom is a government," and the argument begins.

---

[1] Link: http://lesswrong.com/lw/lf/purpose_and_pragmatism/
[2] See https://en.wikipedia.org/wiki/No_true_Scotsman.

Should a "religious" person be defined as someone who has a definite opinion about the existence of at least one God, e.g., assigning a probability lower than 10% or higher than 90% to the existence of Zeus? Or should a "religious" person be defined as someone who has a positive opinion (say, a probability higher than 90%) on the existence of at least one God? In the former case, Stalin was "religious"; in the latter case, Stalin was "not religious."

But this is exactly the wrong way to look at the problem. What you really want to know—what the argument was originally about—is why, at certain points in human history, large groups of people were slaughtered and tortured, ostensibly in the name of an idea. Redefining a word won't change the facts of history one way or the other.

Communism was a complex catastrophe, and there may be no single *why*, no single critical link in the chain of causality. But if I had to suggest an ur-mistake, it would be . . . well, I'll let God say it for me:

> If your brother, the son of your father or of your mother, or your son or daughter, or the spouse whom you embrace, or your most intimate friend, tries to secretly seduce you, saying, "Let us go and serve other gods," unknown to you or your ancestors before you, gods of the peoples surrounding you, whether near you or far away, anywhere throughout the world, you must not consent, **you must not listen to him**; you must show him no pity, you must not spare him or conceal his guilt. No, **you must kill him**, your hand must strike the first blow in putting him to death and the hands of the rest of the people following. You must stone him to death, since he has tried to divert you from Yahweh your God.
>
> —Deuteronomy 13:7–11, emphasis added

This was likewise the rule which Stalin set for Communism, and Hitler for Nazism: if your brother tries to tell you why Marx is wrong, if your son tries to tell you the Jews are not planning world conquest, then do not debate him or set forth your own evidence; do not perform replicable experiments or examine history; but turn him in at once to the secret police.

208

I suggested that one key to resisting an affective death spiral is the principle of "burdensome details"—just *remembering* to question the specific details of each additional nice claim about the Great Idea.[3] This wouldn't get rid of the halo effect, but it would hopefully reduce the resonance to below criticality, so that one nice-sounding claim triggers less than 1.0 additional nice-sounding claims, on average.

The diametric opposite of this advice, which sends the halo effect *supercritical*, is when it feels wrong to argue against *any* positive claim about the Great Idea.

Politics is the mind-killer. Arguments are soldiers. Once you know which side you're on, you must support all favorable claims, and argue against all unfavorable claims. Otherwise it's like giving aid and comfort to the enemy, or stabbing your friends in the back.

If . . .

- . . . you feel that contradicting someone else who makes a flawed nice claim in favor of evolution would be giving aid and comfort to the creationists;

- . . . you feel like you get spiritual credit for each nice thing you say about God, and arguing about it would interfere with your relationship with God;

- . . . you have the distinct sense that the other people in the room will dislike you for "not supporting our troops" if you argue against the latest war;

- . . . saying anything against Communism gets you ~~stoned to death~~ shot;

. . . then the affective death spiral has gone supercritical. It is now a Super Happy Death Spiral.

When it comes to our original question—"What makes the slaughter?"—the key category to pay attention to isn't religion as such. The best distinction I've

---

[3] It's not trivial advice. People often don't remember to do this when they're listening to a futurist sketching amazingly detailed projections about the wonders of tomorrow, let alone when they're thinking about their favorite idea ever.

heard between "supernatural" and "naturalistic" worldviews is that a supernatural worldview asserts the existence of ontologically basic mental substances, like spirits, while a naturalistic worldview reduces mental phenomena to nonmental parts. Focusing on this as the source of the problem buys into religious exceptionalism. Supernaturalist claims are worth distinguishing, because they always turn out to be wrong for fairly fundamental reasons.[4] But it's still just one kind of mistake.

An affective death spiral can nucleate around supernatural beliefs—particularly monotheisms whose pinnacle is a Super Happy Agent, defined primarily by agreeing with any nice statement about it—and particularly meme complexes grown sophisticated enough to assert supernatural punishments for disbelief. But the death spiral can also start around a political innovation, a charismatic leader, belief in racial destiny, or an economic hypothesis. The lesson of history is that affective death spirals are dangerous whether or not they happen to involve supernaturalism. Religion isn't special enough, as a class of mistake, to be the key problem.

Sam Harris came closer when he put the accusing finger on *faith*. If you don't place an appropriate burden of proof on each and every additional nice claim, the affective resonance gets started *very* easily. Look at the poor New Agers. Christianity developed defenses against criticism, arguing for the wonders of faith; New Agers culturally inherit the cached thought that faith is positive, but lack Christianity's exclusionary scripture to keep out competing memes. New Agers end up in happy death spirals around stars, trees, magnets, diets, spells, unicorns . . .

But the affective death spiral turns much deadlier after criticism becomes a sin, or a gaffe, or a crime. There are things in this world that are worth praising greatly, and you can't *flatly* say that praise beyond a certain point is forbidden. But there is *never* an Idea so true that it's wrong to criticize any argument that supports it. Never. Never ever never for ever. *That* is flat. The vast majority of possible beliefs in a nontrivial answer space are false, and likewise, the vast majority of possible *supporting arguments* for a true belief are also false, and not even the happiest idea can change that.

---

[4]See, for example, "Mysterious Answers to Mysterious Questions" in *Map and Territory*.

And it is triple ultra forbidden to respond to criticism with violence. There are a very few injunctions in the human art of rationality that have no ifs, ands, buts, or escape clauses. This is one of them. Bad argument gets counterargument. Does not get bullet. Never. Never ever never for ever.

57

Evaporative Cooling of Group Beliefs

Early studiers of cults were surprised to discover than when cults receive a major shock—a prophecy fails to come true, a moral flaw of the founder is revealed—they often come back stronger than before, with increased belief and fanaticism. The Jehovah's Witnesses placed Armageddon in 1975, based on Biblical calculations; 1975 has come and passed. The Unarian cult, still going strong today, survived the nonappearance of an intergalactic spacefleet on September 27, 1975.

Why would a group belief become *stronger* after encountering crushing counterevidence?

The conventional interpretation of this phenomenon is based on cognitive dissonance. When people have taken "irrevocable" actions in the service of a belief—given away all their property in anticipation of the saucers landing—they cannot possibly admit they were mistaken. The challenge to their belief presents an immense cognitive dissonance; they must find reinforcing thoughts to counter the shock, and so become more fanatical. In this interpretation, the increased group fanaticism is the result of increased individual fanaticism.

I was looking at a Java applet which demonstrates the use of evaporative cooling to form a Bose-Einstein condensate, when it occurred to me that another force entirely might operate to increase fanaticism. Evaporative cooling sets up a potential energy barrier around a collection of hot atoms. Thermal energy is essentially statistical in nature—not all atoms are moving at the exact same speed. The kinetic energy of any given atom varies as the atoms collide with each other. If you set up a potential energy barrier that's just a little higher than the average thermal energy, the workings of chance will give an occasional atom a kinetic energy high enough to escape the trap. When an unusually fast atom escapes, it takes with it an unusually large amount of kinetic energy, and the average energy decreases. The group becomes substantially cooler than the potential energy barrier around it.

In Festinger, Riecken, and Schachter's classic *When Prophecy Fails*, one of the cult members walked out the door immediately after the flying saucer failed to land.[1] Who gets fed up and leaves *first*? An *average* cult member? Or a relatively skeptical member, who previously might have been acting as a voice of moderation, a brake on the more fanatic members?

After the members with the highest kinetic energy escape, the remaining discussions will be between the extreme fanatics on one end and the slightly less extreme fanatics on the other end, with the group consensus somewhere in the "middle."

And what would be the analogy to collapsing to form a Bose-Einstein condensate? Well, there's no real need to stretch the analogy that far. But you may recall that I used a fission chain reaction analogy for the affective death spiral; when a group ejects all its voices of moderation, then all the people encouraging each other, and suppressing dissents, may internally increase in average fanaticism.[2]

When Ayn Rand's long-running affair with Nathaniel Branden was revealed to the Objectivist membership, a substantial fraction of the Objectivist mem-

---

[1] Leon Festinger, Henry W. Riecken, and Stanley Schachter, *When Prophecy Fails: A Social and Psychological Study of a Modern Group That Predicted the Destruction of the World* (Harper-Torchbooks, 1956).

[2] No thermodynamic analogy here, unless someone develops a nuclear weapon that explodes when it gets cold.

bership broke off and followed Branden into espousing an "open system" of Objectivism not bound so tightly to Ayn Rand. Who stayed with Ayn Rand even after the scandal broke? The ones who *really, really* believed in her—and perhaps some of the undecideds, who, after the voices of moderation left, heard arguments from only one side. This may account for how the Ayn Rand Institute is (reportedly) more fanatical after the breakup than the original core group of Objectivists under Branden and Rand.

A few years back, I was on a transhumanist mailing list where a small group espousing "social democratic transhumanism" vitriolically insulted every libertarian on the list. Most libertarians left the mailing list; most of the others gave up on posting. As a result, the remaining group shifted substantially to the left. Was this deliberate? Probably not, because I don't think the perpetrators knew that much psychology.[3] At most, they might have thought to make themselves "bigger fish in a smaller pond."

This is one reason why it's important to be prejudiced in favor of tolerating dissent. Wait until substantially *after* it seems to you justified in ejecting a member from the group, before actually ejecting. If you get rid of the old outliers, the group position will shift, and someone else will become the oddball. If you eject them too, you're well on the way to becoming a Bose-Einstein condensate and, er, exploding.

The flip side: Thomas Kuhn believed that a science has to become a "paradigm," with a shared technical language that excludes outsiders, before it can get any real work done. In the formative stages of a science, according to Kuhn, the adherents go to great pains to make their work comprehensible to outside academics. But (according to Kuhn) a science can only make real progress as a technical discipline once it abandons the requirement of outside accessibility, and scientists working in the paradigm assume familiarity with large cores of technical material in their communications. This sounds cynical, relative to what is usually said about public understanding of science, but I can definitely see a core of truth here.[4]

---

[3] For that matter, I can't recall seeing the evaporative cooling analogy elsewhere, though that doesn't mean it hasn't been noted before.

[4] My own theory of Internet moderation is that you have to be willing to exclude trolls and spam to get a conversation going. You must even be willing to exclude kindly but technically uninformed

folks from technical mailing lists if you want to get any work done. A genuinely open conversation on the Internet degenerates fast.

It's the *articulate* trolls that you should be wary of ejecting, on this theory—they serve the hidden function of legitimizing less extreme disagreements. But you should not have so many articulate trolls that they begin arguing with each other, or begin to dominate conversations. If you have one person around who is the famous Guy Who Disagrees With Everything, anyone with a more reasonable, more moderate disagreement won't look like the sole nail sticking out. This theory of Internet moderation may not have served me too well in practice, so take it with a grain of salt.

58

When None Dare Urge Restraint

One morning, I got out of bed, turned on my computer, and my Netscape email client automatically downloaded that day's news pane. On that particular day, the news was that two hijacked planes had been flown into the World Trade Center.

These were my first three thoughts, in order:

I guess I really am living in the Future.

Thank goodness it wasn't nuclear.

and then

The overreaction to this will be ten times worse than the original event.

A mere factor of "ten times worse" turned out to be a vast understatement. Even I didn't guess how badly things would go. That's the challenge of pessimism; it's *really hard* to aim low enough that you're pleasantly surprised around as often and as much as you're unpleasantly surprised.

Nonetheless, I did realize immediately that everyone everywhere would be saying how awful, how terrible this event was; and that no one would dare to be the voice of restraint, of proportionate response. Initially, on 9/11, it was thought that six thousand people had died. Any politician who had said, "6,000 deaths is 1/8 the annual US casualties from automobile accidents," would have been asked to resign the same hour.

No, 9/11 wasn't a good day. But if *everyone* gets brownie points for emphasizing how much it hurts, and *no one* dares urge restraint in how hard to hit back, then the reaction will be greater than the appropriate level, whatever the appropriate level may be.

This is the even darker mirror of the happy death spiral—the spiral of hate. Anyone who attacks the Enemy is a patriot; and whoever tries to dissect even a single negative claim about the Enemy is a traitor. But just as the vast majority of all complex statements are untrue, the vast majority of negative things you can say about anyone, even the worst person in the world, are untrue.

I think the best illustration was "the suicide hijackers were cowards." Some common sense, please? It takes a little courage to voluntarily fly your plane into a building. Of all their sins, cowardice was not on the list. But I guess anything bad you say about a terrorist, no matter how silly, must be true. Would I get even more brownie points if I accused al-Qaeda of having assassinated John F. Kennedy? Maybe if I accused them of being Stalinists? Really, *cowardice?*

Yes, it matters that the 9/11 hijackers weren't cowards. Not just for understanding the enemy's realistic psychology. There is simply too much damage done by spirals of hate. It is just too dangerous for there to be any target in the world, whether it be the Jews or Adolf Hitler, about whom *saying negative things* trumps *saying accurate things.*

When the defense force contains thousands of aircraft and hundreds of thousands of heavily armed soldiers, one ought to consider that the immune system itself is capable of wreaking more damage than nineteen guys and four nonmilitary airplanes. The US spent billions of dollars and thousands of soldiers' lives shooting off its own foot more effectively than any terrorist group could dream.

If the USA had completely ignored the 9/11 attack—just shrugged and rebuilt the building—it would have been better than the real course of history. But that wasn't a political option. Even if anyone privately guessed that the

217

immune response would be more damaging than the disease, American politicians had no career-preserving choice but to walk straight into al-Qaeda's trap. Whoever argues for a greater response is a patriot. Whoever dissects a patriotic claim is a traitor.

Initially, there were smarter responses to 9/11 than I had guessed. I saw a Congressperson—I forget who—say in front of the cameras, "We have forgotten that the first purpose of government is not the economy, it is not health care, it is defending the country from attack." That widened my eyes, that a politician could say something that wasn't an applause light. The emotional shock must have been very great for a Congressperson to say something that . . . real.

But within two days, the genuine shock faded, and concern-for-image regained total control of the political discourse. Then the spiral of escalation took over completely. Once restraint becomes unspeakable, no matter where the discourse starts out, the level of fury and folly can only rise with time.

59

The Robbers Cave Experiment

Did you ever wonder, when you were a kid, whether your inane "summer camp" actually had some kind of elaborate hidden purpose—say, it was all a science experiment and the "camp counselors" were really researchers observing your behavior?

Me neither.

But we'd have been more paranoid if we'd read "Intergroup Conflict and Co-operation: The Robbers Cave Experiment" by Sherif, Harvey, White, Hood, and Sherif. In this study, the experimental subjects—excuse me, "campers"—were 22 boys between fifth and sixth grade, selected from 22 different schools in Oklahoma City, of stable middle-class Protestant families, doing well in school, median IQ 112. They were as well-adjusted and as similar to each other as the researchers could manage.

The experiment, conducted in the bewildered aftermath of World War II, was meant to investigate the causes—and possible remedies—of intergroup conflict. How would they spark an intergroup conflict to investigate? Well, the 22 boys were divided into two groups of 11 campers, and—

—and that turned out to be quite sufficient.

The researchers' original plans called for the experiment to be conducted in three stages. In Stage 1, each group of campers would settle in, unaware of the other group's existence. Toward the end of Stage 1, the groups would gradually be made aware of each other. In Stage 2, a set of contests and prize competitions would set the two groups at odds.

They needn't have bothered with Stage 2. There was hostility almost from the moment the two groups (christened the Rattlers and the Eagles) became aware of the other group's existence: They were using *our* campground, *our* baseball diamond.

On their first meeting, the two groups began hurling insults. When the contests and prizes were announced, in accordance with pre-established experimental procedure, the intergroup rivalry rose to a fever pitch. Good sportsmanship in the contests was evident for the first two days but rapidly disintegrated.

The Eagles stole the Rattlers' flag and burned it. Rattlers raided the Eagles' cabin and stole the blue jeans of the group leader, which they painted orange and carried as a flag the next day, inscribed with the legend "The Last of the Eagles." The Eagles launched a retaliatory raid on the Rattlers, turning over beds, scattering dirt. Then they returned to their cabin where they entrenched and prepared weapons (socks filled with rocks) in case of a return raid. After the Eagles won the last contest planned for Stage 2, the Rattlers raided their cabin and stole the prizes. This developed into a fistfight that the staff had to shut down for fear of injury. The Eagles, retelling the tale among themselves, turned the whole affair into a magnificent victory—they'd chased the Rattlers "over halfway back to their cabin" (they hadn't).

Each group developed a negative stereotype of Them and a contrasting positive stereotype of Us. The Rattlers swore heavily. The Eagles, after winning one game, concluded that the Eagles had won because of their prayers and the Rattlers had lost because they used cuss-words all the time. The Eagles decided to stop using cuss-words themselves. They also concluded that since the Rattlers swore all the time, it would be wiser not to talk to them. The Eagles developed an image of themselves as proper-and-moral; the Rattlers developed an image of themselves as rough-and-tough.

220

Group members held their noses when members of the other group passed. In Stage 3, the researchers tried to reduce friction between the two groups.

Mere contact (being present without contesting) did not reduce friction between the two groups. Attending pleasant events together—for example, shooting off Fourth of July fireworks—did not reduce friction; instead it developed into a food fight.

Would you care to guess what *did* work?

(Spoiler space . . .)

The boys were informed that there might be a water shortage in the whole camp, due to mysterious trouble with the water system—possibly due to vandals. (The Outside Enemy, one of the oldest tricks in the book.)

The area between the camp and the reservoir would have to be inspected by four search details. (Initially, these search details were composed uniformly of members from each group.) All details would meet up at the water tank if nothing was found. As nothing was found, the groups met at the water tank and observed for themselves that no water was coming from the faucet. The two groups of boys discussed where the problem might lie, pounded the sides of the water tank, discovered a ladder to the top, verified that the water tank was full, and finally found the sack stuffed in the water faucet. All the boys gathered around the faucet to clear it. Suggestions from members of both groups were thrown at the problem and boys from both sides tried to implement them.

When the faucet was finally cleared, the Rattlers, who had canteens, did not object to the Eagles taking a first turn at the faucets (the Eagles didn't have canteens with them). No insults were hurled, not even the customary "Ladies first."

It wasn't the end of the rivalry. There was another food fight, with insults, the next morning. But a few more common tasks, requiring cooperation from both groups—e.g., restarting a stalled truck—did the job. At the end of the trip, the Rattlers used $5 won in a bean-toss contest to buy malts for all the boys in both groups.

The Robbers Cave Experiment illustrates the psychology of hunter-gatherer bands, echoed through time, as perfectly as any experiment ever devised by social science.

Any resemblance to modern politics is just your imagination.

(Sometimes I think humanity's second-greatest need is a supervillain. Maybe I'll go into that line of work after I finish my current job.)

60

Every Cause Wants to Be a Cult

Cade Metz at *The Register* recently alleged that a secret mailing list of Wikipedia's top administrators has become obsessed with banning all critics and possible critics of Wikipedia.[1] Including banning a productive user when one administrator—solely *because* of the productivity—became convinced that the user was a spy sent by *Wikipedia Review*. And that the top people at Wikipedia closed ranks to defend their own.

Is there some deep moral flaw in seeking to systematize the world's knowledge, of the sort that would lead pursuers of that Cause into madness? Perhaps only people with innately totalitarian tendencies would try to become the world's authority on everything—

Correspondence bias alert! If the allegations about Wikipedia are true, they're explained by *ordinary* human nature, not by *extraordinary* human nature.

The ingroup-outgroup dichotomy is part of ordinary human nature. So are happy death spirals and spirals of hate. A Noble Cause doesn't need a deep

---

[1] See "Secret Mailing List Rocks Wikipedia" (http://www.theregister.co.uk/2007/12/04/wikipedia_secret_mailing/) and "Wikipedia Black Helicopters Circle Utah's Traverse Mountain" (http://www.theregister.co.uk/2007/12/06/wikipedia_and_overstock/).

hidden flaw for its adherents to form a cultish in-group. It is sufficient that the adherents be human. Everything else follows naturally, decay by default, like food spoiling in a refrigerator after the electricity goes off.

In the same sense that every thermal differential wants to equalize itself, and every computer program wants to become a collection of ad-hoc patches, every Cause *wants* to be a cult. It's a high-entropy state into which the system trends, an attractor in human psychology. It may have nothing to do with whether the Cause is truly Noble. You might think that a Good Cause would rub off its goodness on every aspect of the people associated with it—that the Cause's followers would also be less susceptible to status games, ingroup-outgroup bias, affective spirals, leader-gods. But believing one true idea won't switch off the halo effect. A noble cause won't make its adherents something other than human. There are plenty of bad ideas that can do plenty of damage—but that's not necessarily what's going on.

Every group of people with an unusual goal—good, bad, or silly—will trend toward the cult attractor unless they make a constant effort to resist it. You can keep your house cooler than the outdoors, but you have to run the air conditioner constantly, and as soon as you turn off the electricity—give up the fight against entropy—things will go back to "normal."

On one notable occasion there was a group that went semicultish whose rallying cry was "Rationality! Reason! Objective reality!" Labeling the Great Idea "rationality" won't protect you any more than putting up a sign over your house that says "Cold!" You still have to run the air conditioner—expend the required energy per unit time to reverse the natural slide into cultishness. Worshipping rationality won't make you sane any more than worshipping gravity enables you to fly. You can't talk to thermodynamics and you can't pray to probability theory. You can *use* it, but not join it as an in-group.[2]

Cultishness is quantitative, not qualitative. The question is not, "Cultish, yes or no?" but, "How much cultishness and where?" Even in Science, which is the archetypal Genuinely Truly Noble Cause, we can readily point to the current frontiers of the war against cult-entropy, where the current battle line creeps

---

[2] For more specifics on how I think Objectivism fell into the cult attractor, see "Guardians of the Truth" (http://lesswrong.com/lw/lz/guardians_of_the_truth/) and "Guardians of Ayn Rand" (http://lesswrong.com/lw/m1/guardians_of_ayn_rand/).

224

forward and back. Are journals more likely to accept articles with a well-known authorial byline, or from an unknown author from a well-known institution, compared to an unknown author from an unknown institution? How much belief is due to authority and how much is from the experiment? Which journals are using blinded reviewers, and how effective is blinded reviewing?

I cite this example, rather than the standard vague accusations of "scientists aren't open to new ideas," because it shows a *battle line*—a place where human psychology is being actively driven back, where accumulated cult-entropy is being pumped out. (Of course, this requires emitting some waste heat.)

This essay is not a catalog of techniques for actively pumping against cultishness. I've described some such techniques before, and I'll discuss more later. Here I just want to point out that the worthiness of the Cause does not mean you can spend any *less* effort in resisting the cult attractor. And that if you can point to current battle lines, it does not mean you confess your Noble Cause unworthy. You might think that if the question were, "Cultish, yes or no?" that you were obliged to answer, "No," or else betray your beloved Cause. But that is like thinking that you should divide engines into "perfectly efficient" and "inefficient," instead of measuring waste.

Contrariwise, if you believe that it was the Inherent Impurity of those Foolish Other Causes that made them go wrong, if you laugh at the folly of "cult victims," if you think that cults are led and populated by mutants, then you will not expend the necessary effort to pump against entropy—to resist being human.

61

Two Cult Koans

A novice rationalist studying under the master Ougi was rebuked by a friend who said, "You spend all this time listening to your master, and talking of 'rational' this and 'rational' that—you have fallen into a cult!"

The novice was deeply disturbed; he heard the words *You have fallen into a cult!* resounding in his ears as he lay in bed that night, and even in his dreams.

The next day, the novice approached Ougi and related the events, and said, "Master, I am constantly consumed by worry that this is all really a cult, and that your teachings are only dogma."

Ougi replied, "If you find a hammer lying in the road and sell it, you may ask a low price or a high one. But if you keep the hammer and use it to drive nails, who can doubt its worth?"

The novice said, "See, now that's just the sort of thing I worry about—your mysterious Zen replies."

Ougi said, "Fine, then, I will speak more plainly, and lay out perfectly reasonable arguments which demonstrate that you have not fallen into a cult. But first you have to wear this silly hat."

Ougi gave the novice a huge brown ten-gallon cowboy hat.

"Er, master . . ." said the novice.

"When I have explained everything to you," said Ougi, "you will see why this was necessary. Or otherwise, you can continue to lie awake nights, wondering whether this is a cult."

The novice put on the cowboy hat.

Ougi said, "How long will you repeat my words and ignore the meaning? Disordered thoughts begin as feelings of attachment to preferred conclusions. You are too anxious about your self-image as a rationalist. You came to me to seek reassurance. If you had been truly curious, not knowing one way or the other, you would have thought of ways to resolve your doubts. Because you needed to resolve your cognitive dissonance, you were willing to put on a silly hat. If I had been an evil man, I could have made you pay a hundred silver coins. When you concentrate on a real-world question, the worth or worthlessness of your understanding will soon become apparent. You are like a swordsman who keeps glancing away to see if anyone might be laughing at him—"

"All *right*," said the novice.

"You asked for the long version," said Ougi.

This novice later succeeded Ougi and became known as Ni no Tachi. Ever after, he would not allow his students to cite his words in their debates, saying, "Use the techniques and do not mention them."

A novice rationalist approached the master Ougi and said, "Master, I worry that our rationality dojo is . . . well . . . a little cultish."

"That is a grave concern," said Ougi.

The novice waited a time, but Ougi said nothing more.

So the novice spoke up again: "I mean, I'm sorry, but having to wear these robes, and the hood—it just seems like we're the bloody Freemasons or something."

"Ah," said Ougi, "the robes and trappings."

"Well, *yes* the robes and trappings," said the novice. "It just seems terribly irrational."

"I will address all your concerns," said the master, "but first you must put on this silly hat." And Ougi drew out a wizard's hat, embroidered with crescents and stars.

The novice took the hat, looked at it, and then burst out in frustration: "*How can this possibly help?*"

"Since you are so concerned about the interactions of clothing with probability theory," Ougi said, "it should not surprise you that you must wear a special hat to understand."

When the novice attained the rank of grad student, he took the name Bouzo and would only discuss rationality while wearing a clown suit.

62

Asch's Conformity Experiment

Solomon Asch, with experiments originally carried out in the 1950s and well-replicated since, highlighted a phenomenon now known as "conformity." In the classic experiment, a subject sees a puzzle like the one in the nearby diagram: Which of the lines A, B, and C is the same size as the line X? Take a moment to determine your own answer . . .

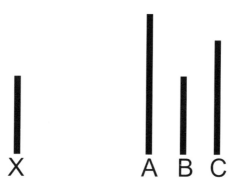

The gotcha is that the subject is seated alongside a number of other people looking at the diagram—seemingly other subjects, actually confederates of the experimenter. The other "subjects" in the experiment, one after the other, say that line C seems to be the same size as X. The real subject is seated next-to-last. How many people, placed in this situation, would say "C"—giving an obviously incorrect answer that agrees with the unanimous answer of the other subjects? What do you think the percentage would be?

Three-quarters of the subjects in Asch's experiment gave a "conforming" answer at least once. A third of the subjects conformed more than half the time.

Interviews after the experiment showed that while most subjects claimed to have not really believed their conforming answers, some said they'd really thought that the conforming option was the correct one.

Asch was disturbed by these results:[1]

> That we have found the tendency to conformity in our society so strong . . . is a matter of concern. It raises questions about our ways of education and about the values that guide our conduct.

It is not a trivial question whether the subjects of Asch's experiments behaved *irrationally*. Robert Aumann's Agreement Theorem shows that honest Bayesians cannot agree to disagree—if they have common knowledge of their probability estimates, they have the same probability estimate. Aumann's Agreement Theorem was proved more than twenty years after Asch's experiments, but it only formalizes and strengthens an intuitively obvious point—other people's beliefs are often legitimate evidence.

If you were looking at a diagram like the one above, but you knew *for a fact* that the other people in the experiment were honest and seeing the same diagram as you, and three other people said that C was the same size as X, then what are the odds that *only you* are the one who's right? I lay claim to no advantage of *visual* reasoning—I don't think I'm better than an average human at judging whether two lines are the same size. In terms of individual

---

[1] Solomon E. Asch, "Studies of Independence and Conformity: A Minority of One Against a Unanimous Majority," *Psychological Monographs* 70 (1956).

230

rationality, I hope I would notice my own severe confusion and then assign >50% probability to the majority vote.

In terms of group rationality, seems to me that the proper thing for an honest rationalist to say is, "How surprising, it *looks* to me like B is the same size as X. But if we're all looking at the same diagram and reporting honestly, I have no reason to believe that my assessment is better than yours." The last sentence is important—it's a much weaker claim of disagreement than, "Oh, *I* see the optical illusion—I understand why you think it's C, of course, but the real answer is B."

So the conforming subjects in these experiments are not *automatically* convicted of irrationality, based on what I've described so far. But as you might expect, the devil is in the details of the experimental results. According to a meta-analysis of over a hundred replications by Smith and Bond . . .[2]

. . . Conformity increases strongly up to 3 confederates, but doesn't increase further up to 10–15 confederates. If people are conforming rationally, then the opinion of 15 other subjects should be substantially stronger evidence than the opinion of 3 other subjects.

Adding a single dissenter—just one other person who gives the correct answer, or even an incorrect answer that's different from the group's incorrect answer—reduces conformity *very* sharply, down to 5–10% of subjects. If you're applying some intuitive version of Aumann's Agreement to think that when 1 person disagrees with 3 people, the 3 are probably right, then in most cases you should be equally willing to think that 2 people will disagree with 6 people.[3] On the other hand, if you've got people who are emotionally nervous about being the odd one out, then it's easy to see how adding a single other person who agrees with you, or even adding a single other person who disagrees with the group, would make you much less nervous.

Unsurprisingly, subjects in the one-dissenter condition did not think their nonconformity had been influenced or enabled by the dissenter. Like the 90% of drivers who think they're ~~above-average~~ in the top 50%, some of them may be right about this, but not all. People are not self-aware of the causes of their

---

[2] Rod Bond and Peter B. Smith, "Culture and Conformity: A Meta-Analysis of Studies Using Asch's (1952b, 1956) Line Judgment Task," *Psychological Bulletin* 119 (1996): 111–137.
[3] This isn't automatically true, but it's true *ceteris paribus*.

conformity or dissent, which weighs against any attempts to argue that the patterns of conformity are rational.[4]

When the single dissenter suddenly switched to *conforming to the group*, subjects' conformity rates went back up to just as high as in the no-dissenter condition. Being the first dissenter is a valuable (and costly!) social service, but you've got to keep it up.

Consistently within and across experiments, all-female groups (a female subject alongside female confederates) conform significantly more often than all-male groups. Around one-half the women conform more than half the time, versus a third of the men. If you argue that the average subject is rational, then apparently women are too agreeable and men are too disagreeable, so neither group is actually *rational* . . .

Ingroup-outgroup manipulations (e.g., a handicapped subject alongside other handicapped subjects) similarly show that conformity is significantly higher among members of an ingroup.

Conformity is lower in the case of blatant diagrams, like the one at the beginning of this essay, versus diagrams where the errors are more subtle. This is hard to explain if (all) the subjects are making a socially rational decision to avoid sticking out.

Finally, Paul Crowley reminds me to note that when subjects can respond in a way that will not be seen by the group, conformity also drops, which also argues against an Aumann interpretation.

---

[4] For example, in the hypothesis that people are socially-rationally choosing to lie in order to not stick out, it appears that (at least some) subjects in the one-dissenter condition do not consciously anticipate the "conscious strategy" they would employ when faced with unanimous opposition.

63

On Expressing Your Concerns

The scary thing about Asch's conformity experiments is that you can get many people to say black is white, if you put them in a room full of other people saying the same thing. The hopeful thing about Asch's conformity experiments is that a single dissenter tremendously drove down the rate of conformity, even if the dissenter was only giving a different wrong answer. And the *wearisome* thing is that dissent was not *learned* over the course of the experiment—when the single dissenter started siding with the group, rates of conformity rose back up.

Being a voice of dissent can bring real benefits to the group. But it also (famously) has a cost. And then you have to keep it up. Plus you could be wrong.

I recently had an interesting experience wherein I began discussing a project with two people who had previously done some planning on their own. I thought they were being too optimistic and made a number of safety-margin-type suggestions for the project. Soon a fourth guy wandered by, who was providing one of the other two with a ride home, and began making suggestions. At this point I had a sudden insight about how groups become overconfident, because whenever I raised a possible problem, the fourth guy would say, "Don't worry, I'm sure we can handle it!" or something similarly reassuring.

An individual, working alone, will have natural doubts. They will think to themselves, "Can I really do XYZ?" because there's nothing impolite about doubting your *own* competence. But when two unconfident people form a group, it is polite to say nice and reassuring things, and impolite to question the other person's competence. Together they become more optimistic than either would be on their own, each one's doubts quelled by the other's seemingly confident reassurance, not realizing that the other person initially had the same inner doubts.

The most fearsome possibility raised by Asch's experiments on conformity is the specter of everyone agreeing with the group, swayed by the confident voices of others, careful not to let their own doubts show—not realizing that others are suppressing similar worries. This is known as "pluralistic ignorance."

Robin Hanson and I have a long-running debate over when, exactly, aspiring rationalists should dare to disagree. I tend toward the widely held position that you have no real choice but to form your own opinions. Robin Hanson advocates a more iconoclastic position, that *you*—not just other people—should consider that others may be wiser. Regardless of our various disputes, we both agree that Aumann's Agreement Theorem extends to imply that common knowledge of a factual disagreement shows *someone* must be irrational.[1] Despite the funny looks we've gotten, we're sticking to our guns about modesty: Forget what everyone tells you about individualism, you *should* pay attention to what other people think.

Ahem. The point is that, for rationalists, disagreeing with the group is serious business. You can't wave it off with, "Everyone is entitled to their own opinion."

I think the most important lesson to take away from Asch's experiments is to distinguish "expressing concern" from "disagreement." Raising a point that others haven't voiced is not a promise to disagree with the group at the end of its discussion.

---

[1] See "The Modesty Argument," http://lesswrong.com/lw/gr/the_modesty_argument/.

The ideal Bayesian's process of convergence involves sharing evidence that is unpredictable to the listener. The Aumann agreement result holds only for *common knowledge*, where you know, I know, you know I know, etc. Hanson's post or paper on "We Can't Foresee to Disagree" provides a picture of how strange it would look to watch ideal rationalists converging on a probability estimate; it doesn't look anything like two bargainers in a marketplace converging on a price.[2]

Unfortunately, there's not much difference *socially* between "expressing concerns" and "disagreement." A group of rationalists might agree to pretend there's a difference, but it's not how human beings are really wired. Once you speak out, you've committed a socially irrevocable act; you've become the nail sticking up, the discord in the comfortable group harmony, and you can't undo that. Anyone insulted by a concern you expressed about their competence to successfully complete task XYZ will probably hold just as much of a grudge afterward if you say, "No problem, I'll go along with the group," at the end.

Asch's experiment shows that the power of dissent to inspire others is real. Asch's experiment shows that the power of conformity is real. If everyone refrains from voicing their private doubts, that will indeed lead groups into madness. But history abounds with lessons on the price of being the first, or even the second, to say that the Emperor has no clothes. Nor are people hardwired to distinguish "expressing a concern" from "disagreement even with common knowledge"; this distinction is a rationalist's artifice. If you read the more cynical brand of self-help books (e.g., Machiavelli's *The Prince*) they will advise you to mask your nonconformity entirely, *not* voice your concerns first and then agree at the end. If you perform the group service of being the one who gives voice to the obvious problems, don't expect the group to thank you for it.

These are the costs and the benefits of dissenting—whether you "disagree" or just "express concern"—and the decision is up to you.

---

[2] Link: http://www.overcomingbias.com/2007/01/we_cant_foresee.html

64

Lonely Dissent

Asch's conformity experiment showed that the presence of a single dissenter tremendously reduced the incidence of "conforming" wrong answers. Individualism is easy, experiment shows, when you have company in your defiance. Every other subject in the room, except one, says that black is white. You become the second person to say that black is black. And it feels glorious: the two of you, lonely and defiant rebels, against the world![1]

But you can only *join* the rebellion after someone, somewhere, becomes the *first* to rebel. Someone has to say that black is black after hearing *everyone* else, one after the other, say that black is white. And that—experiment shows—is a *lot harder*.

Lonely dissent doesn't feel like going to school dressed in black. It feels like going to school wearing a clown suit.

That's the difference between *joining the rebellion* and *leaving the pack*.

If there's one thing I can't stand, it's fakeness—you may have noticed this. Well, lonely dissent has got to be one of the most commonly, most ostentatiously faked characteristics around. Everyone wants to be an iconoclast.

---

[1] Followup interviews showed that subjects in the one-dissenter condition expressed strong feelings of camaraderie with the dissenter—though, of course, they didn't think the presence of the dissenter had influenced their own nonconformity.

I don't mean to degrade the act of joining a rebellion. There are rebellions worth joining. It does take courage to brave the disapproval of your peer group, or perhaps even worse, their shrugs. Needless to say, going to a rock concert is not rebellion. But, for example, vegetarianism is. I'm not a vegetarian myself, but I respect people who are, because I expect it takes a noticeable amount of quiet courage to tell people that hamburgers won't work for dinner.[2]

Still, if you tell people that you're a vegetarian, they'll think they understand your motives (even if they don't). They may disagree. They may be offended if you manage to announce it proudly enough, or for that matter, they may be offended just because they're easily offended. But they know how to relate to you.

When someone wears black to school, the teachers and the other children understand the role thereby being assumed in their society. It's Outside the System—in a very standard way that everyone recognizes and understands. Not, y'know, *actually* outside the system. It's a Challenge to Standard Thinking, of a standard sort, so that people indignantly say, "I can't understand why you—" but don't have to actually think any thoughts they had not thought before. As the saying goes, "Has any of the 'subversive literature' you've read caused you to modify any of your political views?"

What takes *real* courage is braving the outright *incomprehension* of the people around you, when you do something that *isn't* Standard Rebellion #37, something for which they lack a ready-made script. They don't hate you for a rebel. They just think you're, like, weird, and turn away. This prospect generates a much deeper fear. It's the difference between explaining vegetarianism and explaining cryonics. There are other cryonicists in the world, somewhere, but they aren't there next to you. You have to explain it, alone, to people who just think it's *weird*. Not forbidden, but outside bounds that people don't even think about. You're going to get your head frozen? You think that's going to stop you from dying? What do you mean, brain information? Huh? What? Are you *crazy*?

I'm tempted to essay a post facto explanation in evolutionary psychology: You could get together with a small group of friends and walk away from your

---

[2] Albeit that in the Bay Area, people ask as a matter of routine.

hunter-gatherer band, but having to go it *alone* in the forests was probably a death sentence—at least reproductively. We don't reason this out explicitly, but that is not the nature of evolutionary psychology. Joining a rebellion that everyone knows about is scary, but nowhere near as scary as doing something really differently—something that in ancestral times might have concluded, not with the band splitting, but with you being driven out alone.

As the case of cryonics testifies, the fear of thinking *really* different is stronger than the fear of death. Hunter-gatherers had to be ready to face death on a routine basis—hunting large mammals, or just walking around in a world that contained predators. They needed that courage in order to live. Courage to defy the tribe's standard ways of thinking, to entertain thoughts that seem truly weird—well, that probably didn't serve its bearers as well. We don't reason this out explicitly; that's not how evolutionary psychology works. We human beings are just built in such fashion that many more of us go skydiving than sign up for cryonics.

And that's not even the highest courage. There's more than one cryonicist in the world. Only Robert Ettinger had to say it *first*.

To be a *scientific* revolutionary, you've got to be the first person to contradict what everyone else you know is thinking. This is not the only route to scientific greatness; it is rare even among the great. No one can become a scientific revolutionary by trying to imitate revolutionariness. You can only get there by pursuing the correct answer in all things, whether the correct answer is revolutionary or not. But if, in the due course of time—if, having absorbed all the power and wisdom of the knowledge that has already accumulated—if, after all that and a dose of sheer luck, you find your pursuit of mere correctness taking you into new territory . . . *then* you have an opportunity for your courage to fail.

This is the true courage of lonely dissent, which every damn rock band out there tries to fake.

Of course, not everything that takes courage is a good idea. It would take courage to walk off a cliff, but then you would just go splat.

238

The *fear* of lonely dissent is a hindrance to good ideas, but not every dissenting idea is good.[3] Most of the difficulty in having a new true scientific thought is in the "true" part.

It really isn't *necessary* to be different for the sake of being different. If you do things differently only when you see an overwhelmingly good reason, you will have more than enough trouble to last you the rest of your life.

There are a few genuine packs of iconoclasts around. The Church of the SubGenius, for example, seems to genuinely aim at *confusing* the mundanes, not merely offending them. And there are islands of genuine tolerance in the world, such as science fiction conventions. There *are* certain people who have no fear of departing the pack. Many fewer such people really exist, than imagine themselves rebels; but they do exist. And yet scientific revolutionaries are tremendously rarer. Ponder that.

Now *me*, you know, I *really am* an iconoclast. Everyone thinks they are, but with me it's *true*, you see. I would *totally* have worn a clown suit to school. My serious conversations were with books, not with other children.

But if you think you would *totally* wear that clown suit, then don't be too proud of that either! It just means that you need to make an effort in the *opposite direction* to avoid dissenting too easily. That's what I have to do, to correct for my own nature. Other people do have reasons for thinking what they do, and ignoring that completely is as bad as being afraid to contradict them. You wouldn't want to end up as a free thinker. It's not a *virtue*, you see—just a bias either way.

---

[3] See Robin Hanson's "Against Free Thinkers," http://www.overcoming-bias.com/2007/06/against_free_th.html.

65

Cultish Countercultishness

In the modern world, joining a cult is probably one of the worse things that can happen to you. The best-case scenario is that you'll end up in a group of sincere but deluded people, making an honest mistake but otherwise well-behaved, and you'll spend a lot of time and money but end up with nothing to show. Actually, that could describe any failed Silicon Valley startup. Which is supposed to be a hell of a harrowing experience, come to think. So yes, very scary.

Real cults are vastly worse. "Love bombing" as a recruitment technique, targeted at people going through a personal crisis. Sleep deprivation. Induced fatigue from hard labor. Distant communes to isolate the recruit from friends and family. Daily meetings to confess impure thoughts. It's not unusual for cults to take *all* the recruit's money—life savings plus weekly paycheck—forcing them to depend on the cult for food and clothing. Starvation as a punishment for disobedience. Serious brainwashing and serious harm.

With all that taken into account, I should probably sympathize more with people who are terribly nervous, embarking on some odd-seeming endeavor, that *they might be joining a cult.* It should not grate on my nerves. Which it does.

Point one: "Cults" and "non-cults" aren't separated natural kinds like dogs and cats. If you look at any list of cult characteristics, you'll see items that could easily describe political parties and corporations—"group members encouraged to distrust outside criticism as having hidden motives," "hierarchical authoritative structure." I've written on group failure modes like group polarization, happy death spirals, uncriticality, and evaporative cooling, all of which seem to feed on each other. When these failures swirl together and meet, they combine to form a Super-Failure stupider than any of the parts, like Voltron. But this is not a cult *essence*; it is a cult *attractor*.

Dogs are born with dog DNA, and cats are born with cat DNA. In the current world, there is no in-between. (Even with genetic manipulation, it wouldn't be as simple as creating an organism with half dog genes and half cat genes.) It's not like there's a mutually reinforcing set of dog-characteristics, which an individual cat can wander halfway into and become a semidog.

The human mind, as it thinks about categories, seems to prefer essences to attractors. The one wishes to say, "It is a cult," or, "It is not a cult," and then the task of classification is over and done. If you observe that Socrates has ten fingers, wears clothes, and speaks fluent Greek, then you can say, "Socrates is human," and from there deduce, "Socrates is vulnerable to hemlock," without doing specific blood tests to confirm his mortality. You have decided Socrates's humanness once and for all.

But if you observe that a certain group of people seems to exhibit ingroup-outgroup polarization and see a positive halo effect around their Favorite Thing Ever—which could be Objectivism, or vegetarianism, or neural networks—you cannot, *from the evidence gathered so far,* deduce whether they have achieved uncriticality. You cannot deduce whether their main idea is true, or false, or genuinely useful but not quite as useful as they think. *From the information gathered so far,* you cannot deduce whether they are otherwise polite, or if they will lure you into isolation and deprive you of sleep and food. The characteristics of cultness are not all present or all absent.

If you look at online arguments over "X is a cult," "X is not a cult," then one side goes through an online list of cult characteristics and finds one that applies and says, "Therefore it is a cult!" And the defender finds a characteristic that does not apply and says, "Therefore it is not a cult!"

You cannot build up an accurate picture of a group's reasoning dynamic using this kind of essentialism. You've got to pay attention to individual characteristics individually.

Furthermore, reversed stupidity is not intelligence. If you're interested in the central *idea*, not just the implementation group, then smart ideas can have stupid followers. Lots of New Agers talk about "quantum physics," but this is no strike against quantum physics.[1] Along with binary essentialism goes the idea that if you infer that a group is a "cult," therefore their beliefs must be false, because false beliefs are characteristic of cults, just like cats have fur. If you're interested in the idea, then look at the idea, not the people. Cultishness is a characteristic of *groups* more than *hypotheses*.

The second error is that when people nervously ask, "This isn't a cult, is it?" it sounds to me like they're seeking *reassurance of rationality.* The notion of a rationalist not getting too attached to their self-image as a rationalist deserves its own essay.[2] But even without going into detail, surely one can see that *nervously seeking reassurance* is not the best frame of mind in which to evaluate questions of rationality. You will not be genuinely curious or think of ways to fulfill your doubts. Instead, you'll find some online source which says that cults use sleep deprivation to control people, you'll notice that Your-Favorite-Group doesn't use sleep deprivation, and you'll conclude, "It's not a cult. Whew!" If it doesn't have fur, it must not be a cat. Very reassuring.

But every cause wants to be a cult, whether the cause itself is wise or foolish. The ingroup-outgroup dichotomy, etc., are part of human nature, not a special curse of mutants. Rationality is the exception, not the rule. You have to put forth a constant effort to maintain rationality against the natural slide into entropy. If you decide, "It's not a cult!" and sigh with relief, then you will not put forth a continuing effort to push back *ordinary* tendencies toward cultishness. You'll decide the cult-essence is absent, and stop pumping against the entropy of the cult attractor.

---

[1] Of course, stupid ideas can also have stupid followers.
[2] Though see "The Twelve Virtues of Rationality" (at http://yudkowsky.net/rational/virtues/), "Why Truth? And . . . " (in *Map and Territory*), and the two cult koans.

If you are terribly nervous about cultishness, then you will want to deny any hint of any characteristic that resembles a cult. But *any* group with a goal seen in a positive light is at risk for the halo effect, and will have to pump against entropy to avoid an affective death spiral. This is true even for ordinary institutions like political parties—people who think that "liberal values" or "conservative values" can cure cancer, etc. It is true for Silicon Valley startups, both failed and successful. It is true of Mac users and of Linux users. The halo effect doesn't become okay just because everyone does it; if everyone walks off a cliff, you wouldn't too. The error in reasoning is to be fought, not tolerated. But if you're too nervous about, "Are you *sure* this isn't a cult?" then you will be reluctant to see *any* sign of cultishness, because that would imply you're in a cult, and *It's not a cult!!* So you won't see the current battlefields where the *ordinary* tendencies toward cultishness are creeping forward, or being pushed back.

The third mistake in nervously asking, "This isn't a cult, is it?" is that, I strongly suspect, the *nervousness* is there for entirely the wrong reasons.

Why is it that groups which praise their Happy Thing to the stars, encourage members to donate all their money and work in voluntary servitude, and run private compounds in which members are kept tightly secluded, are called "religions" rather than "cults" once they've been around for a few hundred years?

Why is it that most of the people who nervously ask of cryonics, "This isn't a cult, is it?" would not be equally nervous about attending a Republican or Democratic political rally? Ingroup-outgroup dichotomies and happy death spirals can happen in political discussion, in mainstream religions, in sports fandom. If the *nervousness* came from fear of *rationality errors*, people would ask, "This isn't an ingroup-outgroup dichotomy, is it?" about Democratic or Republican political rallies, in just the same fearful tones.

There's a legitimate reason to be less fearful of Libertarianism than of a flying-saucer cult, because Libertarians don't have a reputation for employing sleep deprivation to convert people. But cryonicists don't have a reputation for using sleep deprivation, either. So why be any more worried about having your head frozen after you stop breathing?

I suspect that the *nervousness* is not the fear of believing falsely, or the fear of physical harm. It is the fear of lonely dissent. The nervous feeling that subjects get in Asch's conformity experiment, when all the other subjects (actually confederates) say one after another that line C is the same size as line X, and it looks to the subject like line B is the same size as line X. The fear of leaving the pack.

That's why groups whose beliefs have been around long enough to seem "normal" don't inspire the same nervousness as "cults," though some mainstream religions may also take all your money and send you to a monastery. It's why groups like political parties, that are strongly liable for rationality errors, don't inspire the same nervousness as "cults." The word "cult" isn't being used to symbolize rationality errors; it's being used as a label for something that *seems weird*.

Not every change is an improvement, but every improvement is necessarily a change. That which you want to do better, you have no choice but to do differently. Common wisdom does embody a fair amount of, well, actual wisdom; yes, it makes sense to require an extra burden of proof for weirdness. But the *nervousness* isn't that kind of deliberate, rational consideration. It's the fear of believing something that will make your friends look at you really oddly. And so people ask, "This isn't a *cult*, is it?" in a tone that they would never use for attending a political rally, or for putting up a gigantic Christmas display.

That's the part that bugs me.

It's as if, as soon as you believe anything that your ancestors did not believe, the Cult Fairy comes down from the sky and infuses you with the Essence of Cultness, and the next thing you know, you're all wearing robes and chanting. As if "weird" beliefs are the *direct cause* of the problems, never mind the sleep deprivation and beatings. The harm done by cults—the Heaven's Gate suicide and so on—just goes to show that everyone with an odd belief is crazy; the first and foremost characteristic of "cult members" is that they are Outsiders with Peculiar Ways.

Yes, socially unusual belief puts a group at risk for ingroup-outgroup thinking and evaporative cooling and other problems. But the unusualness is a risk factor, not a disease in itself. Same thing with having a goal that you think is

244

worth accomplishing. Whether or not the belief is true, having a nice goal always puts you at risk of the happy death spiral. But that makes lofty goals a risk factor, not a disease. Some goals are genuinely worth pursuing.[3]

Problem four: The fear of lonely dissent is something that *cults themselves* exploit. Being afraid of your friends looking at you disapprovingly is *exactly the effect that real cults use to convert and keep members*—surrounding converts with wall-to-wall agreement among cult believers.

The fear of strange ideas, the impulse to conformity, has no doubt warned many potential victims away from flying saucer cults. When you're out, it keeps you out. But when you're *in*, it keeps you *in*. Conformity just glues you to wherever you are, whether that's a good place or a bad place.

The one wishes there was some way they could be *sure* that they weren't in a "cult." Some definite, crushing rejoinder to people who looked at them funny. Some way they could know once and for all that they were doing the right thing, without these constant doubts. I believe that's called "need for closure." And—of course—cults exploit that, too.

Hence the phrase "cultish countercultishness."

Living with doubt is not a virtue—the purpose of every doubt is to annihilate itself in success or failure, and a doubt that just hangs around accomplishes nothing. But sometimes a doubt does take a while to annihilate itself. Living with a stack of currently unresolved doubts is an unavoidable fact of life for rationalists. Doubt shouldn't be scary. Otherwise you're going to have to choose between living one heck of a hunted life, or one heck of a stupid one.

If you really, genuinely can't figure out whether a group is a "cult," then you'll just have to choose under conditions of uncertainty. That's what decision theory is all about.

Problem five: Lack of strategic thinking.

I know people who are cautious around ideas like intelligence explosion and superintelligent AI, and they're *also* cautious around political parties and mainstream religions. *Cautious*, not nervous or defensive. These people can see at a glance that singularity-ish ideas aren't currently the nucleus of a full-

---

[3] On the other hand, I see no legitimate reason for sleep deprivation or threatening dissenters with beating, full stop. When a group does this, then whether you call it "cult" or "not-cult," you have directly answered the pragmatic question of whether to join.

blown cult with sleep deprivation, etc. But they worry that it will *become* a cult, because of risk factors like turning the concept of a powerful AI into a Super Happy Agent (an agent defined primarily by agreeing with any nice thing said about it). Just because something isn't a cult now doesn't mean it won't become a cult in the future. Cultishness is an attractor, not an essence.

Does *this* kind of caution annoy me? Hell no. I spend a lot of time worrying about that scenario myself. I try to place my Go stones in advance to block movement in that direction.[4]

People who talk about "rationality" also have an added risk factor. Giving people advice about how to think is an inherently dangerous business. But it is a *risk factor*, not a *disease*.

Both of my favorite Causes are at-risk for cultishness. Yet somehow I get asked, "Are you sure this isn't a cult?" a lot more often when I talk about powerful AIs than when I talk about probability theory and cognitive science. I don't know if one risk factor is higher than the other, but I know which one *sounds weirder* . . .

Problem #6 with asking, "This isn't a cult, is it?" . . .

Just the question itself places me in a very annoying sort of Catch-22. An actual Evil Guru would surely use the one's nervousness against them, and design a plausible elaborate argument explaining Why This Is Not A Cult, and the one would be eager to accept it. Sometimes I get the impression that this is what people *want* me to do! Whenever I try to write about cultishness and how to avoid it, I keep feeling like I'm giving in to that flawed desire—that I am, in the end, providing people with *reassurance*. Even when I tell people that a constant fight against entropy is required.

It feels like I'm making myself a first dissenter in Asch's conformity experiment, telling people, "Yes, line X really is the same as line B, it's okay for you to say so too." They shouldn't need to ask! Or, even worse, it feels like I'm presenting an elaborate argument for Why This Is Not A Cult. It's a *wrong question*.

Just look at the group's reasoning processes for yourself, and decide for yourself whether it's something you want to be part of, once you get rid of the

---

[4] Hence, for example, the series of essays on cultish failures of reasoning.

fear of weirdness. It is your own responsibility to stop yourself from thinking cultishly, no matter which group you currently happen to be operating in.

Cults feed on groupthink, nervousness, desire for reassurance. You cannot make nervousness go away by wishing, and false self-confidence is even worse. But so long as someone needs reassurance—even reassurance about being a rationalist—that will always be a flaw in their armor. A skillful swordsman focuses on the target, rather than glancing away to see if anyone might be laughing. When you know what you're trying to do and why, you'll know whether you're getting it done or not, and whether a group is helping you or hindering you.[5]

---

[5] PS: If the one comes to you and says, "Are you *sure* this isn't a cult?" don't try to explain all these concepts in one breath. You're underestimating inferential distances. The one will say, "Aha, so you're *admitting* you're a cult!" or, "Wait, you're saying I shouldn't worry about joining cults?" or, "So . . . the fear of cults is cultish? That sounds awfully cultish to me."

So the last annoyance factor—#7 if you're keeping count—is that all of this is such a long story to explain.

Part J

Letting Go

66

Singlethink

I remember the exact moment when I began my journey as a rationalist.

It was not while reading *Surely You're Joking, Mr. Feynman* or any existing work upon rationality; for these I simply accepted as obvious. The journey begins when you see a great flaw in your existing art, and discover a drive to improve, to create *new* skills beyond the helpful but inadequate ones you found in books.

In the last moments of my first life, I was fifteen years old, and rehearsing a pleasantly self-righteous memory of a time when I was much younger. My memories this far back are vague; I have a mental image, but I don't remember how old I was exactly. I think I was six or seven, and that the original event happened during summer camp.

What happened originally was that a camp counselor, a teenage male, got us much younger boys to form a line, and proposed the following game: the boy at the end of the line would crawl through our legs, and we would spank him as he went past, and then it would be the turn of the next eight-year-old boy at the end of the line. (Maybe it's just that I've lost my youthful innocence, but I can't help but wonder . . .) I refused to play this game, and was told to go sit in the corner.

This memory—of refusing to spank and be spanked—came to symbolize to me that even at this very early age I had refused to take joy in hurting others. That I would not purchase a spank on another's butt, at the price of a spank on my own; would not pay in hurt for the opportunity to inflict hurt. I had refused to play a negative-sum game.

And then, at the age of fifteen, I suddenly realized that it wasn't true. I *hadn't* refused out of a principled stand against negative-sum games. I found out about the Prisoner's Dilemma pretty early in life, but not at the age of seven. I'd refused simply because I didn't want to get hurt, and standing in the corner was an acceptable price to pay for not getting hurt.

More importantly, I realized that I had *always* known this—that the real memory had *always* been lurking in a corner of my mind, my mental eye glancing at it for a fraction of a second and then looking away.

In my very first step along the Way, *I caught the feeling*—generalized over the subjective experience—and said, "So *that's* what it feels like to shove an unwanted truth into the corner of my mind! Now I'm going to notice every time I do that, and clean out *all* my corners!"

This discipline I named *singlethink*, after Orwell's doublethink. In doublethink, you forget, and then forget you have forgotten. In singlethink, you notice you are forgetting, and then you remember. You hold only a single non-contradictory thought in your mind at once.

"Singlethink" was the first *new* rationalist skill I created, which I had not read about in books. I doubt that it is original in the sense of academic priority, but this is thankfully not required.

Oh, and my fifteen-year-old self liked to name things.

The terrifying depths of the confirmation bias go on and on. Not forever, for the brain is of finite complexity, but long enough that it feels like forever. You keep on discovering (or reading about) new mechanisms by which your brain shoves things out of the way.

But my young self swept out quite a few corners with that first broom.

67

The Importance of Saying "Oops"

I just finished reading a history of Enron's downfall, *The Smartest Guys in the Room*, which hereby wins my award for "Least Appropriate Book Title."

An unsurprising feature of Enron's slow rot and abrupt collapse was that the executive players never admitted to having made a *large* mistake. When catastrophe #247 grew to such an extent that it required an actual policy change, they would say, "Too bad that didn't work out—it was such a good idea—how are we going to hide the problem on our balance sheet?" As opposed to, "It now seems obvious in retrospect that it was a mistake from the beginning." As opposed to, "I've been stupid." There was never a watershed moment, a moment of humbling realization, of acknowledging a *fundamental* problem. After the bankruptcy, Jeff Skilling, the former COO and brief CEO of Enron, declined his own lawyers' advice to take the Fifth Amendment; he testified before Congress that Enron had been a *great* company.

Not every change is an improvement, but every improvement is necessarily a change. If we only admit small local errors, we will only make small local changes. The motivation for a *big* change comes from acknowledging a *big* mistake.

As a child I was raised on equal parts science and science fiction, and from Heinlein to Feynman I learned the tropes of Traditional Rationality: theories must be bold and expose themselves to falsification; be willing to commit the heroic sacrifice of giving up your own ideas when confronted with contrary evidence; play nice in your arguments; try not to deceive yourself; and other fuzzy verbalisms.

A traditional rationalist upbringing tries to produce arguers who will concede to contrary evidence *eventually*—there should be *some* mountain of evidence sufficient to move you. This is not trivial; it distinguishes science from religion. But there is less focus on *speed*, on giving up the fight *as quickly as possible*, integrating evidence *efficiently* so that it only takes a *minimum* of contrary evidence to destroy your cherished belief.

I was raised in Traditional Rationality, and thought myself quite the rationalist. I switched to Bayescraft (Laplace / Jaynes / Tversky / Kahneman) in the aftermath of . . . well, it's a long story. Roughly, I switched because I realized that Traditional Rationality's fuzzy verbal tropes had been insufficient to prevent me from making a large mistake.

After I had finally and fully admitted my mistake, I looked back upon the path that had led me to my Awful Realization. And I saw that I had made a series of small concessions, minimal concessions, grudgingly conceding each millimeter of ground, realizing as little as possible of my mistake on each occasion, admitting failure only in small tolerable nibbles. I could have moved so much faster, I realized, if I had simply screamed *"Oops!"*

And I thought: *I must raise the level of my game.*

There is a *powerful advantage* to admitting you have made a *large* mistake. It's painful. It can also change your whole life.

It is *important* to have the watershed moment, the moment of humbling realization. To acknowledge a *fundamental* problem, not divide it into palatable bite-size mistakes.

Do not indulge in drama and become proud of admitting errors. It is surely superior to get it right the first time. But if you do make an error, better by far to see it all at once. Even hedonically, it is better to take one large loss than many small ones. The alternative is stretching out the battle with yourself over years. The alternative is Enron.

Since then I have watched others making their own series of minimal concessions, grudgingly conceding each millimeter of ground; never confessing a global mistake where a local one will do; always learning as little as possible from each error. What they could fix in one fell swoop voluntarily, they transform into tiny local patches they must be argued into. Never do they say, after confessing one mistake, *I've been a fool.* They do their best to minimize their embarrassment by saying *I was right in principle*, or *It could have worked*, or *I still want to embrace the true essence of whatever-I'm-attached-to.* Defending their pride in this passing moment, they ensure they will again make the same mistake, and again need to defend their pride.

Better to swallow the entire bitter pill in one terrible gulp.

68

The Crackpot Offer

When I was very young—I think thirteen or maybe fourteen—I thought I had found a disproof of Cantor's Diagonal Argument, a famous theorem which demonstrates that the real numbers outnumber the rational numbers. Ah, the dreams of fame and glory that danced in my head!

My idea was that since each whole number can be decomposed into a bag of powers of 2, it was possible to map the whole numbers onto the set of subsets of whole numbers simply by writing out the binary expansion. The number 13, for example, 1101, would map onto {0, 2, 3}. It took a whole week before it occurred to me that perhaps I should *apply* Cantor's Diagonal Argument to my clever construction, and of course it found a counterexample—the binary number (. . . 1111), which does not correspond to any finite whole number.

So I found this counterexample, and saw that my attempted disproof was false, along with my dreams of fame and glory.

I was initially a bit disappointed.

The thought went through my mind: "I'll get that theorem eventually! *Someday* I'll disprove Cantor's Diagonal Argument, even though my first try failed!" I resented the theorem for being obstinately true, for depriving me of my fame and fortune, and I began to look for other disproofs.

And then I realized something. I realized that I had made a mistake, and that, now that I'd spotted my mistake, there was absolutely no reason to suspect the strength of Cantor's Diagonal Argument any more than other major theorems of mathematics.

I saw then very clearly that I was being offered the opportunity to become a math crank, and to spend the rest of my life writing angry letters in green ink to math professors. (I'd read a book once about math cranks.)

I did not wish this to be my future, so I gave a small laugh, and let it go. I waved Cantor's Diagonal Argument on with all good wishes, and I did not question it again.

And I don't remember, now, if I thought this at the time, or if I thought it afterward . . . but what a terribly unfair test to visit upon a child of thirteen. That I had to be that rational, already, at that age, or fail.

The smarter you are, the younger you may be, the first time you have what looks to you like a really revolutionary idea. I was lucky in that I saw the mistake myself; that it did not take another mathematician to point it out to me, and perhaps give me an outside source to blame. I was lucky in that the disproof was simple enough for me to understand. Maybe I would have recovered eventually, otherwise. I've recovered from much worse, as an adult. But if I had gone wrong that early, would I ever have developed that skill?

I wonder how many people writing angry letters in green ink were thirteen when they made that first fatal misstep. I wonder how many were promising minds before then.

I made a mistake. That was all. I was not *really right, deep down*; I did not win a moral victory; I was not displaying ambition or skepticism or any other wondrous virtue; it was not a reasonable error; I was not half right or even the tiniest fraction right. I thought a thought I would never have thought if I had been wiser, and that was all there ever was to it.

If I had been unable to admit this to myself, if I had reinterpreted my mistake as virtuous, if I had insisted on being at least a *little* right for the sake of pride, then I would not have let go. I would have gone on looking for a flaw in the Diagonal Argument. And, sooner or later, I might have found one.

Until you admit you were wrong, you cannot get on with your life; your self-image will still be bound to the old mistake.

Whenever you are tempted to hold on to a thought you would never have thought if you had been wiser, you are being offered the opportunity to become a crackpot—even if you never write any angry letters in green ink. If no one bothers to argue with you, or if you never tell anyone your idea, you may still be a crackpot. It's the *clinging* that defines it.

It's not true. It's not true deep down. It's not half-true or even a little true. It's nothing but a thought you should never have thought. Not every cloud has a silver lining. Human beings make mistakes, and not all of them are disguised successes. Human beings make mistakes; it happens, that's all. Say "oops," and get on with your life.

258

69

Just Lose Hope Already

Casey Serin, a 24-year-old web programmer with no prior experience in real estate, owes banks 2.2 million dollars after lying on mortgage applications in order to simultaneously buy eight different houses in different states. He took cash out of the mortgage (applied for larger amounts than the price of the house) and spent the money on living expenses and real-estate seminars. He was expecting the market to go up, it seems.

That's not even the sad part. The sad part is that *he still hasn't given up.* Casey Serin does not accept defeat. He refuses to declare bankruptcy, or get a job; he still thinks he can make it big in real estate. He went on spending money on seminars. He tried to take out a mortgage on a ninth house. He hasn't *failed*, you see, he's just had a *learning experience.*

That's what happens when you refuse to lose hope.

While this behavior may seem to be merely stupid, it also puts me in mind of two Nobel-Prize-winning economists . . .

. . . namely Merton and Scholes of Long-Term Capital Management.

While LTCM raked in giant profits over its first three years, in 1998 the inefficiences that LTCM were exploiting had started to vanish—other people knew about the trick, so it stopped working.

259

LTCM refused to lose hope. Addicted to 40% annual returns, they borrowed more and more leverage to exploit tinier and tinier margins. When everything started to go wrong for LTCM, they had equity of $4.72 billion, leverage of $124.5 billion, and derivative positions of $1.25 trillion.

Every profession has a different way to be smart—different skills to learn and rules to follow. You might therefore think that the study of "rationality," as a general discipline, wouldn't have much to contribute to real-life success. And yet it seems to me that *how to not be stupid* has a great deal in common across professions. If you set out to teach someone *how to not turn little mistakes into big mistakes*, it's nearly the same art whether in hedge funds or romance, and one of the keys is this: Be ready to admit you lost.

70

The Proper Use of Doubt

Once, when I was holding forth upon the Way, I remarked upon how most organized belief systems exist to *flee from doubt.* A listener replied to me that the Jesuits must be immune from this criticism, because they practice organized doubt: their novices, he said, are told to doubt Christianity; doubt the existence of God; doubt if their calling is real; doubt that they are suitable for perpetual vows of chastity and poverty. And I said: *Ah, but they're supposed to overcome these doubts, right?* He said: *No, they are to doubt that perhaps their doubts may grow and become stronger.*

Googling failed to confirm or refute these allegations. But I find this scenario fascinating, worthy of discussion, regardless of whether it is true or false of Jesuits. *If* the Jesuits practiced deliberate doubt, as described above, would they *therefore* be virtuous as rationalists?

I think I have to concede that the Jesuits, in the (possibly hypothetical) scenario above, would not properly be described as "fleeing from doubt." But the (possibly hypothetical) conduct still strikes me as highly suspicious. To a truly virtuous rationalist, doubt should not be scary. The conduct described above sounds to me like a program of desensitization for something *very* scary, like exposing an arachnophobe to spiders under carefully controlled conditions.

But even so, they are encouraging their novices to doubt—right? Does it matter if their reasons are flawed? Is this not still a worthy deed unto a rationalist?

All curiosity seeks to annihilate itself; there is no curiosity that does not *want* an answer. But if you obtain an answer, if you satisfy your curiosity, then the glorious mystery will no longer be mysterious.

In the same way, every doubt exists in order to annihilate some particular belief. If a doubt fails to destroy its target, the doubt has died unfulfilled—but that is still a resolution, an ending, albeit a sadder one. A doubt that neither destroys itself nor destroys its target might as well have never existed at all. It is the *resolution* of doubts, not the mere act of doubting, which drives the ratchet of rationality forward.

Every improvement is a change, but not every change is an improvement. Every rationalist doubts, but not all doubts are rational. Wearing doubts doesn't make you a rationalist any more than wearing a white medical lab coat makes you a doctor.

A rational doubt comes into existence for a specific reason—you have some specific justification to suspect the belief is wrong. This reason, in turn, implies an avenue of investigation which will either destroy the targeted belief or destroy the doubt. This holds even for highly abstract doubts, like: "I wonder if there might be a simpler hypothesis which also explains this data." In this case you investigate by trying to think of simpler hypotheses. As this search continues longer and longer without fruit, you will think it less and less likely that the next increment of computation will be the one to succeed. Eventually the cost of searching will exceed the expected benefit, and you'll stop searching. At which point you can no longer claim to be *usefully doubting.* A doubt that is not investigated might as well not exist. Every doubt exists to destroy itself, one way or the other. An unresolved doubt is a null-op; it does not turn the wheel, neither forward nor back.

If you really believe a religion (and don't just believe *in* it), then why would you tell your novices to consider doubts that must die unfulfilled? It would be like telling physics students to agonize over whether the twentieth-century revolution might have been a mistake, and that Newtonian mechanics was correct all along. If you don't *really* doubt something, why would you *pretend* that you do?

Because we all want to be seen as rational—and doubting is *widely believed* to be a virtue of a rationalist. But it is not widely understood that you need a particular reason to doubt, or that an unresolved doubt is a null-op. Instead people think it's about *modesty*, a submissive demeanor, maintaining the tribal status hierarchy—almost exactly the same problem as with humility, on which I have previously written. Making a great public display of doubt to convince yourself that you are a rationalist will do around as much good as wearing a lab coat.

To avoid merely professing doubts, in the manner of "Professing and Cheering" (*Map and Territory*), remember:

- A rational doubt exists to destroy its target belief, and if it does not destroy its target it dies unfulfilled.

- A rational doubt arises from some specific reason the belief might be wrong.

- An unresolved doubt is a null-op.

- An uninvestigated doubt might as well not exist.

- You should not be proud of mere doubting, although you can justly be proud when you have just *finished* tearing a cherished belief to shreds.

- Though it may take courage to face your doubts, never forget that *to an ideal mind* doubt would not be scary in the first place.

71

You Can Face Reality

What is true is already so.
Owning up to it doesn't make it worse.
Not being open about it doesn't make it go away.
And because it's true, it is what is there to be interacted with.
Anything untrue isn't there to be lived.
People can stand what is true,
for they are already enduring it.

—*Eugene Gendlin*

✳

72

The Meditation on Curiosity

The first virtue is curiosity.

—"The Twelve Virtues of Rationality"

As rationalists, we are obligated to criticize ourselves and question our beliefs . . . are we not?

Consider what happens to you, on a psychological level, if you begin by saying: "It is my duty to criticize my own beliefs." Roger Zelazny once distinguished between "wanting to be an author" versus "wanting to write." Mark Twain said: "A classic is something that everyone wants to have read and no one wants to read." Criticizing yourself from a sense of duty leaves you *wanting to have investigated*, so that you'll be able to say afterward that your faith is not blind. This is not the same as *wanting to investigate*.

This can lead to motivated stopping of your investigation. You consider an objection, then a counterargument to that objection, then you *stop there*. You repeat this with several objections, until you feel that you have done your duty to investigate, and then you *stop there*. You have achieved your underlying psychological objective: to get rid of the cognitive dissonance that would result from thinking of yourself as a rationalist and yet knowing that you had not tried to criticize your belief. You might call it purchase of rationalist satisfaction—trying to create a "warm glow" of discharged duty.

Afterward, your stated probability level will be high enough to justify your keeping the plans and beliefs you started with, but not so high as to evoke incredulity from yourself or other rationalists.

When you're really curious, you'll gravitate to inquiries that seem most promising of producing shifts in belief, or inquiries that are least like the ones you've tried before. Afterward, your probability distribution likely should *not* look like it did when you started out—shifts should have occurred, whether up or down; and either direction is equally fine to you, if you're genuinely curious.

Contrast this to the subconscious motive of keeping your inquiry on familiar ground, so that you can get your investigation over with quickly, so that you can *have investigated*, and restore the familiar balance on which your familiar old plans and beliefs are based.

As for what I think true curiosity should look like, and the power that it holds, I refer you to the essay "A Fable of Science and Politics" in the first book of this series, *Map and Territory*. The fable showcases the reactions of different characters to an astonishing discovery, with each character's response intended to illustrate different lessons. Ferris, the last character, embodies the power of innocent curiosity: which is lightness, and an eager reaching forth for evidence.

Ursula K. LeGuin wrote: "In innocence there is no strength against evil. But there is strength in it for good."[1] Innocent curiosity may turn innocently awry; and so the training of a rationalist, and its accompanying sophistication, must be dared as a danger if we want to become stronger. Nonetheless we can try to keep the lightness and the eager reaching of innocence.

As it is written in "The Twelve Virtues of Rationality":

> If in your heart you believe you already know, or if in your heart you do not wish to know, then your questioning will be purposeless and your skills without direction. Curiosity seeks to annihilate itself; there is no curiosity that does not want an answer.

---

[1] Ursula K. Le Guin, *The Farthest Shore* (Saga Press, 2001).

266

There just isn't any good substitute for genuine curiosity. "A burning itch to know is higher than a solemn vow to pursue truth." But you can't produce curiosity just by willing it, any more than you can will your foot to feel warm when it feels cold. Sometimes, all we have is our mere solemn vows.

So what can you do with duty? For a start, we can try to take an interest in our dutiful investigations—keep a close eye out for sparks of genuine intrigue, or even genuine ignorance and a desire to resolve it. This goes right along with keeping a special eye out for possibilities that are painful, that you are flinching away from—it's not all negative thinking.

It should also help to meditate on "Conservation of Expected Evidence." For every *new* point of inquiry, for every piece of *unseen* evidence that you suddenly look at, the expected posterior probability should equal your prior probability. In the microprocess of inquiry, your belief should always be evenly poised to shift in either direction. Not every point may suffice to blow the issue wide open—to shift belief from 70% to 30% probability—but if your current belief is 70%, you should be as ready to drop it to 69% as raise it to 71%. You should not think that you know which direction it will go in (on average), because by the laws of probability theory, if you know your destination, you are already there. If you can investigate honestly, so that each *new* point really does have equal potential to shift belief upward or downward, this may help to keep you interested or even curious about the microprocess of inquiry.

If the argument you are considering is *not* new, then why is your attention going here? Is this where you would look if you were genuinely curious? Are you subconsciously criticizing your belief at its strong points, rather than its weak points? Are you rehearsing the evidence?

If you can manage not to rehearse already known support, and you can manage to drop down your belief by one tiny bite at a time from the new evidence, you may even be able to relinquish the belief entirely—to realize from which quarter the winds of evidence are blowing against you.

Another restorative for curiosity is what I have taken to calling the Litany of Tarski, which is really a meta-litany that specializes for each instance (this is only appropriate). For example, if I am tensely wondering whether a locked box contains a diamond, then rather than thinking about all the wonderful consequences if the box does contain a diamond, I can repeat the Litany of Tarski:

> *If the box contains a diamond,*
> *I desire to believe that the box contains a diamond;*
> *If the box does not contain a diamond,*
> *I desire to believe that the box does not contain a diamond;*
> *Let me not become attached to beliefs I may not want.*

Then you should meditate upon the possibility that there is no diamond, and the subsequent advantage that will come to you if you believe there is no diamond, and the subsequent disadvantage if you believe there is a diamond. See also the Litany of Gendlin.

If you can find within yourself the slightest shred of true uncertainty, then guard it like a forester nursing a campfire. If you can make it blaze up into a flame of curiosity, it will make you light and eager, and give purpose to your questioning and direction to your skills.

73

No One Can Exempt You From Rationality's Laws

Traditional Rationality is phrased in terms of *social rules*, with violations interpretable as cheating—as defections from cooperative norms. If you want me to accept a belief from you, you are obligated to provide me with a certain amount of evidence. If you try to get out of it, we all know you're cheating on your obligation. A theory is obligated to make bold predictions for itself, not just steal predictions that other theories have labored to make. A theory is obligated to expose itself to falsification—if it tries to duck out, that's like trying to duck out of a fearsome initiation ritual; you must pay your dues.

Traditional Rationality is phrased similarly to the customs that govern human societies, which makes it easy to pass on by word of mouth. Humans detect social cheating with much greater reliability than isomorphic violations of abstract logical rules. But viewing rationality as a social obligation gives rise to some strange ideas.

For example, one finds religious people defending their beliefs by saying, "Well, *you* can't justify your belief in science!" In other words, "How dare you criticize me for having unjustified beliefs, you hypocrite! You're doing it too!"

To Bayesians, the brain is an engine of accuracy: it processes and concentrates entangled evidence into a map that reflects the territory. The principles of rationality are laws in the same sense as the Second Law of Thermodynamics: obtaining a reliable belief requires a calculable amount of entangled evidence, just as reliably cooling the contents of a refrigerator requires a calculable minimum of free energy.

In principle, the laws of physics are time-reversible, so there's an infinitesimally tiny probability—indistinguishable from zero to all but mathematicians—that a refrigerator will spontaneously cool itself down while generating electricity. There's a slightly larger infinitesimal chance that you could accurately draw a detailed street map of New York without ever visiting, sitting in your living room with your blinds closed and no Internet connection. But I wouldn't hold your breath.

Before you try mapping an unseen territory, pour some water into a cup at room temperature and wait until it spontaneously freezes before proceeding. That way you can be sure the general trick—ignoring infinitesimally tiny probabilities of success—is working properly. You might not realize directly that your map is wrong, especially if you never visit New York; but you can see that water doesn't freeze itself.

If the rules of rationality are social customs, then it may seem to excuse behavior X if you point out that others are doing the same thing. It wouldn't be *fair* to demand evidence from you, if we can't provide it ourselves. We will realize that none of us are better than the rest, and we will relent and mercifully excuse you from your social obligation to provide evidence for your belief. And we'll all live happily ever afterward in liberty, fraternity, and equality.

If the rules of rationality are mathematical laws, then trying to justify evidence-free belief by pointing to someone else doing the same thing will be around as effective as listing thirty reasons why you shouldn't fall off a cliff. Even if we all vote that it's unfair for your refrigerator to need electricity, it still won't run (with probability ~ 1). Even if we all vote that you shouldn't have to visit New York, the map will still be wrong. Lady Nature is famously indifferent to such pleading, and so is Lady Math.

So—to shift back to the social language of Traditional Rationality—don't think you can *get away with* claiming that it's okay to have arbitrary beliefs about XYZ, because other people have arbitrary beliefs too. If two parties to a contract both behave equally poorly, a human judge may decide to impose penalties on neither. But if two engineers design their engines equally poorly, neither engine will work. One design error cannot excuse another. Even if *I'm* doing XYZ wrong, it doesn't help you, or exempt you from the rules; it just means we're both screwed.

As a matter of human law in liberal democracies, everyone is entitled to their own beliefs. As a matter of Nature's law, you are not entitled to accuracy. We don't arrest people for believing weird things, at least not in the wiser countries. But no one can revoke the law that you need evidence to generate *accurate* beliefs. Not even a vote of the whole human species can obtain mercy in the court of Nature.

Physicists don't decide the laws of physics, they just guess what they are. Rationalists don't decide the laws of rationality, we just guess what they are. You cannot "rationalize" anything that is not rational to begin with. If by dint of extraordinary persuasiveness you convince all the physicists in the world that you are exempt from the law of gravity, and you walk off a cliff, you'll fall. Even saying "*We* don't decide" is too anthropomorphic. There is no higher authority that could exempt you. There is only cause and effect.

Remember this, when you plead to be excused just this once. We *can't* excuse you. It isn't up to us.

74

Leave a Line of Retreat

When you surround the enemy

Always allow them an escape route.

They must see that there is

An alternative to death.

> —Sun Tzu, *The Art of War*

Don't raise the pressure, lower the wall.

> —Lois McMaster Bujold, *Komarr*

I recently happened into a conversation with a nonrationalist who had somehow wandered into a local rationalists' gathering. She had just declared (a) her belief in souls and (b) that she didn't believe in cryonics because she believed the soul wouldn't stay with the frozen body. I asked, "But how do you know that?"

From the confusion that flashed on her face, it was pretty clear that this question had never occurred to her. I don't say this in a bad way—she seemed like a nice person without any applied rationality training, just like most of the rest of the human species.

Most of the ensuing conversation was on items already covered on *Overcoming Bias*—if you're *really* curious about something, you probably *can* figure out a good way to test it, try to attain accurate beliefs first and then let your emotions flow from that, that sort of thing. But the conversation reminded me of one notion I haven't covered here yet:

"Make sure," I suggested to her, "that you visualize what the world would be like if there are no souls, and what you would do about that. Don't think about all the reasons that it can't be that way; just accept it as a premise and then visualize the consequences. So that you'll think, 'Well, if there are no souls, I can just sign up for cryonics,' or 'If there is no God, I can just go on being moral anyway,' rather than it being too horrifying to face. As a matter of self-respect, you should try to believe the truth no matter how uncomfortable it is, like I said before; but as a matter of human nature, it helps to make a belief less uncomfortable, *before* you try to evaluate the evidence for it."

The principle behind the technique is simple: as Sun Tzu advises you to do with your enemies, you must do with yourself—leave yourself a line of retreat, so that you will have less trouble retreating. The prospect of losing your job, for example, may seem a lot more scary when you can't even bear to think about it than after you have calculated exactly how long your savings will last, and checked the job market in your area, and otherwise planned out exactly what to do next. Only then will you be ready to *fairly* assess the probability of keeping your job in the planned layoffs next month. Be a true coward, and plan out your retreat in detail—visualize every step—preferably before you first come to the battlefield.

The hope is that it takes less courage to visualize an uncomfortable state of affairs *as a thought experiment*, than to consider *how likely* it is to be true. But then after you do the former, it becomes easier to do the latter.

Remember that Bayesianism is precise—even if a scary proposition really should seem unlikely, it's still important to count up all the evidence, for and against, exactly fairly, to arrive at the rational quantitative probability. Visualizing a scary belief does *not* mean admitting that you think, deep down,

273

it's probably true. You can visualize a scary belief on general principles of good mental housekeeping. "The thought you cannot think controls you more than thoughts you speak aloud"—this happens even if the unthinkable thought is false!

The leave-a-line-of-retreat technique does require a certain minimum of self-honesty to use correctly.

For a start: You must at least be able to admit to yourself *which* ideas scare you, and which ideas you are attached to. But this is a substantially less difficult test than fairly counting the evidence for an idea that scares you. Does it help if I say that I have occasion to use this technique myself? A rationalist does not reject all emotion, after all. There are ideas which scare me, yet I still believe to be false. There are ideas to which I know I am attached, yet I still believe to be true. But I still plan my retreats, not because I'm planning *to* retreat, but because planning my retreat in advance helps me think about the problem without attachment.

But the greater test of self-honesty is to *really* accept the uncomfortable proposition as a premise, and figure out how you would *really* deal with it. When we're faced with an uncomfortable idea, our first impulse is naturally to think of all the reasons why it *can't possibly* be so. And so you will encounter a certain amount of psychological resistance in yourself, if you try to visualize exactly how the world would be, and what you would do about it, if My-Most-Precious-Belief were false, or My-Most-Feared-Belief were true.

Think of all the people who say that without God, morality is impossible.[1] If theists could visualize their *real* reaction to believing as a fact that God did not exist, they could realize that, no, they wouldn't go around slaughtering babies. They could realize that atheists are reacting to the nonexistence of God in pretty much the way they themselves would, if they came to believe that. I say this, to show that it *is* a considerable challenge to visualize the way you *really would* react, to believing the opposite of a tightly held belief.

Plus it's always counterintuitive to realize that, yes, people do get over things. Newly minted quadriplegics are not as sad, six months later, as they expect to be, etc. It can be equally counterintuitive to realize that if the scary belief turned

---

[1] And yes, this topic did come up in the conversation; I'm not offering a strawman.

out to be true, you *would* come to terms with it somehow. Quadriplegics deal, and so would you.

See also the Litany of Gendlin and the Litany of Tarski. What is true is already so; owning up to it doesn't make it worse. You shouldn't be afraid to just *visualize* a world you fear. If that world is already actual, visualizing it won't make it worse; and if it is *not* actual, visualizing it will do no harm. And remember, as you visualize, that if the scary things you're imagining really are true—which they may not be!—then you would, indeed, want to believe it, and you should visualize that too; not believing wouldn't help you.

How many religious people would retain their belief in God if they could *accurately* visualize that hypothetical world in which there was no God and they themselves have become atheists?

Leaving a line of retreat is a powerful technique, but it's not easy. *Honest* visualization doesn't take as much effort as admitting *outright* that God doesn't exist, but it does take an effort.

75

Crisis of Faith

It ain't a true crisis of faith unless things could just as easily go either way.

—Thor Shenkel

Many in this world retain beliefs whose flaws a ten-year-old could point out, *if* that ten-year-old were hearing the beliefs for the first time. These are not subtle errors we're talking about. They would be child's play for an unattached mind to relinquish, if the skepticism of a ten-year-old were applied without evasion. As Premise Checker put it, "Had the idea of god not come along until the scientific age, only an exceptionally weird person would invent such an idea and pretend that it explained anything."[1]

And yet skillful scientific specialists, even the major innovators of a field, even in this very day and age, do not apply that skepticism successfully. Nobel laureate Robert Aumann, of Aumann's Agreement Theorem, is an Orthodox Jew: I feel reasonably confident in venturing that Aumann must, at one point or another, have questioned his faith. And yet he did not doubt successfully. We change our minds less often than we think.

---

[1] See "Occam's Razor" (in *Map and Territory*).

276

This should scare you down to the marrow of your bones. It means you can be a world-class scientist *and* conversant with Bayesian mathematics *and* still fail to reject a belief whose absurdity a fresh-eyed ten-year-old could see. It shows the invincible defensive position which a belief can create for itself, if it has long festered in your mind.

What does it take to defeat an error that has built itself a fortress?

But by the time you *know* it is an error, it is already defeated. The dilemma is not "How can I reject long-held false belief X?" but "How do I know if long-held belief X is false?" Self-honesty is at its most fragile when we're not *sure* which path is the righteous one. And so the question becomes:

> How can we create in ourselves a true crisis of faith, that could just as easily go either way?

Religion is the trial case we can all imagine.[2] But if you have cut off all sympathy and now think of theists as evil mutants, then you won't be able to imagine the real internal trials they face. You won't be able to ask the question:

> What general strategy would a religious person have to follow in order to escape their religion?

I'm sure that some, looking at this challenge, are already rattling off a list of standard atheist talking points—"They would have to admit that there wasn't any Bayesian evidence for God's existence," "They would have to see the moral evasions they were carrying out to excuse God's behavior in the Bible," "They need to learn how to use Occam's Razor—"

WRONG! WRONG WRONG WRONG! This kind of rehearsal, where you just cough up points *you already thought of long before*, is *exactly* the style of thinking that keeps people within their current religions. If you stay with your cached thoughts, if your brain fills in the obvious answer so fast that you can't see originally, you surely will not be able to conduct a crisis of faith.

Maybe it's just a question of not enough people reading *Gödel, Escher, Bach* at a sufficiently young age, but I've noticed that a large fraction of the

---

[2] Readers born to atheist parents have missed out on a fundamental life trial, and must make do with the poor substitute of thinking of their religious friends.

population—even technical folk—have trouble following arguments that go this meta.[3] On my more pessimistic days I wonder if the camel has two humps.

Even when it's explicitly pointed out, some people seemingly *cannot follow the leap* from the object-level "Use Occam's Razor! You have to see that your God is an unnecessary belief!" to the meta-level "Try to stop your mind from completing the pattern the usual way!" Because in the same way that all your rationalist friends talk about Occam's Razor like it's a good thing, and in the same way that Occam's Razor leaps right up into your mind, so too, the obvious friend-approved religious response is "God's ways are mysterious and it is presumptuous to suppose that we can understand them." So for you to think that the *general* strategy to follow is "Use Occam's Razor," would be like a theist saying that the general strategy is to have faith.

"But—but Occam's Razor really is better than faith! That's not like preferring a different flavor of ice cream! Anyone can see, looking at history, that Occamian reasoning has been far more productive than faith—"

Which is all true. But beside the point. The point is that you, saying this, are rattling off a standard justification that's already in your mind. The challenge of a crisis of faith is to handle the case where, possibly, our standard conclusions are *wrong* and our standard justifications are *wrong*. So if the standard justification for X is "Occam's Razor!" and you want to hold a crisis of faith around X, you should be questioning if Occam's Razor really endorses X, if your understanding of Occam's Razor is correct, and—if you want to have sufficiently deep doubts—whether simplicity *is* the sort of criterion that has worked well historically in this case, or could reasonably be *expected* to work, et cetera. If you would advise a religionist to question their belief that "faith" is a good justification for X, then you should advise yourself to put forth an equally strong effort to question your belief that "Occam's Razor" is a good justification for X.[4]

---

[3] See "Archimedes's Chromophone" (http://lesswrong.com/lw/h5/archimedess_chronophone/) and my follow-up (http://lesswrong.com/lw/h6/chronophone_motivations/).

[4] Think of all the people out there who don't understand the Minimum Description Length or Solomonoff induction formulations of Occam's Razor, who think that Occam's Razor outlaws many-worlds or the simulation hypothesis. They would need to question their formulations of Occam's Razor and their notions of why simplicity is a good thing. Whatever X in contention you just justified by saying "Occam's Razor!" is, I bet, not the same level of Occamian slam dunk as gravity.

If "Occam's Razor!" is your usual reply, your standard reply, the reply that all your friends give—then you'd better block your brain from instantly completing that pattern, if you're trying to instigate a true crisis of faith.

Better to think of such rules as, "Imagine what a skeptic would say—and then imagine what they would say to your response—and then imagine what else they might say, that would be harder to answer."

Or, "Try to think the thought that hurts the most."

And above all, the rule:

> Put forth the same level of desperate effort that it would take for a theist to reject their religion.

Because if you *aren't* trying that hard, then—for all *you* know—your head could be stuffed full of nonsense as bad as religion.

Without a convulsive, wrenching effort to be rational, the kind of effort it would take to throw off a religion—then how dare you believe anything, when Robert Aumann believes in God?

Someone (I forget who) once observed that people had only until a certain age to reject their religious faith. Afterward they would have answers to all the objections, and it would be too late. That is the kind of existence you must surpass. This is a test of your strength as a rationalist, and it is very severe; but if you cannot pass it, you will be weaker than a ten-year-old.

But again, by the time you know a belief is an error, it is already defeated. So we're not talking about a desperate, convulsive effort to undo the effects of a religious upbringing, *after* you've come to the conclusion that your religion is wrong. We're talking about a desperate effort to *figure out* if you should be throwing off the chains, or keeping them. Self-honesty is at its most fragile when we don't *know* which path we're supposed to take—that's when rationalizations are not *obviously* sins.

Not every doubt calls for staging an all-out Crisis of Faith. But you should consider it when:

- A belief has long remained in your mind;

- It is surrounded by a cloud of known arguments and refutations;

- You have sunk costs in it (time, money, public declarations);

- The belief has emotional consequences (remember that this does not make it wrong);

- It has gotten mixed up in your personality generally.

None of these warning signs are immediate disproofs. These attributes place a belief at risk for all sorts of dangers, and make it very hard to reject when it *is* wrong. And they hold for Richard Dawkins's belief in evolutionary biology, not just the Pope's Catholicism.

Nor does this mean that we're only talking about different flavors of ice cream. Two beliefs can inspire equally deep emotional attachments without having equal evidential support. The point is not to have shallow beliefs, but to have a map that reflects the territory.

I emphasize this, of course, so that you can admit to yourself, "My belief has these warning signs," without having to say to yourself, "My belief is false."

But what these warning signs *do* mark is a belief that will take *more than an ordinary effort to doubt effectively*. It will take more than an ordinary effort to doubt in such a way that if the belief is in fact false, you will in fact reject it. And where you cannot doubt in this way, you are blind, because your brain will hold the belief unconditionally.[5]

When should you stage a Crisis of Faith?

Again, think of the advice you would give to a theist: If you find yourself feeling a little unstable inwardly, but trying to rationalize reasons the belief is still solid, then you should probably stage a Crisis of Faith. If the belief is as solidly supported as gravity, you needn't bother—but think of all the theists who would desperately want to conclude that God is as solid as gravity. So try to imagine what the skeptics out there would say to your "solid as gravity" argument. Certainly, one reason you might fail at a crisis of faith is that you never really sit down and question in the first place—that you never say, "Here is something I need to put effort into doubting properly."

---

[5] In "What Is Evidence?", collected in *Map and Territory*, I note: when a retina sends the same signal regardless of the photons entering it, we call that eye blind. Blind belief works the same way.

If your thoughts get that complicated, you should go ahead and stage a Crisis of Faith. Don't try to do it haphazardly; don't try it in an ad-hoc spare moment. Don't rush to get it done with quickly, so that you can say, "I have doubted, as I was obliged to do." That wouldn't work for a theist, and it won't work for you either. Rest up the previous day, so you're in good mental condition. Allocate some uninterrupted hours. Find somewhere quiet to sit down. Clear your mind of all standard arguments; try to see from scratch. And make a desperate effort to put forth a true doubt that would destroy a false—and *only* a false—deeply held belief.

Elements of the Crisis of Faith technique have been scattered over many essays:

- Avoiding Your Belief's Real Weak Points—One of the first temptations in a crisis of faith is to doubt the strongest points of your belief, so that you can rehearse your good answers. You need to seek out the most painful spots, not the arguments that are most reassuring to consider.

- The Meditation on Curiosity—Roger Zelazny once distinguished between "wanting to be an author" versus "wanting to write," and there is likewise a distinction between wanting to have investigated and wanting to investigate. It is not enough to say, "It is my duty to criticize my own beliefs"; you must be curious, and only uncertainty can create curiosity. Keeping in mind *conservation of expected evidence* may help you *update yourself incrementally*: for every *single* point that you consider, and each element of new argument and new evidence, you should not expect your beliefs to shift more (on average) in one direction than another. Thus you can be truly curious each time about how it will go.

- Original Seeing—Use Pirsig's technique to prevent standard cached thoughts from rushing in and completing the pattern.

- The Litany of Gendlin and the Litany of Tarski—People can stand what is true, for they are already enduring it. If a belief is true, you will be better off believing it, and if it is false, you will be better off rejecting it. You would advise a religious person to try to visualize fully and deeply

281

the world in which there is no God, and to, without excuses, come to the full understanding that *if* there is no God *then* they will be better off believing there is no God. If one cannot come to accept this on a deep emotional level, one will not be able to have a crisis of faith. So you should put in a sincere effort to visualize the *alternative* to your belief, the way that the best and highest skeptic would want you to visualize it. Think of the effort a religionist would have to put forth to imagine, without corrupting it for their own comfort, an atheist's view of the universe.

- *Tsuyoku Naritai!*—The drive to become stronger.

- The Genetic Heuristic—You should be extremely suspicious if you have many ideas suggested by a source that you now know to be untrustworthy, but by golly, it seems that all the ideas still ended up being right.

- The Importance of Saying "Oops"—It really is less painful to swallow the entire bitter pill in one terrible gulp.

- Singlethink—The opposite of doublethink. See the thoughts you flinch away from, that appear in the corner of your mind for just a moment before you refuse to think them. If you become aware of what you are not thinking, you can think it.

- Affective Death Spirals and Resist the Happy Death Spiral—Affective death spirals are prime generators of false beliefs that it will take a Crisis of Faith to shake loose. But since affective death spirals can also get started around real things that are genuinely nice, you don't have to admit that your belief is a lie, to try and resist the halo effect at every point—refuse false praise even of genuinely nice things. Policy debates should not appear one-sided.

- Hold Off On Proposing Solutions—Don't propose any solutions until the problem has been discussed as thoroughly as possible. Make your mind wait on knowing what its answer will be; and try for five minutes before giving up—both generally, and especially when pursuing the devil's point of view.

And these standard techniques, discussed in this volume or in *Map and Territory*, are particularly relevant:

- The sequence on *the bottom line* and *rationalization*, which explains why it is always wrong to selectively argue one side of a debate.

- *Positive bias, motivated skepticism*, and *motivated stopping*, lest you selectively look for support, selectively look for counter-counterarguments, and selectively stop the argument before it gets dangerous. Missing alternatives are a special case of stopping. A special case of motivated skepticism is fake humility, where you bashfully confess that no one can know something you would rather not know. Don't selectively demand too much authority of counterarguments.

- Beware of *semantic stopsigns, applause lights,* and the choice between *explaining, worshiping, and ignoring* something.

- Feel the weight of *burdensome details*—each detail a separate burden, a point of crisis.

But really, there's rather a lot of relevant material, here and on *Overcoming Bias*. There are ideas I have yet to properly introduce. There is the concept of *isshokenmei*—the *desperate, extraordinary, convulsive effort* to be rational. The effort that it would take to surpass the level of Robert Aumann and all the great scientists throughout history who never broke free of their faiths.

The Crisis of Faith is only the critical point and sudden clash of the longer *isshoukenmei*—the lifelong uncompromising effort to be so incredibly rational that you rise above the level of stupid damn mistakes. It's when you get a chance to use the skills that you've been practicing for so long, all-out against yourself.

I wish you the best of luck against your opponent. Have a wonderful crisis!

Postlude:
The Ritual

THE room in which Jeffreyssai received his non-*beisutsukai* visitors was quietly formal, impeccably appointed in only the most conservative tastes. Sunlight and outside air streamed through a grillwork of polished silver, a few sharp edges making it clear that this wall was not to be opened. The floor and walls were glass, thick enough to distort, to a depth sufficient that it didn't matter what might be underneath. Upon the surfaces of the glass were subtly scratched patterns of no particular meaning, scribed as if by the hand of an artistically inclined child (and this was in fact the case).

Elsewhere in Jeffreyssai's home there were rooms of other style; but this, he had found, was what most outsiders expected of a Bayesian Master, and he chose not to enlighten them otherwise. That quiet amusement was one of life's little joys, after all.

The guest sat across from him, knees on the pillow and heels behind. She was here solely upon the business of her Conspiracy, and her attire showed it: a form-fitting jumpsuit of pink leather with even her hands gloved—all the way to the hood covering her head and hair, though her face lay plain and unconcealed beneath.

And so Jeffreyssai had chosen to receive her in this room.

Jeffreyssai let out a long breath, exhaling. "Are you *sure*?"

"Oh," she said, "and do I have to be *absolutely certain* before my advice can shift your opinions? Does it not suffice that I am a domain expert, and you are not?"

Jeffreyssai's mouth twisted up at the corner in a half-smile. "How do *you* know so much about the rules, anyway? You've never had so much as a Planck length of formal training."

"Do you even need to ask?" she said dryly. "If there's one thing that you *beisutsukai* do love to go on about, it's the reasons why you do things."

Jeffreyssai inwardly winced at the thought of trying to pick up rationality by watching other people talk about it—

"And don't inwardly wince at me like that," she said. "I'm not trying to be a rationalist myself, just trying to win an argument with a rationalist. There's a difference, as I'm sure you tell your students."

Can she really read me that well? Jeffreyssai looked out through the silver grillwork, at the sunlight reflected from the faceted mountainside. Always, always the golden sunlight fell each day, in this place far above the clouds. An unchanging thing, that light. The distant Sun, which that light represented, was in five billion years burned out; but now, in *this* moment, the Sun still shone. And that could never alter. Why wish for things to stay the same way forever, when that wish was already granted as absolutely as any wish could be? The paradox of permanence and impermanence: only in the latter perspective was there any such thing as progress, or loss.

"You have always given me good counsel," Jeffreyssai said. "Unchanging, that has been. Through all the time we've known each other."

She inclined her head, acknowledging. This was true, and there was no need to spell out the implications.

"So," Jeffreyssai said. "Not for the sake of arguing. Only because I want to know the answer. *Are* you sure?" He didn't even see how she could *guess*.

"Pretty sure," she said, "we've been collecting statistics for a long time, and in nine hundred and eighty-five out of a thousand cases like yours—"

Then she laughed at the look on his face. "No, I'm joking. Of course I'm not sure. This thing only you can decide. But I *am* sure that you should go off and do whatever it is you people do—I'm quite sure you have a ritual for it, even if you won't discuss it with outsiders—when you *very seriously consider* abandoning a long-held premise of your existence."

It was hard to argue with that, Jeffreyssai reflected, the more so when a domain expert had told you that you were, in fact, probably wrong.

"I concede," Jeffreyssai said. Coming from his lips, the phrase was spoken with a commanding finality. *There is no need to argue with me any further: you have won.*

288

"Oh, stop it," she said. She rose from her pillow in a single fluid shift without the slightest wasted motion. She didn't flaunt her age, but she didn't conceal it either. She took his outstretched hand, and raised it to her lips for a formal kiss. "Farewell, sensei."

"Farewell?" repeated Jeffreyssai. That signified a higher order of departure than *goodbye*. "I do intend to visit you again, milady; and you are always welcome here."

She walked toward the door without answering. At the doorway she paused, without turning around. "It won't be the same," she said. And then, without the movements seeming the least rushed, she walked away so swiftly it was almost like vanishing.

Jeffreyssai sighed. But at least, from here until the challenge proper, all his actions were prescribed, known quantities.

Leaving that formal reception area, he passed to his arena, and caused to be sent out messengers to his students, telling them that the next day's classes must be improvised in his absence, and that there would be a test later.

And then he did nothing in particular. He read another hundred pages of the textbook he had borrowed; it wasn't very good, but then the book he had loaned out in exchange wasn't very good either. He wandered from room to room of his house, idly checking various storages to see if anything had been stolen (a deck of cards was missing, but that was all). From time to time his thoughts turned to tomorrow's challenge, and he let them drift. Not directing his thoughts at all, only blocking out every thought that had ever *previously* occurred to him; and disallowing any kind of conclusion, or even any thought as to where his thoughts might be trending.

The sun set, and he watched it for a while, mind carefully put in idle. It was a fantastic balancing act to set your mind in idle without having to obsess about it, or exert energy to keep it that way; and years ago he would have sweated over it, but practice had long since made perfect.

The next morning he awoke with the chaos of the night's dreaming fresh in his mind, and, doing his best to preserve the feeling of the chaos as well as its memory, he descended a flight of stairs, then another flight of stairs, then a

289

flight of stairs after that, and finally came to the least fashionable room in his whole house.

It was white. That was pretty much it as far as the color scheme went.

All along a single wall were plaques, which, following the classic and suggested method, a younger Jeffreyssai had very carefully scribed himself, burning the *concepts* into his mind with each touch of the brush that wrote the words. *That which can be destroyed by the truth should be. People can stand what is true, for they are already enduring it. Curiosity seeks to annihilate itself.* Even one small plaque that showed nothing except a red horizontal slash. Symbols could be made to stand for *anything*; a flexibility of visual power that even the Bardic Conspiracy would balk at admitting outright.

Beneath the plaques, two sets of tally marks scratched into the wall. Under the plus column, two marks. Under the minus column, five marks. Seven times he had entered this room; five times he had decided not to change his mind; twice he had exited something of a different person. There was no set ratio prescribed, or set range—that would have been a mockery indeed. But if there were no marks in the plus column after a while, you might as well admit that there was no point in having the room, since you didn't have the ability it stood for. Either that, or you'd been born knowing the truth and right of everything.

Jeffreyssai seated himself, not facing the plaques, but facing away from them, at the featureless white wall. It was better to have no visual distractions.

In his mind, he rehearsed first the meta-mnemonic, and then the various sub-mnemonics referenced, for the seven major principles and sixty-two specific techniques that were most likely to prove needful in the Ritual Of Changing One's Mind. To this, Jeffreyssai added another mnemonic, reminding himself of his own fourteen most embarrassing oversights.

He did not take a deep breath. Regular breathing was best.

And then he asked himself the question.

About the author. Eliezer Yudkowsky is a decision theorist and computer scientist who is known for his work in technological forecasting. As the senior researcher at the Machine Intelligence Research Institute in Berkeley, Yudkowsky helped draft some of the first technical research proposals aimed at better formalizing safety requirements for notional general-purpose artificial intelligence systems. His writings have helped spark a number of ongoing academic and public debates about the long-term impact of AI. Yudkowsky's publications include the *Cambridge Handbook of Artificial Intelligence* chapter "The Ethics of Artificial Intelligence," co-authored with Nick Bostrom, and he has written a number of popular introductions to topics in cognitive science and formal epistemology, such as *Rationality: From AI to Zombies* and *Harry Potter and the Methods of Rationality*.

Made in the USA
San Bernardino, CA
24 May 2018